The Central and East European Economies in the 1990s: Prospects and Constraints

Les économies des pays de l'Est et du Centre de l'Europe dans les années 90 : perspectives et contraintes

Reiner Weichhardt
Editor

Assistant Director
NATO Economics Directorate

The Central and East European Economies in the 1990s: Prospects and Constraints

Colloquium

4-6 April 1990

Brussels

Les économies des pays de l'Est et du Centre de l'Europe dans les années 90 : perspectives et contraintes

Colloque

4-6 avril 1990

Bruxelles

First edition 1990
ISBN 92-845-0057-5

This is the latest in a series bringing together papers presented at the NATO colloquia organised by the NATO Economics Directorate and Office of Information and Press on economic issues in the USSR and Central and East European countries. For further information please write to the Director, Office of Information and Press, NATO, 1110 Brussels, Belgium.

The articles contained in this volume represent the views of the authors and do not necessarily reflect the official opinion or policy of member governments or NATO.

Printed in Belgium by Antilope

Contents

Preface

Reiner Weichhardt
Asst. Director, NATO Economics Directorate

The 1990 NATO Economics Colloquium on "The Central and East European Economies in the 1990s" was both a very timely and difficult undertaking. Due to the unprecedented changes in the region, speakers' evaluations of current developments not only required great analytical skills but also a fair amount of "best guesses". The organisers of the Colloquium are most grateful to contributors for their masterful management of these demanding tasks.

Recent developments in Central and Eastern Europe are difficult to understand without taking into account Gorbachevian perestroika. This is why the Colloquium was initiated by two assessments of the Soviet economy. However, the bulk of the programme focussed on the economies of Central and East European countries incorporating both domestic and external aspects. A main conclusion that could be drawn from the detailed country assessments was: all these countries have entered into a movement towards more market-oriented systems but the scope, depth and pace of the transition processes underway are very different in each individual case. The economic reform movement is particularly strong in Hungary, Poland and Czechoslovakia. Bulgaria is moving at a moderate pace and the post-Ceausescu leadership in Romania has so far been unable to come up with a convincing reform model. The GDR developments are a special case since they are embedded in the ongoing process of overall German unification.

Another result emerging from a number of presentations was that foreign economic relations of Central and East European countries with regard to CMEA (in particular the USSR) and Western countries are becoming increasingly diversified. A special paper elaborated on the expanding relations of Eastern countries with the European Community.

For the first time in the history of the conference the programme included speakers from the East, Professor Bauer (Frankfurt a. M. and Budapest), Professor Bogomolov (Moscow) and Dr. Grela (Warsaw). The contributions of these speakers were of great value and interest and substantially upgraded the quality of the conference.

The assessments and contributions submitted by speakers and reproduced in this book represent the state of knowledge at the time of the Colloquium. Only a few up-dates of papers were possible during the editing process. As a result, some assessments are already overtaken by events. This is the risk editors of such books have presently to live with.

Brussels, August 1990.

The Economies of Central and Eastern Europe at the Beginning of the 1990s

Speech by Ambassador Amedeo de Franchis
Deputy Secretary General of NATO

In comparing current political and economic developments in Central and Eastern Europe with the situation one year ago, we must admit that even in our imagination we would not have predicted the events that have actually occurred. In August 1989 Tadeusz Masowiecki was elected as Prime Minister of Poland and that was part of a trend that has been confirmed by the recent free elections in the GDR and Hungary. No doubt, a main pre-condition for all these changes were Gorbachev's new policies based on glasnost and perestroika. The Alliance wholeheartedly supports such developments. The Allies have moved decisively to help the reformers in Central and Eastern Europe — materially and morally.

What is the impact of the dramatic changes in Central and Eastern Europe on the economies of these countries? No doubt, the badly needed restructuring will require much time to lead to better economic performance. In many cases things will get worse before they start to improve. The health of these economies is not good and all the countries suffer, to greater or lesser degree, from similar systemic problems. Economic growth over recent years has been poor. Monopolistic state industries based on ageing, obsolete equipment, and devoted to an ill-conceived "iron philosophy" of excessive heavy industry concentration, have been unable to produce either the quantity or quality of consumer and investment products demanded. Few manufactured goods can meet world standards and trade has been largely within the CMEA area. Some countries, in particular Poland and Hungary, are burdened with heavy levels of hard currency debt from past policies of misguided investment. Inflation rates, already high in some cases, threaten to accelerate as the imbalance between supply and demand of consumer goods grows. Productivity of agriculture is generally low, even in those countries with adequate supplies of basic food products.

With careful management and adequate support the economies of Central and Eastern Europe can be put on the path to recovery and further growth. Although the imposition of centrally planned command economies has severely damaged the former free market structures, the basic framework and institutional memory remain. Of great importance is the rich reservoir of skilled, industrial labour which is still present, to some degree, in each of the countries. The provision of modern technology to replace the ageing, obsolescent industrial plant should put the needed tools into the workers' hands. Both here and in agriculture, however, the most vital ingredient will be the necessary incentives for more and higher quality work. Only the creation of a market system with democratic, private property rights can ensure this. Elimination of the artificial constraints will lead to greater integration of these economies into the world market. This should bring both benefits and pressures for higher economic performance. Rehabilitation of the economies in Central and Eastern Europe will be difficult and drawn out: in some cases complete reconstruction may be needed. But the basic plans have been laid.

Economic reform began in some countries, such as Hungary and Poland, earlier than in others and has assumed in each country certain unique aspects. However, a common pattern appears to be evolving throughout the region. There is a clear recognition by new leaders that systemic reform is essential, including the reduction if not total elimination of central command methods. Some form of market economy is emerging in each country, both for industry and agriculture. Foreign economic relations are being brought more into balance, with reductions in Soviet and intra-CMEA links balanced by new agreements with the West. Individual enterprises are gaining greater independence in trading and management. Workers are being allowed enlarged roles, including rights to own shares and other private property. Clearly the trend is in the right direction. However, the fate of economic reform is closely bound to political developments and the growth of greater freedom and democracy. We will have to await the ultimate outcome of elections in most countries to know whether the future path will be smooth or whether setbacks will occur.

Le succès des réformes en Europe Centrale et Orientale dépendra, en fin de compte, des peuples et des gouvernements de ces pays. Toutefois, nous pouvons les aider, et nous devons le faire. Quelque 13 milliards d'aide ont déjà été affectés à la Pologne et à la Hongrie par 24 nations occidentales, comme suite aux décisions prises au Sommet du G7 de juillet dernier. D'autres formes d'aide sont prévues, provenant de la Banque Mondiale, du Fonds Monétaire International et, lorsqu'elle aura été créée, de la Banque Européenne de Reconstruction et de Développement. Compte tenu des événements qui sont intervenus dans d'autres pays de l'Est et du Centre de l'Europe, il est maintenant envisagé d'étendre à ceux-ci l'assistance déjà garantie aux précédents. L'on s'efforce de réduire, ou d'éliminer, les restrictions au commerce et d'intégrer, autant que possible, ces pays dans le système économique mondial. En même temps que l'assistance financière, les pays occidentaux peuvent assurer la formation des cadres dans les techniques de management et de commerce. Une grande part de cette aide viendra des entreprises privées, comme il est normal, mais les gouvernements devront assurer la transition ou le complément de ces programmes lorsque cela sera nécessaire.

Bien entendu, la Communauté Européenne exerce une attraction bien compréhensible sur la plupart de ces pays, et l'on a pu lire qu'au cours d'une récente réunion des pays du COMECON à Prague, les délégués tchèques ont estimé souhaitable d'envisager la possibilité, pour les membres de cette Organisation, de rejoindre d'autres groupements économiques tels que l'Association Européenne de Libre Echange ou la CEE. Il est certes prématuré d'émettre de telles hypothèses, mais il n'en demeure pas moins que les relations des pays d'Europe Centrale avec la Communauté constitueront l'un des problèmes essentiels que les Européens auront à résoudre au cours des prochaines années.

Le cas de la République Démocratique allemande est évidemment différent dans la mesure où les préparatifs de "l'Union monétaire, économique et sociale" avec la République Fédérale conduiront tout naturellement ce pays sur la voie de profondes réformes. Celles-ci permettront aux investisseurs occidentaux de développer leurs activités en R.D.A. — alors que ce pays était, jusqu'à l'an dernier, le seul des pays socialistes à rejeter les "Joint Ventures" — et d'améliorer du même coup les conditions de vie d'une population qui ne voyait d'autre remède à la médiocrité de ses conditions d'existence que dans l'exode vers l'Ouest.

La Conférence de Bonn sur la "Coopération Economique en Europe", suite de la réunion CSCE de Vienne, s'achèvera la semaine prochaine. Au cours de cette importante manifestation, l'on aura cherché les moyens de développer et de consolider les réformes à l'Est, d'encourager l'expansion du secteur privé, d'améliorer les conditions de travail, préliminaires indispensables à un accès sans restriction au système économique international. Ce qui confère à la réunion de Bonn un caractère exceptionnel, c'est le fait qu'y participent non seulement des officiels, mais également des hommes d'affaires de l'Est et de l'Ouest. Le cadre de la conférence leur fournit l'occasion de discuter, dans des groupes de travail appropriés, des problèmes économiques présentant un intérêt particulier pour l'Est, tels que les économies d'énergie ou les techniques de marketing.

Allies can and will contribute to strengthen the reform processes under way in the East. Our common goal should be to ensure that strong, viable market economies evolve to support free democratic systems throughout Central and Eastern Europe. Thus will all our interests be promoted in future years. It was said of the Greek goddess Athena that she was "wise in the industries of peace and the art of war". For forty years of cold war this Alliance has been most wise in deterring armed conflict. Now we must apply the same wisdom to the transition to true peace and the construction of a prosperous democratic Central and Eastern Europe.

New Issues in East-West Economic Relations

Luncheon Address by Ambassador Henning Wegener*
Assistant Secretary General for Political Affairs

Looking at the work of the Economics Directorate, and at this Colloquium which is part of its annual work programme, a transformation strikes me. We have always analyzed economic events in the Soviet Union and in the Central and East European countries very soberly, as a small but competent research institute would, not with a direct operational end in mind. And yet, this work somehow had a purpose. It was connected with security, which is not astounding in this place. It explored in depth the relationship between security, defence, and economics. Looking at the East European countries and the Soviet Union, it followed and analysed economic events primarily with the security question in mind. How strong, how effective, how dangerous to our security were these countries becoming? How much economic and technological and engineering prowess was being developed and being transformed into a threat? These were at least underlying questions, and they were explored in all their facets in the daily work, in the confidential and secret notes to the Council, in the inputs which we have received over the years from the specialised services of the 16 member countries. It was not isolated work but one that we linked to a perceived threat, and this we kept very firmly in mind.

While I now look at you, Professor Bogomolov, and at your colleagues from other countries of the Warsaw Treaty Organisation, all of a sudden I realize that our purpose is changing. Not the seriousness of our work, but our analytical approach. There is now a new focus to our work. Now, as this morning's session shows, we are exploring system reform. How do these countries transform themselves for peace? How can they gear up to cooperate with us better? There is still a security link, which I would like to explain.

We see the military threat in Europe receding today, as the age-old security dilemma of the overwhelming conventional and, later, nuclear superiority of the Warsaw Treaty Organisation, mainly the Soviet Union, recedes. We are, with hope and vigour, moving to new shores, a new security equation, as we anticipate arms control agreements which will redimension the role of the military factor in East-West relations. And so we are also redefining our notion of security. We find now that the political underpinnings of security are so much more important in the long run. Let me correct myself — we always knew it.

When NATO enunciated the Harmel Report, the Harmel doctrine as many call it, we already established the relationship between long-term political developments and credible defence. And, in fact, in committing ourselves to both credible defence as an Alliance and a policy of co-operation and dialogue and arms control with our neighbours to the East, we found these two to be mutually supplementary and reinforcing. If our policy of dialogue succeeded better we then thought, more than twenty years ago, that somehow we could redimension our defence effort. And, conversely, since we were strong and united and determined, we could offer our hand for co-operation and dialogue and arms control with confidence from our side. Thus, the political angle of security has always been with us — but now it comes to the fore more strongly. In the light of recent developments, we can give expression even more clearly to our deeply held conviction that free, democratic and prosperous countries will not wage war. The long-term security policy of the Alliance must be to help reform, to help the transformation to freely co-operating countries with freely elected governments, democratic systems, free economic and political choices, and with growth in prosperity, satisfaction and reassurance.

That, then, is very much the new mission of our economic work here, including at this Colloquium — to see how this new security basis, the economic underpinning of a new European security order, shapes up. NATO is uniquely qualified to explore these relationships and aspects. We are the only organization, among the stable structures which the West devised for itself after the Second World War, to ensure that the deficiencies and the pitfalls of the past will not recur. We combine in this building, in the interest of our mutual security, the consideration of military, political and economic matters. We also oversee for the Alliance countries the CSCE process, which includes human rights issues — indeed the way in which countries deal with one another. So I think this Alliance is uniquely qualified to start and to pursue this enquiry. I personally see NATO, in its future, more political role, preparing the security of the world of tomorrow very much by means different from the past. It will have a focal role to play among Western international organizations, no matter how operational and efficient the European Community or OECD might be in their respective domains.

Now let me explore a little more the relationship between security and economics. If it is true that free, democratic, prosperous societies are those that are most peace-prone, then of course we have the greatest interest, to the benefit of our collective security, in drawing in more and more of the countries to the East of us to make sure that the process there supports democracy and that economic growth functions well. Therefore, we should support the reform movement in the East and we should give all the support we can to the fledgling democracies in these countries. Of course, the success of reforms essentially rests with these countries themselves, we cannot substitute for them, we can only marginally tell them what to do. The problem with systemic change is that everything should be changed at once, because a system is defined by the mutual integration of all its parts. Now here arises the real challenge for reform. How do the political and the economic processes, which when flourishing create security in the longer run, develop simultaneously and well synchronized?

Our old assumption was that economic reform could only materialize once political reform had occurred, and indeed what we saw, from our perspective, was the failure of reform movements in many of the East European countries — although some of the economic reforms were basically well designed. They failed because the political structures had remained rigid and the command society did not mobilize those independent forces from which economic fruits could grow.

At present, we see that political reform has been launched, and indeed it is launched in parallel with economic change, because in those Central and East European countries where free elections are being prepared, or have taken place, the process of systemic economic reform is also automatically getting under way with great impetus. But problems do not disappear in spite of this welcome coincidence, and I mention two thoughts in this connection. The first one relates to the difference in time scales. How can the rising expectations and hopes of people that come with the sudden changes, with the more open and more inspiring political process, be reconciled with the economic process which is so painstakingly slow and so unpredictable in its various effects on society and the economy as such? The lack of synchronization between political and economic processes, because of structural differences in time scales, is one of the great problems with which we have to deal. The other one is the inherent, or at least possible, contradiction and competition between political and economic goals. Ideally, re-vamping an economy, in systemic terms, calls for strong medicine, resulting in a rapid but painful cure. Radical reform has its own requirements, no matter what chips fall by the wayside, and regardless of the social havoc that is created.

Which governments democratically elected can proceed to enact such rapid and fundamental cures, and yet remain stable? Where are the compromises? Where are the incompatibilities between popularly elected governments that respond to the political call of new times and the inherent stickinesses and contradictions of a half finished reform? If synchronization cannot be achieved — then the result will be instability, frustration, resentment on the political side, misery on the economic. And that is, I would think — still along my conceptual framework of making long-term security and democracy, political and economic growth coincide — that is where the real challenge lies. I think we have very few means at our disposal to harness the process totally. But we must. The greatest requirement is strength and responsibility of states and credible leaders in the countries which have to go through this difficult passage. And the second one is more co-operation, co-operation to the extent that it can help systemic change. As I have said before, we cannot substitute for reforms, but we can hold out the fruits of our efficient, functioning societies in a spirit of European solidarity to help the process along as swiftly as it can move. What we want to see here, from NATO, is not just security in the narrow sense. We want a new political order in Europe, including the Soviet Union, which we hope to be a prosperous, a great country, high in the hierarchy of States where it belongs, but working with us in co-operation, in peace. Nobody begrudges the Soviet Union its greatness, but we want it to be exercised with responsibility, in peace and in co-operative teamwork with all of us here in Europe, including the United States and Canada.

I hope that these impromptu remarks can generate some fertile additional thoughts in the course of the Colloquium's proceedings.

Notes

* Impromptu, unscripted remarks offered at the 1990 NATO Economics Colloquium Speakers' Luncheon, Wednesday, 4th April, 1990.

Observations liminaires de Jean-Claude Renaud

Directeur des Affaires économiques, OTAN

Au cours de la Conférence de Presse qui a suivi le Colloque de l'an dernier, un journaliste soviétique nous a posé la question de savoir si et quand la Glasnost ferait son apparition dans nos réunions annuelles, autrement dit, si et quand des orateurs des pays socialistes seraient admis à y participer, au même titre que leurs collègues occidentaux. C'est chose faite. Nous avons cette année trois présentateurs venant des pays du Pacte de Varsovie : le Pr. Oleg Bogomolov, de l'Académie des Sciences d'Union soviétique, le Pr. Tamàs Bauer qui, tout en étant Hongrois, enseigne à l'Université de Francfort, et le Dr. Marek Grela, de l'Institut polonais des Affaires Internationales.

Certes, les colloques sur les problèmes de l'Est sont devenus monnaie courante. Il ne s'écoule pas de semaine sans que l'on n'en annonce un ou plusieurs, auxquels participent des experts soviétiques, tchèques, polonais ou hongrois, en attendant les experts roumains et bulgares. J'ai personnellement connu la même floraison de colloques sur les problèmes de l'énergie lors de la crise pétrolière des années 70. Ces réunions sont incontestablement utiles, mais je voudrais souligner qu'en ce qui nous concerne, à l'OTAN, nous n'avons pas attendu la perestroïka pour nous intéresser aux économies des pays de l'Est, dont nous avons commencé à débattre dès l'année 1971. C'est dire que nous avons sans doute dans ce domaine la plus ancienne, sinon la plus riche expérience, comme certains d'entre vous peuvent en témoigner. Nous nous bornons donc à poursuivre dans la voie d'une tradition bien établie, puisque ancienne de près de 20 ans, mais nous nous réjouissons que les conditions présentes nous permettent de discuter désormais en présence et avec la participation de nos collègues de l'Est.

Soviet Economy in Crisis and Transformation

John P. Hardt*

Synopsis

By year's end, the Soviet economy may be deeper in recession with inflation and crises in critical areas, or on its way toward implementation of radical transformation. President Gorbachev, with an independent power base in his Presidential Council and with weaker conservative forces in the nomenklatura, may finally have created the political preconditions for implementation of economic perestroika. Success in weakening resistance to perestroika through democratization may require a new centralized presidential base to carry forward radical programs in marketization, modernization, and global integration. But for Gorbachev to sustain his political base, progress must be made in the crisis areas of economic performance: the value of the rouble, the food supply, health care, environmental quality, housing and hard currency earnings in the global market place. Decline in each of these crisis areas must be arrested and turned around. The promise of improvement in these areas may be sufficient to attract broader support for further implementation of radical economic perestroika.

Alternatively, if the stalemate in perestroika policy continues, the crises are likely to deepen with hyperinflation and severe food and consumer goods shortages. With a confluence of adverse economic trends, national strikes and ethnic disturbances, a regime threatening crisis seems possible.

The Presidency may be the crucial factor in overcoming resistance to implementing perestroika if it provides the fulcrum for leveraging the old Stalinist party system and central bureaucracy. With this independent power base for change, Gorbachev may thus bring about the euthanasia of the nomenklatura class and the ministerial bureaucracy. The unseen hand of the market may replace the seen hand of the micromanaging Party and central bureaucracy.

With a new base of political power, newly centralized economic power in the hands of bankers, macroeconomic forecasters and budgeteers, investment planners, and foreign trade magnates may be established. Learning from the Western economic miracles, the critical marketization and modernization role of such institutions as the Federal Reserve Board may be recognized and implemented with effective staffing in a reasonably short period. With crisis resolution and central regulation of fiscal, monetary, investment and foreign commercial policy, the radical market and modernization reform envisaged by the earlier Abalkin plan may be undertaken.

Domestic reform, providing the basis for monetary stability, more efficient supply of food, health care and other improvements in the quality of life, may be the basis for effective opening of the economy to the global market. A fundamental consideration in effective integration is the expansion of hard currency earnings in the near term. The logical foreign commercial option is use of natural resources in comprehensive long-term foreign contractual arrangements in joint ventures that utilizes the entire energy, forest product and/or food chain. The substantial increases in material based projects in hard currency investment and earning may then finance, perhaps through consortiums, other modernization prospects that could not fund themselves, especially in health care, environmental clean- up, housing and machinery output.

The Soviet Union will find benefits from active participation in international economic organizations, but should keep in mind that responsibilities for adherence to the rules of liberal global institutions call for the opening of all markets and reforms that will benefit the entire global commercial community. Thus, attaining observer status in the GATT, taking a more active role in the ECE; expanding "Basket Two" — the economic part of CSCE; and possibly participating in the Economic part of NATO all hold costs and benefits for the Soviet Union.

(1) Participation in liberal economic institutions such as the GATT may help provide the basis for central economic institution-building and expertise for competing in the global market. It may also assist in reducing barriers to commerce and instituting facilitating mechanisms for expanded trade in areas such as agriculture and textile.

(2) More active involvement by the Soviet Union in the Economic Commission for Europe may help stem the disintegration of the East European commercial system and lead to some restructuring of the CMEA commercial regime through an East European Payments Union and other measures to facilitate integration into the global economy. CMEA may take on the character of a common market by casting off its long time heritage of selective autarky and opening its market to regional comparative advantage. A special regional affinity in the transitional period for East European neighbors may be found, although, in the short run it appears that each CMEA country is intentionally reducing its interregional economic relations.

(3) Adherence to the Final Communique of the Economic CSCE meeting in Bonn indicates a firmer commitment to a process of democratization and marketization. The CSCE review process will encourage opening the Soviet market to external competition that would likely mean some reduced output and employment but foster efficiency in the domestic Soviet economy.

(4) New economic roles for NATO and the Warsaw Pact may facilitate economic integration: inspection and verification of reduction in military programs by economic indicators; coordination of infrastructure buildup in East Europe and the USSR; integrative and coordinating function in programs for improving the environment, health care and housing.

I. *Prologue to Implementation of Economic Perestroika*

From March 1985 Mikhail Gorbachev has gone through a learning process and search for the proper timing and combination of the interrelated parts of perestroika. This was followed by a period of developing the concepts of perestroika[1] with very modest implementation of economic reform.

The learning period 1985-87. Up to the Plenum of June 1987 emphasis was on accelerated growth (uskorenia) and institutional and individual discipline. The economic problems were addressed as resolvable by a perestroika that was based on a precept of more and better use of the traditional institutions of the Party and the government. The heightened growth rate, especially in machine building industry, and the anti-alcohol campaign were the hallmarks of the early perestroika policy. The institutions and the people were to be more productive and sober; a return to the old religion, a kind of Leninist Calvinism. Greater openness (glasnost) was to encourage accountability and responsibility with activation and streamlining of old institutions, but no revolutionary change.

By the June 1987 Plenum, a qualitative change had occurred in Gorbachev's perestroika strategy involving sharp change in the objectives and institutional means of the past. Although not visibly clear at the time to all, Herbert Levine was right in characterizing the 1987 Plenum as the beginning of Act II of perestroika.[2] As in the classic French play, the themes of perestroika are the *donnee* or major themes of Gorbachev's play on perestroika, if one considers the period of Gorbachev's rule metaphorically as a play with the curtain rising in March 1985 when he took power. In that sense Perestroika contained the following themes:

Democratization – Establishment of pluralistic government; the rule of laws and institutions responsive to market forces and the will of the people; enhanced authority for parliamentary institutions; mobility based on performance.

Marketization – Monetary stabilization followed by price reform that would make market measures the criteria for economic activity; breakdown of monopolies; creation of markets for capital, labor and goods; privatization of production.

Modernization – Replacement of low productivity enterprises with more efficient capacity that could compete in the world market; changes in the structure of investment and production (including conversion of defense production).

Integration into the world economy – Expansion of trade and opening to foreign investment; participation in international economic institutions; establishment of meaningful exchange rates; achievement of currency convertibility.

These objectives are complementary, indeed synergistic, but their implementation requires a particular time sequence and resolution of tradeoffs to assure a viable consensus for change on all fronts.

II. *Stalemate, Decline and Crisis in 1988-1980*

Perestroika thus involves democratization, marketization, modernization, and integration into the world economy. In Mr. Gorbachev's view, the international environment required for this comprehensive reform (perestroika) includes arms control and regional crisis resolution (which provide the basis for reduced defense burden), as well as enhanced assistance from the West in facilitating reform. Breaking the stalemate on economic reform apparently has required more domestic political power than supporters of perestroika could muster, as they encountered resistance to replacement of the old administrative control systems with modernizing and marketizing institutions that would facilitate global economic integration. In short, economic reform was being held up by a lack of domestic political and institutional support for the revolutionary requirements of economic perestroika.

Although there have been a number of promising initiatives on reform, they have been followed by equivocation and retreat, resulting in stalemate. The most noteworthy was the introduction of the "Abalkin reforms" followed by an effective retreat to the old management system with the Ryzhkov reforms. In the meantime, economic perestroika has been plagued with the worst of combinations: the weakening of the controls and effectiveness of the old system and the inability to move to a new system. With weakened discipline, output and distribution of industrial and agricultural products has lagged, subsidies and wages have risen dramatically increasing the monetary overhang, and the centrifugal forces of endangered institutions such as the local nomenklatura and ethnic unrest have exacerbated declining quality and quantity of performance.

Jan Vanous at PlanEcon predicts a major economic recession in 1990:[3]

The Soviet economy is headed for a major recession in 1990... realistic Western estimates are likely to put the decline (in Soviet Gross Domestic Product) at 4-5%.

Monetary disequilibrium becomes even more severe... The increase in cash in circulation was up 56% in 1989. Savings in disposable income rose to the highest level in over 30 years. The size of the Soviet internal debt now exceeds 400 billion rubles (43% of GDP).

Inflation reaches a record level. Realistically it now is in the 7-9% range.

The slowdown in industrial production most affects producers goods. In 1990 the growth (gross output of producer goods) is slated to be close to zero.

Grain harvest recovers, but there is trouble in animal husbandry.

Despite stagnant investment volume, the lag in putting capital goods into operation grows. Gross investment in fixed capital was up only 0.5% in 1989.

Large increase in imports of non socialist countries causes the first non socialist trade deficit since 1975-76. The size of Soviet gross hard currency debt reached an estimated $58 billion at the end of 1989, up from $49.5 billion at the end of 1988.

Without radical change in policy and management of the economy, Vanous projects serious economic decline; however, I would argue that he understates the crisis by not highlighting the areas of crucial importance to social satisfaction: food, health care, environment, housing, and their medium of exchange — the rouble.

The lack of implementation and initiation of economic progress has made the promise of eventual improvement less credible and the fruits of economic policies have been bitter and negative: less food on the shelves, falling health care performance, deteriorating environment, inadequate housing and a close-to-useless currency. As Gorbachev looks toward the decade of the nineties, the political basis of perestroika seems to be moving into place while key elements of performance in economic perestroika are in crisis. These crises will need to be resolved if perestroika is to survive and proceed into the economic transition. These areas of material decline may be measured in both objective terms (as Vanous does) and subjective terms, that is, as critical indicators for Ivan Ivanovich in measuring whether perestroika is good for him and his family:

Reduced availability and quality of food and the lengthening of queues for scarce products available. Other subsistence items such as soap have joined the long list of deficit consumer goods. Under current projections there is little evidence to suggest improvement without radical change.

Health care has reached crisis stage with indicators such as absence of sanitary syringes, minimum materials for feminine hygiene and inadequate surgical supplies contributing to an environment of desperation in health care, also, increased awareness of problems from Chernobyl, other industrial disasters has fed mistrust, even anger.

Environment as measured by clean air, water and other minimum norms of environmental quality is also perceived by many as an escalating crisis. Indeed, as Murray Feshbach documents, "the current Soviet leadership has been compelled to recognize the destructive impact of a deficient health care system and serious ecological neglect" ... according to Zaslavskaya, "a shortfall in correcting (these) social problems would profoundly undermine the prospects for success of Gorbachev's *perestroika*."[4]

Housing also has substantial economic and social value. The quality of housing, always low by Western norms, has decreased with quality of housing environment, e.g., TV, appliances and maintenance.

Rouble value as increased monetary overhang and more inflation suggest close to zero liquidity — "who wants to hold roubles" — would even be exceeded. The social and psychological impact of hyperinflation and a near valueless currency is difficult to calculate.

With the crises in other economic and social areas these add up to a potentiality of a general political crisis. Were one to raise the prospects of a general strike of railroad workers, coal miners or oil field workers, for example, and food riots, the transformation of economic crisis to a general political crisis seems more credible than at any time in the past. Disturbances and lack of economic stability in the ethnic minority regions might provide a natural spark to the economic tinder.

III. *A Turning Point (Perekhod) in Perestroika*

Presidency, power and prospects for crisis resolution

In taking the Presidency, Mikhail Gorbachev may have the platform, the will and the opportunity to break the stalemate on implementing effective, radical economic reform. This appears to be his rationale as expressed in his acceptance speech of March 15, 1990,[5] and repeated on several occasions since then.

While the four elements of perestroika are complementary and synergistic, they are also competitive and involve tradeoffs. The democratization of the central governance organs by emergence of an increasingly independent legislature — the Chamber of Deputies and Supreme Soviet — has fostered support for radical perestroika. Pluralism, openness and increased sense of political accountability has made the social dissatisfaction in the declining economic performance more poignant; therefore action and results are needed. Economic reform measures may be facilitated by political and ideological changes in property rights, and a retreat from Party dominance of all political, social and economic functions at the center and in the localities. These political changes were adopted during the 1990 session of the legislature and the January Plenum of the Party, and the regional elections promise to further weaken the political base for opposition to radical economic reform. However, the central power needed to introduce programs of economic austerity as preconditions for marketization and modernization may, in the transition, require a new form of political centralism — a strong presidency — and a new form of economic centralism — a strong central banking, macroeconomic forecasting and strategic coordination function, and a newly centralized foreign economic function. The requirement of a strong political position necessary to establish newly centralized economic powers and unpopular austerity programs may partially explain Gorbachev's insistence on taking to himself a strong presidency, supported by the parliament, with broad powers to carry out an economic and political purpose that would not in all its components be popular. This may be likened to de Gaulle's use of a broad plebiscite to establish himself in the strong presidential position necessary to force the ending of the Algerian War, military demobilization, and unpopular domestic economic reforms in France. A strong presidency, may for example, allow Gorbachev to move toward an unpopular and difficult currency stabilization program leading toward rouble convertibility, reordering of investment, employment planning and management, and a redirection of commercial relations. For these transitional efforts, a new form of economic centralism is arguably necessary. It would be focussed on a central banker, macroeconomic forecasters and on a strong foreign commercial chief, perhaps based or established under the presidency. Experience in Poland, Czechoslovakia and Hungary suggests that an effective beginning in modern economic institution building is possible with promising early results. For example, staff and authority for economists such as Abalkin, Petrakov, and Shatalin could be effective if free from ministerial and Party bureaucratic control.

President Gorbachev has recently been pressing political change in the Soviet Union as a precondition for revolutionary economic changes. While the political and ideological basis for a combination of top down and bottom up change has been building, each of the economic underpinnings of perestroika — marketization, modernization, and integration into the world economy — are still on the drawing board.

The Bush-Gorbachev Summit and CPSU Congress in May-June 1990 could also provide further pressure and selective support for change to deal with these crises. While these crises have been evident for some time and it appears that Gorbachev recognized their serious and essential relationship to the success of perestroika, he has not acted effectively.

Preconditions for comprehensive reform: The recognition of economic crisis, not just serious problems of transition, led Gorbachev to turn to his domestic and foreign economic advisors for advice. The economists' prescription was the Abalkin reform plan of Fall 1989.[6] This plan called for rapid and revolutionary steps in a transition toward a market economy from 1990-1995.

Ownership: Transfer of ownership of factories and farms to joint stock companies, leased and mixed ownership farms with bankruptcy action for failing enterprises.

Financial recovery: Sharp reduction toward elimination of subsidies and budget defaults and movement toward a real interest rate in a newly created financial market; sharp cuts in central investment, especially for defense; institutional changes involving establishment of a tax and banking system and a stock exchange.

Price reform and movement toward a market: Immediate introduction of wholesale, followed by retail, price reform.

Foreign investment: Sharp relaxation of restrictions on foreign investment, establishment of special economic zones, integration in global financial market and creation of a basis for rouble convertibility.

No sooner had these plans for revolutionary change in the economy been announced, than second thoughts began to set in and a second version of the strategy for the 13th Five-Year Plan period, the Ryzhkov reform, program was adopted instead. It may be that the political basis for the Abalkin plan was deemed inadequate, the process of transition was deemed too risky in terms of meeting immediate needs of economic crises and consequently the risk of failure was too great.[7] In this sense, the Ryzhkov Plan may be considered a holding action, i.e., a decision to delay comprehensive reform until a firm political basis could be laid to try to increase the prospects of success while reducing the danger of failure.[8]

The Chamber of Deputies vote on March 13, 1990 on the new powers for the Presidency may have provided the political framework for a crisis-management program enabling decisive steps toward a transitional Abalkin type reform program. The Presidential Council could be the vehicle for new central economic administration. At the same time the Polish experience of January-February 1990 in stabilizing their currency may have been instructive and encouraging. A short term crisis managing program almost inevitably involves a new form of centralization. In this, Gorbachev sees the strengthened role of the Presidency to be essential. Where Polish initial success in stabilization through austerity was based on trust in the central Solidarity leadership, Soviet control of incomes policy might require strong presidential power capable to develop a consensus with the newly influential legislature. The new plan needed would logically include more performance measures than the earlier plan — the pain would be more bearable if performance generating citizen satisfaction were assured. The full outlines of an economic transition and crisis control program have not emerged to date, but such a program could well include some of the following ingredients:[9]

1. A new federal compact to allow for substantial states rights for decentralized economic activities in farm and factory while retaining all-union control of currency, strategic industries and infrastructure, and central features of Western commerce.
2. A drastic stabilization program based on control of the monetary supply, income policy control — especially wage control — sharp reduction of subsidies and neutralization of the monetary overhang. Establishment of a rouble domestically convertible to dollars with a stabilization fund to maintain its new level would complete the parallel with the Polish program. Returning health to the rouble would be a substantial accomplishment.
3. A drastic program to ensure increased supplies of good food, critical health care items, serious efforts to improve environmental quality, and significantly improved housing conditions would be politically valuable in gaining support for perestroika and a vital basis for moving back toward the full transition plan of Abalkin. These concrete improvements may well be pursued by centralized, reprioritized and more effective control of a food chain with substantial marshalling of resources to overcome bottlenecks and key imports to support the debottlenecking and incentive efforts. Evidence by the July Party Congress of a credible prospect for more supplies of food, key medical supplies and consumer durables would be psychologically important in support of perestroika, and provide a popular support basis for introducing the new reform plan announcement in the summer of 1990.
4. A sharp expansion of the National Conversion Program ("guns to butter") to utilize comprehensive control of investment, physical assets and manpower including both military and civilian programs would provide some visible short term fruits of a "peace dividend". A shift of military builders and military transport to the food chain with central control of the combined assets would be one example. Use of the drafted manpower for national service in the health care, environment and housing sectors might be another example of centralized control of assets that would promise meaningful economic results.[10] While costly modernization as well as expansion of defense forces are being deferred or dropped the conversion of military assets to civilian programs must be

directed to be effective.

5. A targeted foreign commercial offensive to bring in direct foreign investment and control of the "bankable assets" the Soviets have in natural resources, e.g. oil and gas, paper and pulp timber and arable land might provide substantial and immediate increases in hard currency and provide for substantially improved domestic performance. The increased hard currency income from direct foreign investment and earnings could provide a financially sound basis for expanded key imports in food processing, health care, housing, environment, etc., that could be repaid from predictable future hard currency earnings. The Chevron control of the oil energy chain from exploration to pump using access to both onshore and offshore North Caspian fields in Kazakhstan within the context of the American Trade Consortium would be an example of such a revolutionary change in Soviet foreign commercial policy. The example of use of foreign ownership by General Electric in Hungary's foreign commercial strategy making foreign capital, technology and management expertise available may provide some assurance of political success for the USSR in a natural resource based foreign economic strategy.

The fruits of such a crisis management program, if successful, would be to provide a strengthened rouble, improved food supplies, enhanced health care, improved housing, and the redirection of foreign economic policies in a way that would provide a basis for hope in establishing a future competitive position in the world market.

There are reasons for doubting success, however, in this newly centralized economic crisis management strategy. Soviet central management of economic affairs has not provided grounds for confidence in the past. The goal is to move to a market based economic system and a case can be made that this goal is not furthered by recentralization with different priorities and tools. Yet, given current economic and political realities in the USSR and the enormity of changes necessary for integration into a world market, preparatory measures utilizing the central economic powers of the Soviet state may be prudent. The danger is, of course, that centralized transitional measures can become entrenched and deter the transition to control through the market mechanism. At the same time, the partial success of the cooperatives in demonstrating market instincts of people and the potential conversion of professionals to competition in a new market environment suggest the yet to be demonstrated capacity of old believers to be converted.

Realization of a newly centralized economic crisis management program need not be a return to the old administrative control system of the past. The illustrative five-step program would not call for production engineers and physical output control of planning and management. Central bankers, business managers of the food chain, macroeconomic forecasters and market regulators, and foreign commercial entrepreneurs could be the transitional central bureaucracy. Gorbachev does not need the old style production engineers but new monetary, financial and business controllers. Political consolidation of Gorbachev's power in a strong presidency, with further support from local governance revolutions unseating the old nomenklatura system in the regions through spring elections, and implementation of new ownership relations and demonopolization efforts and a cooperative pact between Gorbachev and Yeltsin might then provide a favorable environment for adoption of the transitional Abalkin/Shatalin/Petrakov plan in the months ahead. The illustrative crisis management program would, in effect, be a preparation for the Abalkin/Shatalin/Petrakov plan, designed to provide an improved political environment through a centralized economic regulatory mechanism for crisis resolution to make the transition to economic perestroika sustainable. But in 1990 the moment of truth appears to have arrived. In Gorbachev's classic drama on Perestroika the *de'nouement* has been reached.

Global integration in perestroika: the resource based consortium option

Negotiations of a new US-USSR commercial relationship through a trade agreement with the United States, direct investment agreement and revised arrangement on debt settlement, especially a Lend Lease settlement, could either facilitate or discourage such a transitional crisis management program depending on the correlation of programs encouraged with transformation needs, e.g., improved environment, housing, and health care. While the US-Soviet trade agreement may be more narrowly cast to provide for a signable document at or soon after the June Summit, negotiation of a bilateral investment agreement and revised terms of the Lend Lease settlement might provide more leverage for American encouragement of radical economic reforms. Foreign ownership or effective control through long term leases that provide the same degree of assurance of efficient management would improve prospects of US enterprise commitments to large scale, long term commitments. The likely contractual arrangement with consortia approach illustrates some of the mutual advantages of complete system control for both sides. If trade consortia secured sufficient control to merit the exploitation of major Soviet oil fields necessary for large investment, and brought to the world level of efficiency all parts of the petroleum chain from exploration through field management to refining, a major new model for US-Soviet joint ventures would be established. Marketing the incremental value of output over traditional Soviet management of the North Caspian fields might mean an addition, in hard currency, to the Soviet trade balance of tens of billions of dollars over a decade.

If this revolutionary concept, theoretically credible in the petroleum chain, were applied to other natural resources, the results might be equally significant and mutually advantageous. Take the case of pulp and paper timber product resources in East Siberia. Favorable terms of long term leases or foreign ownership might thaw some of the development plans of rich East Siberian resources intended to be opened by the Baikal Amur railroad project but frozen by Gorbachev's "European industry first" policy on investment. American or other Western paper product multinationals might be willing to bid on long term leases for prime pulp timber tracts if they could have long term control and profitable lease terms. The Soviets might be willing to negotiate if the auction price for such tracts were high enough and bonds were arranged to assure maintenance of resource renewability throughout the lease period.

Applied to arable land the results might be equally profitable. If a substantial tract of prime arable land were leased on a long term basis, say in the black soil area of the Ukraine, to an American agribusiness multinational within a trade consortium, one could imagine a modern agribusiness efficiently producing meat for the Soviet market and export. It might even link with a fast-food outlet such as McDonald's to introduce the entire Western type of food chain process to the Soviet Union. Here, again, some bond to assure maintenance of land fertility and environment and a reasonable market price for the leases would be essential.

Long term leases and/or foreign ownership seem to be consistent with the process of foreign commercial reform under the Abalkin/Shatalin/ Petrakov plan but not explicitly proposed. Foreign control of crop land would be especially sensitive. However, building on the consortium example, the Soviet leadership might be encouraged by the Bush-Gorbachev Summit and/or through negotiations of the direct investment agreement to take these logical steps in developing a new first phase foreign commercial strategy. In this way substantial expansion of access to convertible currency, direct technology and management transfer and a significant increase of profits to both sides might be assured.

Soviet leaders and citizens have traditionally opposed natural resource leasing to foreigners on historical grounds. Examples include the role of foreign concessions in the development of the Baku oil fields prior to the Revolution and foreign military intervention to recapture those concessions during the Civil War of 1918-20 and other vilified instances of foreign resources control under socialist direction. Increased participation of regional interests has raised the importance of environmental concerns, e.g., in the North Caspian Kazakh republic development of oil. In Western direct investment negotiations some special emphasis may be given to these environmental issues. Using environmental norms modeled on US legislation, bonds might be established to assure compliance with US levels of environmental and renewable resource protection, e.g., controlled logging of timber areas. Soviet regional resource planners might also want to use those agreements to set aside certain acreage to preserve areas important to watersheds and for public park use.

In discussions on resumption of Lend Lease payments both sides have reasons to revise the earlier terms: as our waiver of Jackson-Vanik will not meet the restricted MFN tariff privilege requirement we have asked the Soviets for a reinterpretation of the earlier agreement; Soviet payment schedules, in turn, would be greatly accelerated to meet the final payment date of the year 2001. In a reconstitution of the schedule of Lend Lease payments closer to a level of the Soviet ability to pay, we might consider some debt for financing exchanges or debt for nature swaps. We could imagine Soviet government funding through debt conversion, health care system improvements and joint projects that could assist in dealing with global environmental problems. Mutually desirable exchanges in technical areas such as desalinization programs, library and archive exchanges and a wide range of scientific, cultural and politically cooperative efforts might be facilitated. Exchanges between parliamentarians could be likewise expanded. Even mutually developed environmental projects for Eastern Europe providing Soviet gas as a substitute for coal or nuclear power could be considered.

Such arrangements, however, would appear to forego revenues to the United States and amount to foreign aid at a time of budget stringency at home. They would however, parallel policies of debt rescheduling and conversion provided to Poland and considered for other East European countries. Were the United States to see earlier payment in programs of clear, concrete interests flexibility on the repayment schedule might be merited.

Some revolutionary approach to the crises areas of stabilizing the rouble, food, health care, environment and housing may well be necessary to sustain the complex process of transition under perestroika toward marketization, modernization, democratization and integration into the world economy. Facilitating joint ventures in developing Soviet natural resources might provide needed hard currency to improve not only efficiency in resource sectors but also fund projects in health care, environment and housing.

Integration into the international economic organizations

Integration into the global market and international economic organizations has costs and benefits to the Soviet perestroika process. Withdrawing or changing old organizations such as CMEA may involve restructuring rather than elimination. Moreover, the benefits are balanced by costs and accountability. Time sequencing of change can also tip the cost-benefit relationship.

With progress toward domestic transformation and integration into the world market, active participation in the International Economic Organizations (IEOs) can take on greater meaning. Thus, as the Soviet Union moves toward observer status in the General Agreement on Tariffs and Trade (GATT), it may not only benefit from knowledge of the global trading community but may have to moderate its commercial behavior to conform to multilateral norms. The Soviet Union was granted observer status to GATT at its meeting of May 16, 1990. While able to participate in the general activities — monthly meetings, standing committees, receive GATT documents — the USSR will not be permitted to contribute or participate in the Uruguay Rounds discussions or vote in the regular proceedings. As it moves toward membership in GATT, the responsibilities as well as privileges may become clearer. Each member must open its economy to commerce unrestricted by trade barriers and regulated by market prices with freer access to all other GATT member markets. Competition from the global market may help domestic reform efforts to demonopolize if properly sequenced with domestic reform, the demonopolization effort could be facilitated. A transitional period over the decade for freer global trade in agricultural products and textiles may favor some Soviet and East European exporters.

When the Uruguay Round winds up it proceedings in Brussels in December 1990 and proceeds toward approval and implementation in 1991, the organization may be substantially different than in the past. If the reformers of GATT get their way it would be transformed into a global commercial institution with new powers for dispute resolution and compliance with agreements. If services and institutional property concerns are added to GATT's agenda their comprehension may be virtually as wide as current accounts in the balance of payments. If more enforcement powers are added perhaps in a new organization, the long delayed International Trade Organization, the GATT will change from a forum in which nations may raise, discuss and settle disputes on trade to a commercial institution. The original ITO promised mechanisms for integration of non-market economics; GATT did not. There will clearly be more pressures for the Soviet Union to become more open, more transparent in reporting, and move toward full foreign currency convertibility.

The Economic Commission for Europe of the United Nations, also with Soviet and East European membership, calls for measures to facilitate technical and grant aid to East Europe.[11] In the current analysis ECE has proposed that they address problems that may be important in debt reduction and credit flows, reduced export controls of CoCom, and improved market access as important to performance. In calling for the creation of a Central European Payments Union, modeled on the West European Payments Union of the 1950s, the ECE drew attention to the needs of East European *transition* toward a system of free trade and multilateral settlements. In such a process, the rapid shift of the Soviet Union to hard currency trade with other CMEA members in January 1991 and the sharp deterioration of East Europe's terms of trade with the USSR might be brought into question. While repeal of the Brezhnev doctrine and encouragement of perestroika in East Europe is helpful politically to East Europe, Soviet's current economic policies of sudden shift for East Europe to hard currency in trade with the USSR would result in a substantial transfer of resources from East Europe to the Soviet Union at a time of critical need in East Europe. Whereas the Soviet call for opening of CMEA trade and shift to convertible currency trade is consistent with GATT principles, the lack of a transition period for easing out of soft goods trade with the Soviet Union would also lead to substantial unemployment and reduced output in the East European economic sectors accustomed to exporting to the Soviet market. Besides, it does not serve Soviet needs to phase out East European commerce too rapidly.

Indeed, there are, objective reasons for contributing to a new, market oriented perestroika and comprehensive reform in the Soviet Union and East Europe:[12]

Mutual interests in the transition to a hard currency regime. Much of the output of Eastern Europe and the Soviet Union has developed to meet the needs of the CMEA market. East European machinery and Soviet materials, other than oil and gas, can not be readily sold for convertible currency. A transition process of modernization and labor force retraining may be facilitated by a step by step withdrawal from soft goods trade within CMEA.

Comparative advantages and mutual interests in regional relations will probably come from the process of marketization and democratization. The newly democratic and market oriented countries may find more interregional interests than they now perceive in the process of integration with Western Europe and the global economy.

ECE also notes the importance of debt reduction to East Europe, e.g., postponement of interest payment by Poland for 1990, saving hard currency payments of $5 billion dwarfs the total aid of G-24. However, if the full financing of Polish debt servicing is not eased by March 1991 when the rescheduled debt servicing resumes, Poland's Western commerce will be overwhelmed by debt servicing. In the interim the Soviet Union has not declared a moratorium on Poland's 5 billion rouble debt to the USSR and is pursuing payment.

ECE also suggest establishing a mechanism for monitoring the effects of CoCom on Eastern economies. The Soviet Union may wish to play an active role in this process. As the CoCom expected at its June 6, 1990 meeting to shift to "core" military control programs while decontrolling many computers, telecommunications equipment and machine tools key to infrastructure development; this use of "high fences over narrow grounds" may make this ECE monitoring more manageable.

Where ECE may play a useful role in monitoring the impact of continued CoCom controls, NATO may play a monitoring role that facilitates reduction of controls as agreement by Soviet and Americans on inspection and verification of imports of possible dual use is developed in response to Soviet offers of external access to domestic users. In this context, new roles for the military organizations of the North Atlantic and European Community may be helpful in facilitating the process of perestroika within agreed policies of export control and transformation. Several may be briefly sketched out:

Economic verification of the defense build-down on a reciprocal basis could be useful in encouraging and building confidence in the implementation of arms control agreements, unilateral reductions and reduced allocation of resources to military programs. The skills in these organizations might be especially useful for enhancing programs of confidence building.

Infrastructure buildup of the Soviet Union and East Europe would be a critical aspect of economic modernization. All forms of transport and communications are areas of expertise of these institutions that may be drawn on to coordinate and provide advice to East-West and bilateral programs of infrastructure improvement.

Environment, health care and housing programs. Military forces may be used especially by conversion of the drafted manpower to national service to perform the labor intensive needs of the socially important programs.

Military administration is well organized and equipped to provide the construction and transport facilities to meet these social needs. Such alternative use of manpower could also reduce the problem of transitional unemployment.

Of course Japan, a member of CoCom but not of NATO, and the Advanced Asian Industrial Economies (South Korea, Republic of China, Hong Kong) would have to be associated with this process to make verification and monitoring a useful mechanism for all critical export controls.

Notably, the Soviet Union at Bonn CSCE meeting of 35 nations on economic co-operation in Europe agreed to a remarkable statement on the desirability of democratization, marketization, modernization, and integration into the world economy.[13] These general objectives were joined by many specific commitments on privatization, use of market forces, acceptance of national treatment and the protection of intellectual property. Soviet agreement to the principles and specific measures for transformation formalizes its commitment to perestroika and transformation in Eastern Europe. Marketization based on private property and prospects of foreign ownership and private capital flows and commerce as an engine of transformation reinforce a new, radical Soviet foreign economic strategy in line with Western experience. Moreover, these agreements may facilitate bilateral commercial agreements and joint ventures more in line with liberal, open market practices. While the CSCE process provides many benefits to the Soviet Union through integration into the global economy, these too are joined by responsibilities for openness and a liberal reform regime.

Graduation of East European and the Soviet economy into the European Community and closer relations with the OECD likewise provide both benefits and responsibilities. Joining the global market and the international economic institutions is not an honorific process of club membership for the Soviet Union but an active involvement in a dynamic global economy. Thus, participation by the Soviet Union in international economic organizations may encourage integration into the global market and foster competition in their domestic market, but the benefits also carry responsibilities and costs that may be borne in structural unemployment and other costs of transition.

Notes

*The views expressed are those of the author and not necessarily those of the Congressional Research Service or the Library of Congress. Comments by Academican Bogomolov, the first Soviet to speak to the NATO Economics Colloqium, were in part a response to this paper. Selected reference will be made to his paper to appear in the annual volume and the *NATO REVIEW.* (These references will be Bogomolov, NATO).

1. Joint Economic Committee, *Gorbachev's Economic Plans,* Part I and II, December 1987. See John P. Hardt and Sheila Heslin, *Perestroika: A Sustainable Process of Change,* Commentary by Oleg Bogomolov. Occasional Paper of Group of Thirty, October 1989.
2. *Gorbachev's Economic Plans,* op. cit. Cf. Gennadiy Zoteyev, "Perestroika as a Strategy of the Transition Period: A View From Within". Presented at the American Economic

Association, December 1989. Oleg Bogomolov, Director of the Institute of World Socialist Economies, defines perestroika more broadly than mine, calling for the above noted elements of perestroika while adding "ideological diversity; the restatement of liberty and humanism as universal human values". See Bogomolov, NATO, *op. cit.*

3. Jan Vanous (editor) "Soviet Economic Performance in 1989: Prelude to a Major Recession This Year", *PlanEcon,* Vol. VI, N. 7-8, February 21, 1990. 40 pages. Cf. "The Soviet Economy Stumbles Badly in 1989" by the Central Intelligence Agency and Defense Intelligence Agency, presented to the Joint Economic Committee, April 20, 1990.
4. See forthcoming Murray Feshbach, *Economics of Health and Environment in the USSR: Implications for Civilian and Military Sectors,* Basic Books, 1990. Tatyana Zaslavskaya, currently head of the All-Union Center for Study of Public Opinion, is a long time supporter of Gorbachev's perestroika.
5. *Pravda,* March 16, 1990.
6. See *Ekomicheskaya gazeta,* N° 43, October 1989, pp. 4-7. Cf. Ed A. Hewett, "Perestroika Plus": The Abalkin Reforms. *PlanEcon Report,* N°. 48-49, Volume V, December 1, 1989.
7. Padma Desai of Columbia University seems to view this type retreat as politically logical. Padma Desai, *Perestroika in Perspective, The Design and Dilemmas of Soviet Reform,* Princeton University Press, 1989, pp. 138. Cf. John Tedstrom, "The Soviet Economy: Planning for the 1990s". *Radio Liberty Report on the USSR,* Volume 1, Number 51, December 22, 1989, pp.1-7
8. Chairman of the Council of Ministers, Nikolai Ryzhkov, overrode his Deputy Minister Abalkin with a modified plan for the 13th Five-Year Plan that retained the general perestroika objectives of the Abalkin Plan but little of the specific plans for implementation. Thereafter, Gorbachev appointed Nikolai Petrakov, a radical reformer, as his personal economic adviser.
9. Plans apparently approved March 11 instructed Abalkin to produce draft laws and decrees by May 1, 1990. Further major monetary, fiscal and organizational reform is to take effect by July 1, 1990. Nikolai Petrakov is said to have told Interfax that the reform program is closely related to the current program in Poland. Gorbachev and another presidential advisor Shatalin indicated that the Soviet Union was not appropriate for the "shock" treatment. Probably performance would have to precede trust. C.f. CIA-DIA submission to the Joint Economic Commitee on Soviet economy, *op. cit.* Bogomolov describes a comprehensive monetary stabilization program and judges currency reform as essential, albeit unpopular. See also Pavel Bunich, "The Reform Has Been Announced But Not Yet Launched" *Narodnyi deputat* (Peoples Deputy) N°. 4, 1990, pp. 53.59. A reform group working for both Gorbachev and Yeltsin was tasked to develop a 500 day reform program by 3 September 1990.
10. Leonid Vid (Deputy Director of Gosplan), "Guns into Butter, Soviet Style" with commentary by John P. Hardt, *Bulletin of Atomic Scientists,* January 1990. John Tedstrom, "USSR-Managing the Conversion of the Defense Industry". *Socialism. Perestroika and the Dilemmas of Soviet Economic Reform.* Westview Press, 1990 (forthcoming).
11. ECE, *Economic Survey of Europe in 1989-1990,* April 1990, focused in this issue on "A Marshall Plan for Eastern Europe?" Cf. Eastern Europe: "Long Road Ahead to Economic Well-Being", a paper by the Central Intelligence Agency presented to the Subcommittee on Technology and National Security of the Joint Economic Commitee. May 16, 1990.
12. C.f. Marie Lavigne's paper from this symposium. "Economic Relations Between Eastern Europe and the USSR: Bilateral Ties versus Multilateral Cooperation".
13. Final Communique of the Conference on Economic Co-operation in Europe, Bonn, Federal Republic of Germany, April 11, 1990.

The Soviet Economy on the Eve of the 1990s: Prospects for International Cooperation*

Oleg Bogomolov

Until 1989, the administrative system of the Soviet Union underwent only partial changes. The basic principles remained intact: the dominance of the Communist party, the dominance of the state form of ownership and the monopoly of Marxism in ideological life. Now we are entering a period when the old social system is being dismantled and a new one established. Perhaps not everybody will agree with my conclusions about our country, but it is a matter of fact that we are entering such a period. The principle features of the new system will be a market economy with diverse forms of ownership, all with equality; free enterprise and competition; broad democracy and glasnost; political pluralism, including the existence of several parties, a Parliament, with parliamentary opposition; ideological diversity; the reinstatement of liberty and humanism as universal human values; and an opening to the outside world.

Perestroika in the Soviet Union has already been in progress for about five years. Changes have coloured different spheres of social life, but perhaps the most radical shifts have taken place in the public consciousness and in the understanding by society of its past and of those problems that it still has to solve. The people are full of expectations and take a lively interest in the press and television. However, there has as yet been no real improvement in their lives. As one of our humourists says, today it is more interesting to read in the Soviet Union than to live. The feeling of disappointment and of deceived hopes is growing among the population.

The results of 1989 point to aggravation of the economic crisis. The growing difficulties of supply and the deterioration in the quality of life have caused strikes in many regions of the country. The problems of relations between different ethnic groups have become more acute, mostly as a result of economic difficulties. A redistribution of budget investment in favour of housing, health care, education, light industry and food industries has not yet produced tangible results. There has been no radical improvement in agriculture. The per capita output of foodstuffs is not increasing, and the country still depends on 40 to 50 million tonnes of grain imports annually.

Miscalculation in the Concept of Perestroika

The success of perestroika depends on the extent to which several negative phenomena are brought under control. These are inflation, the shadow economy which nourishes corruption and criminality, and the state budget which has, for a long time, been in deficit, a deficit which this year is expected to amount to 100 billion roubles, or 10-11 % of GNP. This is a consequence of a rapid growth of expenditures and a considerable reduction in budgetary revenues. The trade balance has declined, principally as a result of the fall in prices of Soviet exports, but also due to mismanagement. The budget deficit is compensated by the issue of money and credit, *not* backed by goods and services.

The public wants to spend its money on the commodities it requires but is unable to find them on the market. The amount of so-called "hot" money is huge, about 200 billion roubles. Despite state control, retail prices are increasing by 4 to 5% a year, and the growing inflation is revealed by shortages, by the disappearance of one commodity after another from the consumer market. Of course, the transition from totalitarianism to democracy and from a command economy to a market economy cannot be effected painlessly. The burden of problems accumulated over many years is still very heavy, but many difficulties could have been avoided if miscalculations had not been made in the concept of perestroika and its practical realization, which has been inconsistent and indecisive.

We began to introduce market principles and the self-financing of industrial enterprises without the prior formation of the necessary environment, which would include a genuine wholesale trade market, full value money, a sound price system and appropriate tax and credit regulations. A reduction of subsidies to loss-making enterprises was also needed. The result — they did not get off to an effective start but instead created additional inflationary pressures.

It would have been wiser to have started from the other end — agriculture — with the emancipation of the agricultural producer from bureaucratic control and with more freedom of economic activity on the land. This would have called for the leasing of the land or its transfer to family and co-operative farms, together with a gradual reduction in obligatory deliveries of agricultural products to the state, and their replacement with a system of free trade.

We have delayed the reform of the federal structure of our state, which remains unitarian. We call our state a federation, but in the real sense, it is not, it is a unitarian state which needs to be reformed. A form of economic relations between the central and local authorities, designed to give greater independence to management at republic, area and regional levels, has become especially urgent. The principle of equivalence should be more fully applied and strictly observed in inter-regional exchange, but this is not the case to date.

The heart of the money-credit system and the body of a domestic market do not now exist but have to be created. This is intended to be brought about by means of cuts in budget expenditures: the military budget, some major investment programmes, subsidies to loss-making enterprises, management expenses, and so on. Then also through the sale and lease of some kinds of state property, creation of small and medium sized enterprises, apartments and land auctions. A more strict control of the growth of cash payments to the population will be effected, but the main hopes are pinned on a higher output of foodstuffs and industrial consumer goods for the population.

Insufficient Economic Programme

The government worked out a special programme of reform of the Soviet economy which was approved by the Congress of Peoples' Deputies. I voted against this programme because I found it insufficient. The envisaged measures aiming at an increase in retail turnover are not realistic. Radical measures should be adopted in order to bring an equilibrium between money and commodity supply on the domestic market. This requires truly radical measures which now, I hope, will be undertaken by the new President. We still cherish an illusion that under the system of administrative distribution, which uses quasi-money, we can create a market. But little significant change can take place without material incentives and enterpreneurship motives and competition. Creation of sound and fully convertible money is the most important step on the road to the creation of true markets and to the introduction of economic incentives for higher output and greater production and efficiency.

We are faced with a vicious circle. We need to give incentives for better and more productive work — we do not have other means of increasing production because we have limited investment funds, while the possibility of getting credit from abroad is very limited. So we can count only on our own efforts, and we can indeed produce much more with the same capacities and on the same basis but it is necessary to give material incentives to the workers. But we cannot give them material incentives because our consumer market is completely destroyed and our currency devalued. How can we break this vicious circle?

I think only radical measures can help us, in spite of our leaders' statements that we shall not undertake currency reform without consultations with the population or that we can solve problems without such drastic measures. In my view, we need some kind of currency reform and price reform, and I hope that now such measures are under preparation and the new President will proceed more resolutely than the government has done these past months.

Our main reserves lie in the awakening of a true interest in a more productive labour force. Its higher performance, with clarification of changed relations in ownership, market, discipline and competition, is where real opportunities of increasing consumption, through our own efforts, lie. People and labour collectives should not rely on the state alone, as they are accustomed to do, to make us happy. Today, it is the state which is unable to do much to guarantee the distribution and supply of goods to the entire population, according to their needs.

It is probable that the transition from one type of economy to another will be associated with some costs and temporary losses which the people will have to pay. From the introduction of a market economy we can expect an additional impulse for inflation and an increase in unemployment. That is why the transition strategy must include measures and social guarantees minimizing the negative social impact of economic reform, especially for our low income groups. Such measures are now in the stage of discussion and preparation.

We are facing very difficult problems and are now at the turning point. We can manage many of our problems if we proceed more definitely and resolutely, but we have not much time to do all this because the population is now losing patience. To be patient under such conditions is not easy without a sense of humour. That is why I will conclude with a joke. An old woman comes to the capital to visit her son who is a very big boss. Sitting in the kitchen and talking about perestroika, the old woman asks her son "Tell me, my son, was the revolution made by the common people or by the scholars?". The son replies, "What a stupid question! Of course the revolution was made by the common people. If the scholars had made the revolution, they would have first tried it on rats!"

* This article was first published in the NATO Review, No. 3, June 1990.

Le cas bulgare : des réformes économiques inachevées

Marie-Claude Maurel

Synopsis

En Bulgarie, les réformes apparaissent vouées à l'inachèvement. Pas plus que les réformes précédentes, la "restructuration" lancée à partir de 1986 n'est parvenue à son terme. Sans projet cohérent et sans programmation établie, la mise en œuvre des réformes a été improvisée. La direction bulgare, vieillie et usée, au sein de laquelle les conservateurs maintenaient de solides positions, ne pouvait pleinement s'engager dans un processus de réforme dont les principes mêmes remettaient en cause son mode d'exercice du pouvoir et de gestion de l'économie.

La première partie retrace ce qu'ont été les velléités de la "version bulgare de la perestroïka", à travers un calendrier de réformes précipité et chaotique. Pratiquant l'art de la fuite en avant et du faire semblant, les dirigeants bulgares ont successivement mis en chantier trois versions du "nouveau mécanisme économique", tout à fait exemplaires des réformes avortées du 1er janvier, phénomène bien connu en Europe de l'Est.

La deuxième partie souligne l'écart appréciable entre les intentions affichées et les restructurations effectivement engagées. Une manœuvre de grande ampleur a été entreprise pour promouvoir une "nouvelle qualité de la croissance économique". Quelques principes guident la restructuration : assouplissement de la planification centrale, transfert du pouvoir de décision économique aux entreprises, instauration de mécanismes économiques susceptibles de renforcer la responsabilité des entreprises et leur compétitivité. Mais en matière d'autogestion et de démocratisation, la plupart des changements restent formels. L'exemple de l'agriculture montre comment d'incessantes réformes ont aggravé la désorganisation.

La dernière partie conclut que la restructuration est mal engagée. Dans une situation économique critique, un rapport de forces politique indécis prolonge indûment l'attente d'une transition.

I. *Introduction*

En Bulgarie, les réformes apparaissent vouées à l'inachèvement. Depuis plus de trois décennies, la réforme permanente spécifie le mode d'existence même du socialisme bulgare. Dès que l'expérimentation d'une réforme se heurte à quelques difficultés, ou qu'elle génère des effets contradictoires, une autre prend le relais sans que les leçons de l'échec aient toujours été analysées. Pas davantage que les précédentes, la réforme lancée à partir de 1986 sous le terme générique de "restructuration" (pereoustroïstvo) n'est parvenue à son terme, bien que ses objectifs aient été à plusieurs reprises reformulés. Le fait certain, clairement mis en évidence par le limogeage de T. Jivkov, en novembre 1989, c'est que la restructuration impliquait un changement radical et authentique de politique auquel l'ancienne direction bulgare n'adhérait pas.

Dans l'état présent de l'évolution de ce pays, il est difficile de faire le point sur le degré d'avancement de la restructuration. D'une part, parce qu'il n'y a jamais eu de projet cohérent, encore moins de modèle de référence, d'autre part, parce que la mise en œuvre des réformes a été improvisée, et développée sans programmation établie, au gré de l'évolution des rapports de forces au sein de la sphère dirigeante bulgare.

Dans ces conditions, les responsables n'ont réussi à maîtriser ni le processus réformateur, ni les contradictions apparues entre anciens et nouveaux éléments du système de gestion. Toutefois, si la réforme des mécanismes économiques est encore très incomplète, des modifications décisives ont été apportées au mode de fonctionnement du système économique. Celui-ci est engagé dans une transition au terme d'autant plus incertain, que la gravité de la situation économique, jusqu'ici masquée par l'opacité d'une information statistique truquée, est brutalement révélée : détérioration des résultats de l'activité productive, alourdissement de la dette extérieure, dont le niveau par habitant est comparable à celui de la Pologne, inflation avouée de l'ordre de 10 %, témoignent de l'ampleur d'une crise à laquelle les conditions d'application des réformes ne sont pas étrangères.

II. *Les vélleités de la "Pereoustroistvo"*

Au cours des trois dernières années, les réformes économiques ont pris un cours nouveau, accéléré et chaotique. Ce double caractère découle de ce que l'on pourrait appeler le zèle "suiviste" des dirigeants bulgares à l'égard de leurs homologues soviétiques, de leurs réticences de fond par rapport à une réforme gorbatchevienne qui, à l'inverse des précédentes, s'annonçait radicale et globale. Ces deux points méritent d'être précisés.

Les responsables bulgares ne sont jamais en retard d'une réforme.[1] La chronologie des réformes mises en œuvre dans les deux pays, au cours des trois dernières décennies, révèle une évidente symétrie : mêmes temps forts et mêmes reflux.

L'expérience des "sovnarkhoz" de l'époque krouchtchevienne a servi de modèle à la déconcentration territoriale du système de gestion bulgare, entre 1959 et 1963. L'expérimentation des méthodes de gestion économique (1966-1969) est le pendant de la grande réforme soviétique lancée par Kossyguine. Comme cette dernière, la réforme bulgare s'accompagne d'un mouvement de recentralisation, sous la forme du rétablissement des ministères techniques, et de la création des unions économiques d'Etat. La décennie soixante-dix est marquée en Bulgarie, comme en Union soviétique, par une transformation du système de gestion dans le sens d'une supercentralisation, avec la création d'une dizaine de complexes économiques nationaux et des regroupements qui tendent vers une liquidation progressive de l'autonomie des entreprises. Ces échecs successifs procèdent des mêmes défauts : manque de cohérence et inefficacité de réajustements partiels, incompatibilité des méthodes de régulation économiques avec le maintien d'une logique centralisatrice.

La direction bulgare, dont l'ardeur réformatrice a sans doute été réanimée par la visite de M. Gorbatchev à Sofia en octobre 1985, ne pouvait manquer de suivre l'exemple soviétique. Entre la mise en chantier de la restructuration soviétique et l'adoption des premières mesures réformatrices en Bulgarie, il y a tout au plus un décalage de quelques mois, que les dirigeants bulgares s'efforceront de réduire par une avalanche de réorganisations tous azimuts. Mais le parallèle entre les deux expériences s'arrête là. La source d'inspiration est commune, mais la "perestroïka" se veut une réforme radicale et globale, articulant l'économique et le politique, tandis que la "pereoustroïstvo" n'en est qu'une version édulcorée, même si elle lui emprunte son habillage conceptuel.

La direction bulgare, vieillie et usée par plus de trente ans d'exercice autoritaire du pouvoir, et au sein de laquelle le courant conservateur maintenait de solides positions, ne pouvait pleinement s'engager dans un processus de réformes qui remettait en cause son mode de gestion de l'économie et de la société. Si comme tout semble l'indiquer, les dirigeants bulgares ont cherché, en jouant les "bons élèves", à donner le change pour se maintenir au pouvoir le plus longtemps possible, il ne faut pas chercher de stratégie cohérente là où il n'y a qu'une série d'opérations tactiques destinées à désamorcer la critique. Cet éclairage étant donné, on peut tenter de dérouler les phases du processus en mentionnant le risque de conférer une cohérence factice, et à posteriori, à un dispositif de réformes qui ne relevait pas d'un projet clairement établi.

La réforme est lancée sans avoir fait l'objet d'une déclaration d'intention et d'un échéancier. C'est a posteriori que les exégèses officielles prendront pour référence le discours de T. Jivkov au plénum du C.C. du PCB des 28 et 29 juillet 1987, sous la dénomination pompeuse de "conception" de juillet. Mais à cette date certains éléments de la réforme avaient déjà été mis en place.[2] Les prémices du branle-bas réformateur se manifestent dès le début de 1986. La création d'un Conseil économique destiné à assumer la direction stratégique de l'économie, prélude à la suppression des ministères de branches et à leur remplacement par quatre Conseils ministériels aux attributions mal définies. En mars, après des années de préparation et de débat, un nouveau code du travail est adopté. Dans ce document figurent les concepts-clés d'"autogestion", de "démocratisation", de "restructuration" et d'"approche économique", sur lesquels le XIIIe Congrès du PCB, réuni en avril de la même année, met tout particulèrement l'accent.

Une nouvelle étape est franchie lors du plénum du C.C. du PCB en décembre 1986. L'adoption du "règlement sur l'activité économique" jette les bases législatives du nouveau système économique (décret n° 71 du 29 décembre 1986).[3] Dénommées "Organisations économiques autogérées", les entreprises sont désormais responsables de leur propre gestion. Dotées de l'autonomie financière, elles fixent leurs objectifs, planifient leur activité, et doivent assurer leur autofinancement. Les organes économiques centraux ont pour mission d'élaborer la stratégie économique, d'organiser et de coordonner la gestion. Ils doivent progressivement substituer aux directives administratives divers "leviers économiques" destinés à intéresser les entreprises aux résultats de leur gestion.

La réforme modifie la nature et le rôle de la planification centrale et accorde une place décisive aux instruments de contrôle indirects. C'est tout l'environnement économique de l'activité des entreprises qui doit être transformé par la réforme des prix, des salaires, du système fiscal, de l'organisation commerciale et bancaire. Dans sa version initiale, le règlement de l'activité économique trace le cadre général des réformes mais reste flou, voire confus, sur bien des points.

L'introduction de cette réforme en janvier 1987 inaugure une année d'intense activité législative et réglementaire et plus encore de profonds bouleversements des structures de gestion, tant au niveau du gouvernement central, qu'aux divers échelons de l'administration territoriale. Les changements organisationnels prennent le pas et connaissent alors une brutale accélération.

Le processus de réforme s'empare de toutes les sphères de la vie publique et l'accent est mis sur l'autogestion, en tant que principe de base et mécanisme de la restructuration. Dans la nouvelle conception bulgare, l'autogestion ne fait pas seulement référence à l'autonomie comptable et financière mais inclut la reconnaissance des droits des collectifs de travail en matière de gestion des entreprises. Le principe de l'élection des organes responsables (Conseil économique et direction) par l'assemblée des travailleurs introduit par le code du travail, est mis en œuvre dans les entreprises. Un nouveau pas est franchi lorsqu'il est décidé de remettre aux collectifs l'exploitation et la gestion de la propriété socialiste (29 avril 1987). La mesure est étendue aux communes, c'est-à-dire aux unités administratives de base, auxquelles l'assemblée nationale confère le statut de "communautés autogérées" (7 juillet 1987).

Quelques semaines plus tard, lors du plénum du C.C. du PCB (28-29 juillet 1987), le secrétaire général T. Jivkov propose un programme politique et économique destiné à promouvoir une société communiste autogérée ("Pour un modèle de société approprié à la nouvelle réalité historique"). Reprenant les mesures économiques déjà adoptées, il trace le cadre général de la restructuration. Ces propositions n'apportent guère d'éclaircissement sur la manière de promouvoir "l'intensification" de l'économie en introduisant des éléments limités du mécanisme de marché, mais en conservant à la planification sa position centrale.

Les propositions politiques les plus importantes concernent en fait l'annonce de changements réorganisant la structure du gouvernement central et celle de l'administration territoriale. L'une d'entre elles, qui prévoyait la suppression du Conseil d'Etat et des Conseils ministériels et leur remplacement par un unique et mystérieux organe d'Etat, restera sans lendemain.

Dans la foulée, les grandes lignes de la réorganisation sont rendues publiques (le 14 août 1989 dans le "*Rabotnicesko delo*") et le 18 août, l'assemblée nationale approuve, à l'issue d'un bref débat, une série d'importantes mesures.[4] Loin d'aller dans le sens annoncé lors du plénum de juillet, la réorganisation du gouvernement central semble indiquer un retour aux principes soutenant l'administration antérieurement à 1985. L'abolition des Conseils ministériels, accusés d'avoir entretenu une administration pléthorique et d'avoir fait obstacle à la restructuration, signe l'échec de la tentative de rationalisation des structures centrales. Ils sont remplacés par cinq ministères : de l'Economie et de la Planification, des Relations économiques extérieures, de l'Agriculture et des Forêts, de la Culture, de la Science et de l'Education, de la Santé publique et des Affaires sociales. C'est le ministère de l'Economie et de la Planification qui détient les plus grands pouvoirs. "Il applique la politique d'Etat, et est chargé par la direction de la coordination et du contrôle de l'activité économique". Il reprend sous son autorité les responsabilités dévolues au Comité d'Etat pour la Recherche et la Technologie. En septembre 1987, des "Associations", chargées d'animer la politique des grands secteurs industriels sont organisées. Leur rôle est de concilier les intérêts de l'Etat (leurs présidents participent au Conseil des ministres pour les affaires de leur compétence) et ceux des entreprises adhérentes (les "organisations économiques autogérées"). Ces "Associations" doivent promouvoir une politique commune en matière de technologie, d'investissement et de commercialisation.

En redistribuant les cartes par un jeu de promotions et de rétrogradations parmi les membres de la sphère dirigeante, ces remaniements n'ont-ils pas également et de manière plus significative une fonction instrumentale ?

Au même moment, la réforme de l'administration territoriale entraîne, elle aussi, une vague de mutations dans l'appareil politico-administratif de niveau intermédiaire. Présentée comme une décentralisation administrative, la réforme territoriale supprime les anciens départements (okrag), au nombre de 28, et les regroupe en 9 régions (oblast). La commune (obchina), qualifiée de "communauté autogérée"[5] devient l'unité administrative fondamentale, au profit de laquelle est opéré un transfert de compétences. Gestionnaire de la propriété socialiste, l'administration locale devient responsable de l'emploi, du logement, de l'approvisionnement alimentaire, etc. Après l'adoption de la loi (26 août 1987), la réforme est entrée immédiatement en application. Des directions régionales provisoires ont été désignées dans les jours qui ont suivi, sans attendre les élections prévues pour le mois de février. La rapidité du changement, l'absence de concertation, la réorganisation ayant été opérée par le haut, conduisent à s'interroger sur la portée d'une "démocratisation", impulsée par le pouvoir central, et qui sème une confusion certaine dans les rangs du personnel politique de l'échelon intermédiaire.[6]

En dehors de ces changements organisationnels, la réforme a peu progressé. Les nouvelles structures apparaissent un cadre vide, tant que certaines conditions économiques et psychologiques ne sont pas réunies. D'une part le transfert de la propriété socialiste aux collectifs de base semble avoir posé des difficultés,[7] d'autre part le règlement de l'activité économique, mis en œuvre au début de 1987, a laissé en dehors de son champ d'application des aspects aussi importants que les prix, les impôts et les salaires. La nécessité d'introduire ces réformes est évoquée lors du plénum du C.C. de novembre 1987, mais elles ne semblent pas avoir fait l'objet de préparation très avancée.[8]

C'est un "nouveau mécanisme économique" encore incomplet qui est relancé au début de 1988. En janvier 1988, un "nouveau règlement sur l'activité économique" remplace celui introduit l'année précédente, dont l'application s'était avérée difficile, en raison notamment de son ambiguïté. Les dispositions du nouveau texte de loi ne remettent pas en cause les orientations antérieures sur l'autonomie et l'autogestion, qui encourageaient la recherche du profit et la concurrence entre les entreprises. Des règlements particuliers concernant les salaires, les prix, la qualité, ainsi qu'une réforme de la fiscalité, complètent le dispositif.[9]

Après le remue-ménage qui avait caractérisé la première phase de la restructuration, 1988 est l'année des petits pas. Les responsables bulgares continuent à ne se préoccuper que de la dimension économique de la restructuration, laissant en dehors du champ de celle-ci la plupart des secteurs de la vie politique, sociale et culturelle, tandis que le soutien officiel à la "glasnost" apparaît de pure forme.[10]

Lors du plénum de décembre 1988, T. Jivkov admet l'existence de sérieuses difficultés dans la mise en œuvre du processus de restructuration, en raison du "manque d'expérience" de la direction bulgare.[11] Le transfert de la gestion de la propriété socialiste aux collectifs de base a échoué dans son objectif essentiel de réanimer le sens de la responsabilité des travailleurs. Il en a été de même en ce qui concerne les régions et les communes. Dans l'analyse de ce fiasco, aucune mention n'est faite de la dégradation des performances économiques, ou de l'aggravation des pénuries puisque, bien au contraire, T. Jivkov met en avant des données tout à fait irréalistes sur la réalisation des plans.

Pratiquant l'art de la fuite en avant, les réformateurs bulgares mettent en chantier une troisième version du nouveau mécanisme économique.[12] Ce décret (ukaz) qui, notons-le au passage, revêt une forme légale supérieure à celles des actes normatifs antérieurs (postanovlenia), innove substantiellement en imposant la création de firmes (ou sociétés) comme formes d'organisation de base de l'activité économique. Plusieurs formes juridiques sont envisagées: sociétés par actions, sociétés à responsabilité limitée, sociétés à responsabilité illimitée et sociétés individuelles. L'autonomie devient totale et l'autogestion, la règle de base. Plusieurs dispositions témoignent que l'on veut aller plus loin dans la direction de l'économie de marché: le système des commandes d'Etat est assoupli, les rapports avec l'étranger sont libérés, la concurrence est encouragée, mais la sanction de cette nouvelle liberté est la faillite de l'entreprise en cas de mauvaise gestion. En outre, le décret inclut des dispositions plus attractives en ce qui concerne les investissements étrangers (en remplacement de la réglementation adoptée en juillet 1987). Pour renforcer l'intérêt très modéré des entreprises étrangères à venir investir en Bulgarie, un décret d'août 1989 autorise la transformation des entreprises d'Etat en sociétés par actions dans lesquelles les étrangers pourraient détenir des parts(jusqu'à 20% sans autorisation du ministère de l'Economie).

Pas davantage que les mesures précédentes, ces dispositions plus libérales ne parviennent à relancer une restructuration qui s'enlise dans les petits pas. Une enième fois en juillet 1989, dans un rapport au Politburo, T. Jivkov dénonce la faible efficience de l'économie bulgare, la médiocre qualité des produits et la lenteur du progrès technologique. Fait sans précédent, il plaide en faveur de l'introduction progressive d'un mécanisme de convertibilité de la monnaie, seule issue pour disposer à terme d'un instrument d'information économique efficace.[13]

Engagée à contrecœur et sans conviction par une direction autoritaire opposée à toute réelle démocratisation de la société, la réforme bulgare est constituée de pièces et de morceaux, de demi-mesures qui ne définissent pas un environnement économique suffisamment cohérent et incitatif pour modifier le comportement des acteurs économiques.

III. *Intentions et réalités*

Entre les intentions affichées et les restructurations effectivement engagées, l'écart est grand. Les principes de la réforme sont loin de s'être traduits dans les faits lorsque même ils ont été mis en application. Cette distance n'est pas la moindre des difficultés quand on cherche à apprécier la réalité des réformes.

Il est clair que l'on a entrepris une manœuvre de grande ampleur pour promouvoir une "nouvelle qualité de la croissance économique", à travers un nouveau mode de gestion du système économique, fondé sur l'autogestion. Quelques principes guident la restructuration: assouplissement de la planification et réduction du centralisme, transfert du pouvoir de décision économique aux entreprises, instauration de mécanismes économiques susceptibles de renforcer la responsabilité des entreprises et leur compétitivité.[14]

— Une planification assouplie.

La planification n'est plus impérative. Le projet de plan, qui est préparé par le ministère de l'Economie et de la Planification, est transmis aux "Associations" et aux entreprises pour information. Il intègre tout un système de régulateurs économiques destinés à fournir aux entreprises les données nécessaires à l'élaboration de leur propre plan. La coordination entre les intérêts de l'Etat (macro-économiques) et ceux des agents économiques doit procéder d'un "dialogue" entre le ministère et les entreprises. En réalité ce n'est pas là le seul moyen d'établir la jonction entre les deux niveaux de planification. C'est, d'une part, la fonction même des régulateurs qui doivent générer des comportements économiques susceptibles de répondre aux objectifs de la planification. C'est, d'autre part, le fait que la rupture avec la planification impérative n'est pas totale. Il y a maintien des "commandes d'Etat" pour un nombre déterminé de produits essentiels et pour quelques projets importants. Les "commandes d'Etat", qui peuvent faire l'objet d'adjudications de manière à placer les entreprises en compétition, sont acceptées par contrat par les entreprises.

En réalité, au moins dans la période de transition, le système de planification s'apparente à un système dual couplant planification impérative et indicative. Les commandes d'Etat sont appelées à voir leur part se réduire au fur et à mesure que l'équilibre sur le marché sera atteint. Depuis 1989, ces commandes d'Etat ne peuvent accaparer plus des deux tiers des capacités de production d'une entreprise.

— La logique de l'autofinancement.

La logique de l'autofinancement implique de réformer le système bancaire d'une part, le système budgétaire d'autre part.

En accord avec les principes de décentralisation des responsabilités et d'autonomie financière des entreprises, la réforme du système bancaire et du mécanisme de crédit a pour but de rapprocher la banque de l'entreprise et de donner les moyens à celle-ci de sa politique financière. Un nouveau système bancaire à deux niveaux a été établi en mai 1987 comprenant une banque nationale et huit banques commerciales. Les actionnaires de ces banques sont la Banque nationale de Bulgarie, pour 50% de leur capital, et les entreprises de leur secteur de compétence (correspondant en gros aux "Associations"). Bien qu'en application du principe de compétitivité, les banques soient autorisées à travailler avec n'importe quelle entreprise, et réciproquement, leur domaine de compétence est dans la pratique limité au secteur industriel auquel elles se rattachent. Leur activité porte sur toutes les opérations bancaires classiques liées à l'activité des entreprises, et notamment l'octroi de crédits en leva ou en devises. Fait nouveau, le crédit doit devenir l'une des sources de financement des investissements et du capital circulant. Un système de crédits d'Etat à long terme a été introduit pour financer les projets d'investissement des secteurs d'activité particulièrement capitalistiques.

Le financement budgétaire était jusqu'en 1987 la principale source de formation du capital. La réforme engagée depuis lors a eu pour objectif de réduire la centralisation/redistribution des profits. L'objectif est de diminuer les prélèvements sur les entreprises, de manière à leur garantir des ressources propres afin de donner corps à la logique de l'autonomie comptable intégrale. Elle a pour contrepartie une réduction du financement budgétaire de l'investissement.

Une première étape a porté sur la diminution du niveau moyen de l'impôt sur le profit (de 61% en 1987 à 51% en 1988). Mais il y a encore des entreprises qui se voient prélever jusqu'à 70 et même 80% de leur profit, ce qui rend impossible tout autofinancement. Un système de prélèvement fiscal sur les ressources utilisées (travail et capital), selon des normes uniformes, a été établi à titre transitoire pour 1988-1990. Cette mesure doit faire pression sur les entreprises pour qu'elles fassent un meilleur usage de leurs ressources. Une réforme est en préparation pour substituer à ces prélèvements une taxe à la valeur ajoutée (à l'horizon 1991).

— La réforme des prix de gros.

L'ensemble du dispositif réformiste est directement conditionné par une refonte du mécanisme des prix.

Les réformes ont adopté une approche gradualiste, consistant à réviser les prix de gros dans un premier temps (1988-1990) sans modifier les prix de détail dont l'ajustement n'interviendrait qu'en 1991. La révision des prix de gros doit prendre pour base les actuels prix à l'exportation sur le marché international. L'établissement d'un lien direct entre ceux-ci et les prix en vigueur sur le marché intérieur a pour objectif d'introduire une référence à la compétitivité internationale dans l'économie nationale. On peut s'interroger sur la signification d'un tel alignement tant que ces prix sont exprimés en leva, monnaie dont la convertibilité n'est toujours pas assurée.

Deux catégories de prix sont distinguées: des prix fixés centralement (alignés sur les prix du marché international) pour les produits stratégiques et les produits déficitaires, des prix contractuels, établis plus librement entre producteurs et utilisateurs, mais qui ne peuvent excéder les prix d'exportation.

Quelques exceptions à la nouvelle règle de formation des prix sont admises pour les produits agricoles, les produits de l'industrie de transformation dont la modernisation technologique doit être temporairement subventionnée. Entre le miroir déformé du système des prix administrés et une vérité des prix totalement alignée sur le niveau international, les réformateurs ont choisi une voie médiane. Mais ce compromis repose sur des prix convertis en leva par application d'un taux de change tout à fait arbitraire.

La réforme s'accompagne de la volonté d'une intégration plus grande de l'économie nationale dans le système économique mondial. L'impératif de la compétitivité est une orientation nouvelle. Le développement des échanges avec les pays socialistes et les relations de coopération ne suffisent plus, c'est désormais vers les pays occidentaux que doivent se tourner les entreprises bulgares pour tenter de réduire l'écart technologique. Cette orientation transparaît à travers le concept de prix international déjà évoqué, et se traduit par des dispositions plus libérales qui permettent aux entreprises de négocier directement avec les partenaires étrangers sans autorisation préalable du ministère du Commerce extérieur. Par ailleurs, les banques commerciales, qui ont vocation à devenir de véritables banques d'affaires, ont reçu la possibilité de s'associer à des partenaires étrangers, pour des activités conjointes, et notamment la constitution de banques en commun.

L'investissement étranger est fortement encouragé, car il permet à la fois d'acquérir de nouvelles technologies et de réduire les sorties en devises. C'est dans ce domaine que la réforme bulgare apparaît la plus spectaculaire, puisque simultanément la législation nouvelle autorise les investissements étrangers, sous forme d'entreprises conjointes, et que sont créées des zones franches. La réglementation sur les investissements étrangers (ordonnance du 28 mars 1980), qui a fait l'objet d'une première refonte en juillet 1987, a été remplacée en janvier 1989 par un nouveau texte inclus dans le décret sur l'activité économique. Plus attractives pour les capitaux étrangers, les nouvelles dispositions prévoient des garanties appropriées (l'égalité de traitement entre nationaux et étrangers, la protection de l'Etat) et des conditions plus avantageuses, concernant le transfert des profits, l'allègement, voire l'exonération, d'impôt.

Pour compléter le dispositif, deux zones franches ont été établies, à Roussé et à Vidin sur le Danube. Les facilités offertes concernent principalement l'exonération des droits et taxes sur les produits importés et exportés par les entreprises qui s'y installeront. Le succès de cette ouverture vers l'extérieur apparaît encore très limité. Les investisseurs demeurent réservés puisque seulement 23 sociétés mixtes à capitaux occidentaux ont été créées, ce qui est peu en comparaison des créations en Hongrie (800), en URSS (792) ou en Pologne (442).[15] Aucune entreprise ne s'est encore installée dans les deux zones franches.

Les réformes ont sensiblement modifié le statut de l'entreprise socialiste devenue "organisation économique autogérée", les conditions de son activité économique et son mode de fonctionnement interne.[16] Si l'on perçoit bien la portée conceptuelle des changements opérés par l'introduction des principes de l'autogestion, en revanche leur signification pratique est beaucoup plus difficile à appréhender. En théorie, le dispositif de la réforme a considérablement étendu l'autonomie économique des entreprises, leur pouvoir de décision, en matière de planification comme en ce qui concerne le choix de leurs partenaires (fournisseurs et clients), des organismes bancaires de service et de prêt, etc. En contrepartie, l'entreprise doit faire face à ses engagements, la sanction de son autonomie étant la faillite. Le transfert du pouvoir de décision économique pose très directement la question des relations de propriété. La cession du droit de gestion de la propriété des moyens de production aux collectifs de travailleurs ne résoud rien sur le fond. Sans doute libère-t-elle l'Etat de sa responsabilité en tant que gestionnaire, mais lui conserve sa responsabilité de propriétaire, un propriétaire qui a délégué le droit d'usage à un collectif. La décision a été prise pour tenter de dépasser le sentiment d'aliénation des travailleurs face à la propriété d'Etat, en plaçant les travailleurs dans des conditions telles qu'ils se sentent responsables, voire "maîtres", de leur outil de travail et se comportent à son égard comme de véritables propriétaires. Ce transfert opéré sur la base d'un contrat n'est pas exempt d'ambiguïté, et sa mise en œuvre semble avoir posé des difficultés, comme l'indique le fait que plusieurs décrets aient été nécessaires.

Le passage à "l'autogestion" est associé à une "démocratisation" au sein de l'entreprise. Devenu en quelque sorte gérant de son entreprise, le collectif des travailleurs est désormais associé à la prise de décision. Le principe de l'élection des responsables dans l'entreprise (jusque-là le directeur était nommé par le ministère de tutelle) a été introduit. L'assemblée des travailleurs délègue à un organe exécutif, une direction élue, la responsabilité des fonctions opératoires de gestion. Les diverses questions concernant l'élaboration de la stratégie et des plans de production, l'organisation interne de l'entreprise, les qualifications et les salaires, l'affectation entre les différents fonds de stimulation, l'émulation, les règles de sécurité, etc... sont du ressort d'un conseil économique élu (par l'assemblée générale), qui se réunit à intervalles réguliers.

La plupart des innovations introduites ont un caractère formel, elles ne remettent pas en cause la structure hiérarchique au sein de l'entreprise, n'apportent pas de remède décisif à l'absence de contre-pouvoir tant que Parti et syndicat conservent leurs rôles traditionnels, tout particulièrement celui de sélectionner les candidats aux fonctions de responsabilité. La participation des travailleurs à la gestion reste encore bien timide et formelle, et laisse en suspens des questions qui ne manqueront pas de se poser avec plus d'acuité lorsqu'une logique d'économie de marché se dessinera plus clairement.

La réforme semble particulièrement tâtonner dans le domaine de la rémunération du travail. Pour contrer la démotivation du travail, stimuler la productivité, il est admis que la rémunération dépende de la quantité, et plus encore de la qualité, du travail fourni. Elaborée en 1988, une nouvelle grille de salaires comportant trois catégories (ouvriers, spécialistes diplômés de l'enseignement supérieur, gestionnaires) et pour chacune d'entre elles trois niveaux de rémunération, devrait servir de base pour la fixation des salaires, les primes restant liées aux performances réalisées.

Trois ans après son lancement, la réforme n'a pas encore fait sentir ses effets bénéfiques. Certains défauts de l'ancien système de gestion n'ont pas disparu et bloquent la logique du processus de restructuration.

– Les "Associations" n'ont pas modifié leurs fonctions en conformité avec l'esprit de la réforme. Elles interviennent comme des organes de direction administrative et restreignent de fait l'autonomie des entreprises adhérentes. Elles continuent à leur affecter les commandes d'Etat, à déterminer les normes pour l'établissement du fonds de salaires, par exemple.

– Les commandes d'Etat perpétuent l'existence des indices obligatoires, et maintiennent un régime de planification centralisée dominant.

– L'incomplète réforme des prix engendre une incohérence certaine qui perturbe l'équilibre financier des entreprises.

– Il apparaît douteux que les prélèvements sur les ressources mises à la disposition de l'entreprise (taxes sur les facteurs de production) remplissent une fonction régulatrice.

– D'une manière générale la réforme n'a pas réussi à entamer le caractère monopoliste de l'économie.

C'est l'une des originalités de la réforme bulgare d'avoir tenté de coupler décentralisation administrative et restructuration économique.[17]

Les changements introduits en 1987 dans la structure administrative du territoire bulgare s'inscrivent dans un processus de refonte dont la première étape avait été engagée en 1979 avec le regroupement des anciennes unités administratives de base (au nombre de 1374) au sein de circonscriptions élargies, au nombre de 291, baptisées "systèmes de peuplement". Les responsables de la planification territoriale, chargés de l'élaboration du nouveau découpage, avaient cherché à établir les limites administratives sur des critères économiques, la "commune" (obchina) devant servir de cadre au développement d'un "système de peuplement", forme d'organisation territoriale, dotée d'une base économique propre. La réforme de 1979 reconnaissait aux organes locaux du pouvoir d'Etat des compétences élargies en matière de coordination et de gestion des activités économiques, sociales et culturelles, mais sans que soit modifié leur lien de subordination par rapport à l'échelon supérieur ("okrag" ou département). La suppression de cet échelon, son remplacement par une structure territoriale élargie ("oblast" ou région) et le renforcement simultané des compétences de l'échelon communal, constituent l'axe essentiel de la réforme effectuée à l'été 1987.

La réforme de l'administration territoriale se présente comme un transfert de haut en bas de la pyramide de certaines fonctions. La suppression de l'échelon intermédiaire doit permettre de fortifier la base, en laissant les communes exercer leurs nouveaux droits en matière d'autogestion.

Dans sa version bulgare, "l'autogestion" ne s'oppose pas au principe du centralisme démocratique, sur lequel reste fondé le système politique et social. Elle doit être entendue comme une déconcentration, un transfert de responsabilité, une nouvelle définition du rapport entre centralisation et décentralisation dans la gestion sociale. Cela se traduit par une limitation des indices fixés et des questions réglées par les organes centraux, et une délégation de compétences aux organes locaux, mieux à même de résoudre les affaires relatives à la production et à la satisfaction des besoins de la population.

Le règlement sur l'autogestion des commautés autogérées établit un nouveau partage des compétences entre les divers échelons territoriaux et définit les fonctions respectives des régions ("oblast") et des communes ("obchina").[18]

La région, "communauté autogérée de la population des communes", est en quelque sorte une association de communes dont les compétences se limitent à l'exercice de fonctions de coordination, de régulation de l'activité des communes. Elle a pour mission de transmettre la stratégie économique nationale et de veiller à l'exécution de la politique d'Etat. La commune reçoit une double définition, "unité administrative territoriale fondamentale", elle est une "communauté autogérée par la population". La formulation juridique exprime la nouvelle conception qui sous-tend l'autogestion, notamment la cession de l'exploitation de la propriété socialiste aux communautés.

"Le territoire des communes comprend les localités et leurs finages, les fonds productifs, les ouvrages d'ingéniérie technique, les équipements sociaux ainsi que la totalité du fonds d'urbanisme" (article 9/2/).

"La population est propriétaire du territoire de la commune et le sujet qui gère la propriété socialiste" (article 9/3/).

Les citoyens deviennent les gestionnaires de leur territoire. Notons toutefois que les articles suivants ne reprennent pas la population comme sujet, mais la commune, entité collective plutôt abstraite, administrée par son conseil. Le texte réglementaire accorde une place significative aux nouvelles formes de "démocratisation": organisation de sessions publiques du Conseil communal, participation des citoyens aux délibérations, consultations sous forme de référendums, ou dans le cadre d'assemblées générales.

Le pouvoir "délégué", exercé au nom du peuple, doit se muer en pouvoir par le peuple. Ces nouvelles dispositions qui, à l'évidence, ont valeur de propagande, cherchent à responsabiliser la population, mais ne lui donnent aucune garantie nouvelle pour contrôler le Conseil et exercer une influence réelle sur les affaires locales.

Si les droits du Conseil communal sont élargis, ses obligations et ses responsabilités aussi. L'administration locale est responsable de l'utilisation efficiente des ressources, garante du plein emploi, de l'approvisionnement alimentaire, de l'organisation des services à la population, de la construction des logements, de l'amélioration des infrastructures.

Une véritable autogestion locale implique l'application du principe de l'autofinancement. Le changement des règles du fonctionnement budgétaire doit permettre d'assurer des ressources nouvelles aux collectivités locales. C'est le rôle du système fiscal, mis en place par la réforme, d'alimenter les budgets de l'Etat et des collectivités locales. Les entreprises versent sous forme d'une taxe, établie selon des normes, une contribution au budget local.

Mais une complète autogestion suppose aussi une certaine capacité de la collectivité locale à promouvoir son propre développement en investissant dans la réalisation d'équipements ou le lancement d'activités nouvelles. Aux termes du "nouveau règlement sur l'activité économique" de janvier 1989, les communes ont désormais le droit de fonder des sociétés par actions dans les divers secteurs de l'activité économique, de manière à accroître les recettes communales et à assurer un meilleur approvisionnement en biens et en services à la population locale. Toutes les communes n'auront pas les forces matérielles et humaines pour développer cette nouvelle fonction entrepreneuriale, et l'on peut craindre une aggravation des déséquilibres territoriaux existants.[19]

IV. *L'Agriculture, l'exemple d'un secteur en pleine confusion*

Depuis deux décennies l'agriculture bulgare est en proie à de brutales et incessantes réorganisations de ses structures de gestion. Les dernières réformes ont achevé de semer la confusion et le désarroi parmi les responsables du secteur, de renforcer le scepticisme et la désillusion dans les rangs des travailleurs.

Les dirigeants bulgares n'ont évité aucun des excès des politiques d'intégration agro-industrielle communes à la plupart des pays de l'Est. Dans la décennie soixante-dix, le modèle industrialiste (fondé sur les principes de concentration et de spécialisation de la production) a été ici appliqué sans discernement et sans nuances. Nulle part ailleurs la concentration des structures foncières n'a atteint un tel niveau. Au début des années soixante-dix les "complexes agro-industriels", dont le sigle bulgare est A.P.K., ont pris la place des exploitations d'Etat et des coopératives de production existantes. Huit cents unités de production ont été regroupées au sein d'un petit nombre (143 en 1977) de complexes de très grandes dimensions (en moyenne 24500 hectares et 5500 travailleurs). La concentration horizontale a largement pris le pas sur l'intégration verticale. L'intention de spécialiser ces complexes est restée lettre morte et une minorité d'entre eux seulement comprenaient des unités de transformation agro-alimentaire.[20] Ces complexes géants, étendus sur le territoire de plusieurs villages, se sont révélés difficiles à gérer. Dès 1978 un processus de déconcentration était engagé de manière à ce que la superficie des complexes correspondît au territoire des unités administratives (ou "systèmes de peuplement") mises en place au même moment.[21] Aux unités géantes, organisées selon un principe sectoriel, font place des complexes deux fois moins étendus (au nombre de 292 en 1982), subdivisés en brigades à base territoriale. A partir de 1982, un nouveau type de brigade, dite "contractuelle" (dogovor), est expérimenté, qui tend à faire de ce collectif le niveau de gestion opérationnelle du travail. En 1987, l'adoption de la réforme mettant en place les "organisations économiques autogérées" a posé la question de savoir quelle place réserver aux "complexes"(A.P.K.) dans le nouvel organigramme des structures de gestion. Ils ont perdu leur statut d'entreprise pour se transformer en "Unions" de brigades, ces dernières devenant des "entreprises économiques autogérées" à part entière, auxquelles s'appliquaient les principes de l'autonomie comptable et de l'autofinancement. En tant que "collectifs de travail", les brigades sont devenues responsables de la gestion des terres et des moyens de production, qui leur ont été remis pour réaliser leur activité productive (en application de la décision de transférer aux collectifs les droits de gérer les entreprises, prise en avril 1987). Ces brigades fixent leurs objectifs de production, en tenant compte des indices de planification obligatoires,[22] déterminent leur activité de spécialisation. Elles peuvent contracter des emprunts auprès des organismes bancaires. En vertu du principe de l'intéressement matériel, les conseils de brigade ont le droit de moduler les salaires, établis selon les normes en usage, en fonction des résultats de chaque équipe de travailleurs.

Le "complexe agro-industriel" a été vidé de son contenu pour devenir une structure administrative aux fonctions mal définies : transmission des indices de planification, organisation des services à la production (agronomique, vétérinaire, etc...), diffusion de l'innovation et du progrès technique, auprès de ses adhérents.

Pour tenter d'apporter une solution aux graves problèmes de main-d'œuvre dont souffre l'agriculture,[23] les autorités bulgares ont généralisé un nouveau mode de gestion et de rémunération du travail sur une base contractuelle (système de l'"accord"). Ce système est fondé sur un contrat qui lie la rémunération finale du collectif de travail au résultat de la production. Cette formule du travail à forfait est appliquée à une grande variété de formes d'organisation du travail (sous unités de brigades, équipes ou groupes, familles, individus) selon les contraintes spécifiques à la nature de la production ou au type de l'opération.[24]

En septembre 1988, dans un memorandum adressé au Politburo,[25] T. Jivkov confirmait dans ses grandes lignes la réorganisation en cours dans l'agriculture. Il reprenait à son compte l'une des importantes innovations proposées par Gorbatchev en juillet 1988, à savoir la location à bail ("arenda") des terres, et évoquait la possibilité de l'étendre à diverses formes d'organisation du travail. Aucune mention n'était faite ni du contrat de travail à forfait, ni des lopins individuels. Encore obscure, la restructuration de ce secteur devait faire l'objet d'un plénum du C.C. du PCB.

Les derniers développements, véritables concessions à la "pereoustroistvo", sont intervenus en mai 1989 sous la forme d'un décret du Conseil des ministres sur "l'utilisation de la terre et la réalisation d'activités agricoles".[26] La confusion est cette fois-ci totale. Toute une série de dispositions sont prévues pour réinstituer des exploitations agricoles collectives, mais aussi pour créer de véritables exploitations agricoles individuelles exerçant une activité sur une terre en propriété, louée à ferme ou cédée, et utilisant des moyens de production (bâtiments, machines, équipements) qui peuvent appartenir en propre à l'exploitant. La nouvelle législation fait une place au système du contrat de travail, ainsi qu'au contrat de location. Il est trop tôt pour apprécier l'accueil réservé à ces nouvelles formes d'organisation du travail en agriculture, par les responsables des divers échelons administratifs, et par les travailleurs auxquels un nouveau champ d'initiative est offert. Notons toutefois que des compétences étendues en matière d'affectation des terres qui sont conférées à des Commissions, au niveau central, comme à l'échelon communal, permettront un contrôle de l'usage de la terre. Dans l'esprit des réformateurs, c'est une fraction résiduelle de la terre qui pourra faire l'objet d'une exploitation individuelle.

Ces réformes vont dans le sens d'une "décollectivisation" progressive de l'agriculture qui passe par une étape préalable de "décollectivisation" du travail et d'une partie des moyens de production, qui réinstaure une affectation territoriale du travail, sans jusqu'à présent se traduire par une "désocialisation" de la terre (c'est-à-dire sans remettre en question la propriété sociale de la terre).

V. *Dans l'attente de la transition*

Par rapport aux Etats voisins de l'Europe de l'Est, la Bulgarie apparaît en situation singulière. Non seulement la transition n'est pas amorcée, mais sa direction reste encore inconnue. Sans doute le limogeage de T. Jivkov, le 10 novembre 1989, a-t-il mis un terme aux formes d'autoritarisme les plus excessives, ainsi qu'à une "stagnation" économique prolongée sous couvert de parodie réformatrice. Mais les perspectives d'évolution demeurent très incertaines. Dans l'attente d'élections légitimatrices en mai 1990, la direction du Parti communiste bulgare, qui conserve le pouvoir bien en mains, s'est refusée à opter pour une stratégie de rupture avec le socialisme. Le nouveau chef du PCB, Petar Mladenov, a déclaré que la restructuration "*ne pouvait se réaliser, uniquement et exclusivement, que dans le cadre du socialisme, au nom du socialisme et sur la voie du socialisme".*[27] Son programme, tel qu'il ressort des orientations du XIVe Congrès du PCB, apparaît sur le plan politique pour le moins minimaliste (réforme des structures du Parti, renonciation au rôle dirigeant, acceptation du multipartisme), tandis que sur le plan économique, il adopte un profil bas, se bornant à annoncer un programme de stabilisation économique. Si "l'état des lieux" en Bulgarie n'est comparable ni à la vision d'apocalypse de la Roumanie, ni à la perte de substance de la R.D.A., il est suffisamment critique pour éviter tout atermoiement dans la mise en œuvre d'un projet cohérent de transition. Mais le rapport de forces entre les "conservateurs", dont les plus durs ont été écartés de la direction du Parti et du gouvernement,[28] et les réformistes, dont le retour au pouvoir est très partiel,[29] s'annonce indécis. Le réveil de la société civile est encore bien timide pour qu'une opposition embryonnaire et peu structurée puisse peser dans l'immédiat pour obtenir des changements radicaux.

Introduite à contrecœur, la restructuration bulgare apparaît, au terme de trois années d'expérimentation, mal engagée.

Réticent à l'égard de la réforme gorbatchevienne, T. Jivkov n'a jamais couru le risque de déplaire à la direction soviétique en s'y opposant de front. Mais avec l'appui des conservateurs, il a tenu à garder le processus de la restructuration sous son contrôle. D'une part en conservant la haute main sur la désignation des responsables aux postes-clés (la promotion de Stoïan Ovcharov au ministère de l'Economie et de la Planification, en août 1987, par exemple), l'éviction des réformateurs les plus acquis au changement (Tchoudomir Alexandrov en juillet 1988), ainsi que sur la redistribution des positions au sein de l'appareil de niveau intermédiaire. D'autre part, en pratiquant des réformes en trompe-l'œil, annoncées à grand renfort de documents et de projets ambitieux, dont la mise en œuvre se trouvait systématiquement retardée, ou privée de signification par l'adoption de mesures transitoires aux effets contradictoires.

Mais surtout l'esprit de la perestroïka est resté strictement cantonné à la sphère économique, l'ouverture de la vie politique et culturelle se réduisant à une caricature de "démocratisation" sans aucune "transparence". Ce freinage des réformes laisse la Bulgarie mal préparée pour affronter une transition qui s'avère inéluctable dès lors que les partenaires traditionnels et le principal d'entre eux, l'Union soviétique, s'y sont engagés.

On se bornera à évoquer un seul exemple de retard pris par la Bulgarie, et qui peut se révéler bientôt comme une contrainte, la très faible diversification des formes de propriété. La plupart des dispositions réformatrices qui auraient pu hâter des réajustements dans le sens d'une pluralité sont restées sans effet. En Bulgarie, la propriété d'Etat règne sans partage. Presque toutes les activités de l'industrie, de la construction, des transports, du commerce et des services relèvent du secteur d'Etat. Les formes de propriété collective sont faiblement représentées, notamment les coopératives qui ont fait les frais d'une approche particulièrement dogmatique. Il en a été ainsi des coopératives de production agricole que l'on cherche aujourd'hui à rétablir après un processus d'étatisation forcené.

Certains économistes se prononcent en faveur du développement de la forme coopérative dans laquelle ils voient un support approprié au développement des petites et moyennes entreprises, une catégorie qui fait gravement défaut à un appareil industriel bulgare très fortement concentré. Or ces dernières années, le mouvement en faveur de la création de petites et moyennes entreprises n'a pas emprunté cette voie. On s'est borné à expérimenter de nouvelles formes de gestion au sein du secteur d'Etat, simples divisions semi-autonomes formellement détachées des grandes entreprises, le plus souvent pour saisir l'opportunité d'un environnement régulateur favorable.[30] Le secteur privé joue encore un rôle négligeable, représentant à peine 6 % du produit social global, principalement dans l'agriculture et les services. Jusqu'à l'adoption du décret de janvier 1989, la législation interdisait le recours au travail salarié. Depuis cette date, des "firmes de citoyens" peuvent être librement créées et embaucher jusqu'à dix personnes. La Bulgarie n'a rien connu de comparable au mouvement de relance de l'initiative privée en Hongrie, en Pologne, ou même en R.D.A.. Il est significatif que les premières tentatives pour mettre aux enchères la gérance-location de fonds de commerce ou de services par des entrepreneurs privés, aient échoué en décembre 1987.[31] En dépit des possibilités offertes par le nouveau système de petites entreprises "semi-privées", les conditions se révélèrent trop contraignantes et fiscalement peu attrayantes. Le développement embryonnaire du secteur privé peut freiner le passage à une économie de marché, faute d'un groupe de petits entrepreneurs individuels en mesure de mobiliser des capitaux, un savoir-faire, voire une expérience entrepreneuriale. A la différence de la Hongrie ou de la Pologne, la "seconde économie" est trop faiblement structurée pour constituer une pépinière d'entrepreneurs privés.

Une deuxième série de contraintes hypothèque la restructuration de l'économie bulgare. Elles ont trait au ralentissement de la croissance, à l'aggravation du déséquilibre des échanges, à la progression de l'endettement. L'image officielle d'une économie dynamique n'est plus qu'un mythe à ranger au magasin des accessoires inutiles. Depuis quelques années, les observateurs[32] avaient noté une distorsion accrue entre les indicateurs de la croissance économique, exprimés en termes monétaires, qui révélaient une progression, et les résultats de production en quantités physiques qui ne cessaient de se dégrader dans des secteurs aussi importants que la production agricole, le charbon, l'acier, le ciment, les chariots à moteur, les autobus, les moissonneuses-batteuses, etc... Ce recul n'est-il pas le signe même de l'échec du nouveau mécanisme économique à stimuler efficacité et productivité ?

La détérioration des échanges extérieurs est une autre preuve du manque de compétitivité de l'économie bulgare. Principalement orientée vers les pays du C.A.E.M. et notamment l'URSS, avec laquelle elle réalise 57,3 % de ses importations et 61 % de ses exportations, l'économie bulgare enregistre un déficit croissant de ses échanges en devises fortes, avec les pays occidentaux. La réduction des achats de technologies occidentales permettrait de rétablir l'équilibre commercial, mais freinerait la modernisation d'un appareil de production en grande partie obsolète et faiblement compétitif.

L'évolution des divers ratios d'endettement atteste d'une dégradation continue dans ce domaine.[33] Avec un endettement supérieur à 7 milliards de dollars, la Bulgarie a atteint à la fin de 1988 un seuil critique, les réserves ne dépassant pas 1 milliard de dollars cette année-là. 45 % des gains commerciaux annuels en devises fortes étaient consacrés au service de la dette.[34] A cet état de fait inquiétant, il faut ajouter qu'il est douteux que la Bulgarie parvienne dans un proche futur à attirer des capitaux étrangers pour créer des sociétés mixtes.

Face à une situation économique désastreuse, le pouvoir politique, qui souffre d'une grave crise de légitimation, faute d'avoir réussi à former un gouvernement d'entente nationale, n'est pas en mesure d'adopter une stratégie claire pour hâter la transition qui s'impose.

Notes

1. Pour une analyse rétrospective des réformes économiques en Bulgarie, voir Vassil Vassilev, Crises et réformes économiques en Bulgarie. *Le Courrier des Pays de l'Est,* n° 269, janvier 1983, pp. 10-39
2. Discours de T. Jivkov au plénum du C.C. du PCB (28-29 juillet 1987). *Rabotnicesko Delo,* 29 juillet 1987. "CC Plenum Proposes Major Political Changes". *Radio Free Europe Research.* Bulgarian Situation Report/7-21 August 1987.
3. Tiraspolsky A, "Bulgarie 1986-1990: la perestroïka". *Le Courrier des Pays de l'Est* n° 316, mars 1987, pp.65-69.
4. "National Assembly approves further major Government changes". *RFER* Bulgarian SR/ 7-21 August 1987.
5. "Municipalities Proclaimed to be "self managing", *RFER* Bulgarian SR/7-21 August 1987.
6. "New Regional System introduced", "Problem and Controversies over the New Regional System", *RFER* Bulgarian SR/8-16 September 1987.
7. Ces difficultés semblent indiquées par le fait qu'un second décret ministériel ait dû être adopté en décembre 1987, après qu'un décret similaire ait été introduit en juillet. Cf. *Darzhaven Vesnik,* n° 59, 31 juillet 1987, *Rabotnicesko Delo,* 19 décembre 1987.
8. "A big stride or a small step in Economic Reform?" *RFER* Bulgarian SR/1-18 January 1988.
9. Les réformes économiques en Bulgarie. Note du Conseiller Economique et Commercial, n° 09/88, Ambassade de France en Bulgarie.
10. "The National Party Conference: some themes from the first day", "The National Party Conference. An extravagant anticlimax?" *RFER* Bulgarian SR/2-11 February 1988.
11. "A New Deal in Economic Restructuring", *RFER* Bulgarian SR/1-3 February 1989.
12. Décret n° 56 de janvier 1989 sur "l'Activité économique" (*J.O.* du 9 janvier 1989). Arrêté n° 2 du 15 février 1989 "Règlement d'application du décret sur l'Activité économique".
13. "Toward genuine Economic Reform or mock Perestroika? *RFER* Bulgarian SR/8-1 September 1989.
14. Pour une présentation des principes de la réforme économique bulgare, voir Angelov I. Framework of the Bulgarian economic reform, Chapter 1. pp. 13-19, ainsi que Stoilov S. Goals of Bulgarian macro-economic policy and means for their achievment, Chapter 3, pp.159-167, in *Economic Commission for Europe Economic Studies,* n° 1, 1989.
15. Données au 1er octobre, citées par *Le Monde,* 2 février 1990, p. 35.
16. Aroio Z., Role and Functioning of the enterprise. The enterprise in the people's Republic of Bulgaria, pp. 85-92, in *Economic Reforms in the European centrally planned Economies,* United Nations Economic Commission for Europe Economic Studies, n° 1, 1989.
17. Une analyse plus approfondie de cette réforme a été publiée par Maurel M-C. Un succédané de la perestroika: la nouvelle réforme territoriale en Bulgarie, in *Le Courrier des Pays de l'Est* n° 338, mars 1989. Pour une approche comparative des réformes administratives en Europe de l'Est, voir Maurel M-C., Administrative Reforms in Eastern Europe: an overview, Chapter 7, pp. 111-123, in *Territory an Administration in Europe* ed by Bennet R., Pinter Publishers, London and New York 1989.
18. "Vremenen Pravilnik za samoupravlenieto territorialnite obchanosti". Conseil des ministres, Sofia, 18 décembre 1987.
19. Grigorov N., Régions et pouvoirs régionaux en République populaire de Bulgarie, pp.37-41, in *Radvany J. et Rey V. (sous la direction de), Régions et pouvoirs régionaux en Europe de l'Est et en URSS,* Masson, Paris, 1989.
20. 60 "complexes agro-industriels" sur 297 intègrent des unités de transformation agro-alimentaire, 17% de l'ensemble de leurs activités est de nature industrielle. Les complexes scientifiques et industriels associant instituts de recherche, combinats agro-alimentaires et filiales agricoles, tel celui de Plovdiv (30 000 hectares et 15 000 travailleurs) sont des exceptions.
21. Maurel M-C, Rey V., Volle J-P, Planification et gestion du territoire en Bulgarie: la réforme des systèmes de peuplement, pp. 40-44, in *Le Courrier des Pays de l'Est,* n° 269, janvier 1983.
22. Ils concernent les 4 productions dont le rôle est déterminant: lait, viande, céréales, betteraves à sucre.

23. Il s'agit du manque de travailleurs résultant d'un exode rural prolongé, et qui se révèle particulièrement critique au moment des récoltes, d'où l'appel aux écoliers, étudiants et ouvriers citadins. La faible qualification d'une main-d'œuvre vieillissante, féminisée, l'absence de motivation rendent compte de la médiocre productivité du travail agricole.
24. Dans le complexe agro-industriel de Veliko Tarnovo, le système de l'"accord" fonctionne à l'échelle des équipes, des individus (cultures de tomates, élevage bovin). Le système de l'"accord" est également appliqué aux travailleurs saisonniers lors des vendanges (complexe viti-vinicole de Ljaskovets, ou de la cueillette des cerises (Veliko Tarnovo). Observations recueillies lors d'une mission d'étude, effectuée en juin 1988, dans le cadre des conventions d'échanges entre le CNRS et l'Académie des Sciences de Bulgarie.
25. Publié le 28 septembre 1988 par le Rabotnicesko Delo, et analysé in "Agriculture to be reorganized again and land leased privately". *RFER* Bulgarian SR/11-15 novembre 1989.
26. Décret n° 922 du 19 mai 1989.
27. Discours d'ouverture prononcé par Petar Mladenov au plénum du CC du PCB le 10 novembre 1989. *Le Monde,* 12-13 novembre 1989.
28. Lors du remaniement du Bureau politique, le 8 décembre 1989, plusieurs partisans de T. Jivkov ont perdu leurs fonctions: Yordan Yotov, Pentcho Koubadinski, Ivan Panev, Natcho Papazov. Le changement le plus significatif réside dans le départ du premier ministre Gueorgui Atanassov et son remplacement par Andreï Loukanov, considéré comme le chef de file des réformateurs, dans les premiers jours de février 1990.
29. Cependant, dès le 9 février, trois réformistes récemment élus ont quitté la direction du PCB. Voir *Le Monde,* 8 décembre 1989, 3 février 1990, 11 février 1990.
30. Voir l'étude de McIntyre R.J.. The small enterprise and agricultural initiatives in Bulgaria: institutional invention without Reform, in *Soviet Studies,* vol XL. n° 4, October 1988, 602-615, et le commentaire de Wyzan M.L. The small enterprise and agricultural initiatives in Bulgaria: a comment on Robert J. McIntyre, in *Soviet Studies,* n° 4, October 1989.
31. "Why the Auctioning of semiprivate Business failed", *RFER* Bulgarian SR/2-11 February 1988.
32. Tiraspolsky A. La Bulgarie en 1987: une croissance en trompe-l'œil. *Le Courrier des Pays de l'Est,* n° 329, mai 1988, pp. 51-55. La Bulgarie en 1988 : croissance douteuse et réforme sans glasnost. *Le Courrier des Pays de l'Est* n° 339, Avril 1989.
33. Voir l'étude de Broclawski J.P. L'endettement des pays de l'Est. *Le Courrier des Pays de l'Est* n° 341, juin- juillet 1989, pp. 33-43.
34. Tiraspolsky A. 1989. *Op.cit.*

Czechoslovakia: Current Issues

Franz-Lothar Altmann

Synopsis

The report of the Czechoslovak Federal Statistical Office (FSU) on social and economic development in 1989 was distinctly shorter than usual, and was to a great extent a "settling accounts" with deficiencies of past economic policy. In short it points to some major negative outcomes, e.g. the deterioration of the terms of trade by 30% between 1970 and 1989, the fact that in 1960 kilogram prices for Czechoslovak export products reached half the average world market prices, whereas in 1989 it was only one fourth, or the truth that almost one million persons had incomes of less than 1,000 Czechoslovak crowns per month, clearly below the social minimum.

Economic growth in 1989 stagnated, with only 1.7% nominal increase of gross national income. If one considers the quasi-official rate of inflation of 3-4% which was admitted by Prime Minister Čalfa (officially the cost of living index rose by only 1.8%), then economic growth was negative, and so was real income growth of the population.

Already the old government (Adamec) had foreseen major "restructurings" of the economic mechanism starting on 1 January 1990. This has been partly taken over by the new Čalfa government, as e.g. the banking reform, the new foreign currency law, and some price changes. However, the real fundamental changes will occur only when a number of law amendments (laws on state enterprises, cooperatives, joint-stock companies, private entrepreneurship, and on joint ventures) have passed parliament, planned for the second half of March 1990.

The Czechoslovak government will try to smooth the transition to a market economy, without accompanying inflation, by applying a strict anti-inflationary monetary policy: the amended budget for 1990 foresees even a surplus after reducing expenses for defence, state administration, and social organizations like the Communist Party. The government did not plan to cut all subsidies nor to free all prices at once, in order to avoid excessive negative impacts on employment and on the standard of living. However, the newly approved government (after the June elections) tends rather to follow an accelerated reform path with quick privatization and prices totally liberalized by 1 January 1991. There are still reserves in the Czechoslovak economy, and the economic pressure is by far not yet comparable with that of the neighbouring CMEA countries. But for how long?

I. *Economic Performance*

The annual report for 1989 economic development was shorter than usual and it contained no comparisons with plan figures nor with results in previous years. Among the reasons were the rather unfavourable performance in 1989 and the fact that statistics for previous years' developments are not reliable.

The main performance indicators include:
- Nominal gross national income: +1.7% (1988: +2.8%).
- Nominal monetary incomes of the population: +3.3%.
- Retail trade turnover, nominal: +3.7%.
- Retail prices: +1.4%; index of standard of living: +1.8%. The list of retail prices increased in 1989 indicates that these figures do not reflect real price hikes. Prime Minister Čalfa also admitted in February 1990 that inflation lay between 3 and 4%!

Therefore real economic growth was negative, and real incomes stagnated or even decreased. According to the Federal Statistical Office (FSÚ), 320,000 households with 908,000 persons (6% of the population) had monthly incomes of less than 1,000 crowns per head. This is at the border of social poverty (average monthly income in the state and cooperative sector in 1989: 3,218 crowns).

In the report there was also much more openness and criticism of the old system and its negative performance. Examples include:
- A statement that the ČSSR had lived on the account of future generations: the average age of machinery and equipment is 11 years with 57% of it totally written off.
- Industrial production increased in 1989 only by 0.9% and it fell in engineering, in particular in heavy engineering, the electrotechnical and chemical industries. This was partly due to a sharp drop in East European and Soviet demand for Czechoslovak investment goods and arms deliveries. Exports of the latter also decreased for the LDCs.
- Discussion began on the future of the nuclear power programme. In Témelin (South Bohemia, near the Austrian border) the construction of two of the planned four blocs (VVER 1000) was stopped in January 1990. It is not know whether it is a "thinking pause" of six months (as officially declared) or for good. In fact, Témelin is already delayed by 21 months due to financing difficulties and late investment deliveries (PM Čalfa in March 1990).
- In some important plants there were manpower problems after the Havel amnesty in January 1990 of prison inmates with working obligations (Škoda, Liaz, Zetor Brno, Preciosa Jablonec, Kladno mines). Of 11,000 prisoners only 1,700 remained in production work.
- Living conditions have clearly deteriorated: at the beginning of the 1960s Czechoslovakia was just behind the world leader, Sweden, in life expectancy: a gap of four years for men and 2.6 years for women. Today the gap is eight years for men and six years for women against number one Japan.

In general the low competitiveness of Czechoslovak products is criticised on account of their technical backwardness. The terms of trade deteriorated between 1970 and 1989 by 30 percentage points. Only vis-à-vis the USSR have they improved somewhat since 1986. In 1960 the per kilogram prices for Czech export products reached half of the world market average level: in 1989 this indicator had fallen to only one fourth.

Looking at present performance, we see that Czechoslovakia still has a very open economy. More than 35% of national income is related to foreign trade. After the introduction of a unified rate of exchange the former extremely high share of CMEA trade (almost 80% in the mid-1980s, due to an overrating of the transferable rouble) fell in 1989 to 69%. At the beginning of January 1990 a further devaluation of the crown against hard currencies (by 18.6%) was carried out and a revaluation vis-à-vis the transferable rouble (Trb). The share of CMEA trade is estimated now, for entire 1990, to reach only 54%!

In 1989 foreign trade increased only by 2%, as CMEA trade decreased by 2.2% (EX -4.7%; IM +0.4%) (USSR trade: -5.2%, share 30%). Trade with the West increased by 9.8% (EX +13.6%; IM +6.1%), and the FRG became Czechoslovakia's second most important trade partner. The unfavourable commodity structure in trade with the West (i.e. in exports) continues with engineering products having just a 13% share, consumer goods (industrial) a 20% share, food products a 7% share, but raw materials and semi-finished products accounting for 60%!

Gross indebtedness in hard currencies reached $7.4 billion at the end of November 1989. Assets are estimated at $1.5 billion but these are considered partly irretrievable (LDCs).

Assets with the socialist countries amount to 43.5 billion crowns (approximately 4.4 billion Trb.)

A short term deterioration may result from changes in the accounting system within the CMEA, as trade is changed from Trb to hard currency at world market prices. This may result in higher prices for Soviet raw materials and lower prices or falling demand for Czech machinery.

There have been some cuts in Soviet oil deliveries already due to "technical problems": in January 1990 -20%!

Czechoslovakia plans a step-by-step reduction of trade in arms and weapons: the ČSSR was the seventh largest arms exporter in the world in 1989.

In the medium and long term, like other reforming and democratizing East European countries, Czechoslovakia plans a reorientation towards the Western trade area. Czechoslovakia has applied for membership in the IMF and World Bank (15 January 1990) and has declared its desire to join the EC as a full member after first becoming an associated member. The government has already passed a resolution to drop Czechoslovak norms and technical specifications and to turn to the application of EC norms and directives.

II. *Economic Reform*

Since 1978 there have been recurring attempts to "improve" or "reconstruct" the centrally administered system of a planned economy. In mid-1987 a new round of "restructuring of the economic mechanism" started:

1988 through 1990 was seen as a preparation period with 1 January 1991 as the date for putting into force the new regulations. This date was advanced by one year already by Prime Minister Adamec, not because progress of restructuring was faster than expected, but because accomplishment was retarded and diluted by administration and party bureaucracy. They pretended that restructuring was successful, citing democratization in the enterprises, dissolution of the associations, reorganization and relative reduction of the ministry apparatus. The retardation was facilitated by the relative stability of the economy. Over the years functional adjustments and gradual abolishment of the greatest absurdities of the original aggressive planning system, and a changeover to defensive planning took place. The clear power position of the central planning bureaucracy was replaced gradually by a complicatedly structured coalition of interests of enterprises, middle management, ministries, state planning commission, and other central organs. In the end the powerful state enterprises dominated in this coalition, due to their information monopoly.

A major real reform step was the transition to a *two-level banking system* on 1 January 1990. The Czech State Bank was relieved of its commercial functions and reduced to a central (issuing) bank. The following new banks were set up:

– Bank of Commerce (Prague), (Komerčnú banka).
– General Credit Bank (Bratislava), (Všeobečná úvěrová banka).
– Investment Bank (Investičnú banka).
– Czechoslovak Trading Bank (Cz. obchodnú banka).
– Entrepreneurial Bank (Živnostenská banka).
– Czech and Slovak State Savings Banks (Česká a Slovenská státni spořitelna).

New banks and savings banks may be generated as joint-stock companies, cooperatives or joint ventures with foreign participation. In principle banks should operate universally, but a specialized bank for agriculture, Agrobank, has already been founded as the first non-state bank in Czechoslovakia since World War II. A share of 30% foreign capital is expected, probably from the Austrian Crédit Agricole, (Österreichische Raiffeisenbank e.a.). Furthermore, foreign banks may now open representations in Czechoslovakia.

Step-by-step *wholesale prices* have been already changed (mainly raised) in previous years. A new round of wholesale price increases was launched in January 1990, but still retail prices have remained relatively untouched. Since the beginning of 1989 *unified rates of exchange* for commercial transactions have existed, replacing the former system of diversified coefficients. After the devaluation on 8 January 1990 against Western currencies and the revaluation against Eastern currencies, the difference between Rb/Kčs and US $/Kčs is substantial. At present one Rb equals 10 Kčs, and one US $ equals 17 Kčs (the official tourist rate of exchange is 1 US $ = 36 Kčs, i.e. rather close to the black market rate). In July 1989 the first hard currency auction took place. Enterprises can trade once per month at prices several times higher than the official ones. At the beginning of this year *12 new foreign trade stockholding companies* were founded. These are – in contrast to the already existing 12 FT stockholding companies – responsible only to their stockholders (i.e. production enterprises).

In January 1990 an Economic Council was established in the Federal Government, headed directly by the then Deputy Prime Minister Komárek. There were five working groups to amend or draft legislation on:

- state enterprises
- cooperatives
- stockholding companies
- private entrepreneurship
- economic cooperation with foreign countries.

Certain draft laws have been forwarded to parliament after approval by the Council of Ministers. (Note: the draft laws listed below were expected to pass parliament by the end of March 1990, to come into force 1 April. In fact it took until mid-April before the parliament passed several laws).

The *draft law on state enterprises,* compared wth the previous (1988) one, was one-half shorter, included the principle of self-financing, there is no reference to the state plan and workers' pure self-administration is dead, but participation will be secured. State enterprises may be founded by a central state organ (e.g. ministry) or a (local) national committee. In principle foreign trade activities are permitted. Three types of state enterprises were foreseen:

- state enterprises with management participation of the founder
- state enterprises for public services
- state enterprises with self-administration (more rights for the enterprise council, but still direct surveillance by the founder). This type was expunged by the parliament.

Depending on the type, the management should consist of the enterprise council and the board of directors (1st type) or the director. Until the end of 1990 the founders can merge their enterprise with others, and they can also split it up or even liquidate it. As V. Klaus stated, there will be no state guarantee for survival of enterprises (20 March 1990). The main goal is demonopolization of Czech industry by the end of 1990.

The *draft law on stockholding companies* (corporations), resembles the West German and Austrian legislation:

- founders can be corporate (including the state) or natural (single) persons
- shares may be registered or bearer shares, preference shares and employee shares are as well possible as convertible bonds
- corporations with foreign majority are not allowed to purchase majority shares in other stockholding companies in Czechoslovakia (in order to protect them from foreign holding companies).

The *law on private entrepreneurship* (in force since May 1, 1990) provides for no limitations on the number of employees or on acquisition of property for production purposes. There are no duties vis-à-vis the state plan, but the obligation to maintain correct accountability is included. Earned foreign currency can be put into currency accounts (according to the new foreign currency law) and/or used for purchases abroad. Twelve activities are exempt as state monopolies (e.g. production of alcohol and cigarettes) or where specific legislation is in preparation (lawyers, health services, etc.).

The *law on joint ventures* (1 January 1989) already allowed foreign capital majority and currency retransfers. Amendments being prepared will improve conditions, as e.g. tax exemptions. Profits earned in domestic currency (Kčs) may be traded at currency auctions into hard currency in order to be then transferred.

III. *Actual Economic Policy Measures*

Price policy so far (i.e. until April 1990) consisted mainly of changes (increases) in wholesale prices, in order to force enterprises to use raw materials and energy more economically. In order to avoid rapid inflation and unemployment, a cautious dismantling of subsidies had been planned before total liberalization of retail prices took place. However, on 29 March 1990, the Czech Ministry of Agriculture already announced freeing of prices for food products in three rather quick steps: 1 June 1990, 1 October 1990, and 1 January 1991.

Fiscal policy of the new government consists mainly of a revision of the state budget for 1990: instead of 10 billion Kčs deficit now there is to be five billion Kčs surplus!

Regarding the CMEA trade-accounting system, on 22 March 1990 the Minister of Finance announced Czechoslovakia's withdrawal from the system of mutual currency agreements.

IV. *Assessment*

In spring 1990 intensive discussions were under way in Prague concerning further proceedings. The principle options were either a shock therapy (V. Klaus) or a softer, socially protected reform (Komárek). Still Czechoslovakia has more economic reserves than the other CMEA countries (GDR included), and therefore the immediate pressure is not yet comparable with the situation in neighbouring countries.

In the meantime the group of radical reformers was reappointed to the government after the first free elections of 8 and 9 June, 1990. Komárek has left the government and Klaus and Dlouhy are trying to speed up the reform process. The parliament will have to pass a number of new economic laws, since many of those passed by the interim parliament in the spring of 1990 were in fact only provisional.

The two major issues at the moment are privatization and price liberalization. The government will attempt to break up huge state enterprises into smaller companies. Some will remain in state ownership, as e.g. electricity, telecommunication, steel works and the weapons industry, others shall be transformed into joint stock companies until the end of 1990. It is still a major point of discussion, how these joint stock companies then shall be privatized, i.e. sold to private persons.

Concerning wholesale and retail prices the principle policy of the government has changed completely. The new time schedule foresees now the full liberalization of all prices already by 1 January 1991. The first major step already happened on 7 July 1990, mainly for food, the next will come on 1 October 1990. A so-called internal convertibility of the domestic currency, the crown, is planned for the beginning of 1991 which means that enterprises but not private persons will then be able to purchase foreign currency for their import requirements at the banks.

Among the approximately 240 new laws the new (two years) parliament is scheduled to approve altogether, the most difficult task will be the preparation of a new constitution for the now ČSFR. In particular the two republics demand much more economic and political independence. Whether this claim will ease or rather complicate the implementation of the next major reform steps remains an open question.

GDR: Current Issues *

Doris Cornelsen

Synopsis

About a year ago, the following topic was planned for this paper: "GDR: An Orthodox But Still Working Model". At that time, the GDR was virtually in last place among the countries of Eastern Europe in attempts to reform basic systems. Now it has overtaken this group: a rapid transition to a market economy is agreed, currency union, social union and economic union with the Federal Republic of Germany are all within reach.

This development has happened very quickly, though clear stages can still be recognised. After the political "turning point" and the fall of the Wall on 9th November 1989, it was the goal of all groups in politics and economics to renew socialism and develop an efficient combination of plan and market. Not long after this, the conviction that high economic efficiency can only be achieved in a market economy gained acceptance. Models like the "Socialist Market Economy" or "Market-Oriented Planned Economy" were rejected. At this stage, however, discussion still centred on a cautious transition accompanied by supporting measures. The final stage of this process was then the demand for economic unification with the Federal Republic of Germany.

I. *Currency Union*

In February 1990, the Federal Government decided to offer the GDR currency union, i.e. replacement of the East German Mark with the D-Mark. The assessment of the prospects for currency union is disputed among economists. Another model for the transition to a market economy meets with great approval, even now: the model based on independent development in the GDR, with a separate currency and an exchange rate with a tendency to slightly undervalue the East German Mark. This model is supported by the evidence from foreign trade theory that a catching-up process is easier if exports are stimulated by devaluation. Although this position has now been overtaken by political decisions, its misgivings should be taken seriously.

Those in favour of currency union essentially use three arguments:

1. Currency union will force a change in the economic system. The difficulties with reforms in the other countries of Eastern Europe can largely be attributed to the hesitancy and half-heartedness of those reforms. In the GDR, monetary unity will require quick and radical reforms.
2. Currency union and reforms will give Western firms the security they need. It will be more likely that the numerous cooperation projects and

joint ventures now under consideration will be converted into action.

3. The decisive argument is the psychological effect of monetary unity. The D-mark is a symbol of success for most citizens of the GDR. Therefore, the introduction of the D-mark will bring a high degree of motivation with it.

The state treaty has now fixed the rules for the exchange rate D-Mark: Mark DDR, coming into effect on the 1st of July:

1. Wages will be changed with the rate 1:1. This can certainly be only a guideline for a very short time. After this the level and structure of incomes will depend on the situation of the economy and the negotiations to come. In the beginning the situation of the workers in the GDR will depend on the development of prices. Prices of basic goods will increase, because they are heavily subsidised and the subsidies will be deleted. Some industrial goods are heavily taxed, the prices will decrease after their deletion. All together, the typical GDR "shopping basket" will be more expensive in the future. This is true especially for lower income groups.
2. The savings accounts (160 billion Mark end of 1989) will be changed differently. The rate 1:1 is applied only to a part of it (2,000 Mark for children up to 14 years old, 4,000 Mark for adults up to 59 years old, 6,000 Mark for older people). The remaining accounts will be converted by thc rate 2:1.
3. The debts (260 billion Mark) and the assets (60 billion Mark) of the firms will be converted 2:1.

The risks involved with monetary unity should not be ignored. After currency union, the firms of the GDR will be confronted with the competition of Western markets immediately and without a transition period, not only in the area of exports, but also on the domestic market. So efficiency and competitiveness are crucial points in the whole context. A precise assessment is almost impossible: today you can find many pessimistic and some optimistic statements.

II. *Statistics*

There is still no new Statistical Yearbook for the GDR; all reviews arc still dependent on the data published before the "turning point".

Statistics from the GDR have frequently been received with great reservation hitherto. The published statistics of the GDR were extremely meagre. A great deal of data, generally taken for granted, was missing, such as data on the interdependence of foreign trade. Other series were not very informative, because they were limited to quotas or indexes. A large amount of information was withheld for political reasons, but broader statistical reporting is now in preparation, and many series of statistics which were once kept secret are already accessible.

A number of puzzles concerning the reliability of statistics have been solved. GDR researchers in the West were always convinced that the State Central Administration for Statistics (now the Statistical Office of the GDR) was not consciously distorting or manipulating the figures. Statisticians in the GDR have now confirmed this assessment. There is also new information on the reliability of the primary statistical material. The statistical reports by firms in the GDR were identical to their target fulfilment reports. Therefore, it was not out of the question that systematic faults were included in the primary material. The Statistical Office now attaches great importance to the ascertainment that its control bodies and check calculations, as well as the very high penalties imposed when false statements were discovered, were a sure remedy for such distortions.

The situation is different in the case of price adjustment, in particular with regard to the methodically difficult problem of dealing with new products. The State Central Administration never kept its own price statistics, but relied on the information provided by firms. Prices for new or further developed products were probably entered too high in the real series. This effect was compounded by the fact that firms were required to realise a prescribed quota of new products per year. These plan indicators were generally fulfilled, with the price increases possible for "new products" being exploited in many cases, even though this was not justified by either the degree of novelty or improvement in quality of the products. The real growth shown by the statistics was therefore exaggerated by an unknown percentage, particularly in recent years. The Statistical Office has now admitted these systematic errors, and systematic price monitoring is planned.

Nor has the problem of the comparability of the statistics been eliminated. Comparability is now to be established in terms of the definitions, terms and demarcations used, even for the past. The overall national accounts, for example, are going over to the concept customary in the West, the System of National Accounts (SNA), and the first results are available. The system used in the West is also to be adopted in industrial reporting. More serious is the problem of appraisal. The East German Mark is a purely internal currency, there is no economically based exchange rate, prices are set autonomously. This makes it impossible to compare statistical values expressed in East German Marks internationally. This problem is what makes appraisal of the international competitiveness of the GDR so difficult.

III. *Outlines*

A number of problems relating to basic structures could already be recognised using the overall national accounts published previously. Thus we discussed the problem of the falling investment ratio in this forum in 1986. The detailed information now available illustrates developments since the start of the 1970s even more clearly (Table I).

1. Macroeconomic growth has declined in stages.
2. In the 1970s there was a balance in the growth in produced national income and in used national income. Domestic use exceeded domestic production (both at 1985 prices) considerably, however, resulting in substantial deficits in foreign trade. After the strong-man act aimed at reducing the deficit in the 1980s, the national income used stagnated for a few years.

3. The ratio between accumulation (investments) and consumption has been shifting systematically since 1971 at the expense of investments.
4. Growth in the area of consumption was led by state consumption. Private consumption also rose, though this was a very contradictory process. Subsidies on basic needs increased to an exceptional extent (Table II); the supply of higher value goods became short. The decision to raise the standard of living of the population ("main task") taken at the 8th Party Congress of the SED (Socialist Unity Party of Germany) in 1971 was a failure in practical terms: it proved to be a burden on investment, caused high state expenditure on subsidies and, in view of changing needs and the short supply of higher value products, generated no motivation in the population.
5. Falling investment affected investments in the productive sector in particular. Investments in the "non-productive sector", on the other hand, rose in both absolute and relative terms. Housing, in particular, was promoted, but other important areas, such as health, education and tourism, were very much neglected.

This shows that many of the structural problems now faced by the GDR have their origins in the proportions laid down by economic policy since the early 1970s.

IV. *Population, Employment and Earnings*

At the end of 1989, the GDR had a population of 16.4 million. Losses resulting from emigration in the period 1984-1988 were about 150,000. A further 350,000 emigrants left in 1989. There have been about 175,000 emigrants in the first four months of 1990.

The age structure in the GDR is similar to that in the Federal Republic of Germany. The higher proportion of the population in infancy in the GDR is striking, however. The GDR has succeeded in increasing the birth rate by means of measures aimed at promoting parenthood.

Participation in employment in the GDR is very high by international standards. In terms of the population of working age (men: 15 to under 65; women: 15 to under 60), 81% of women and 85% of men were gainfully employed in 1988. The workforce has a high level of qualifications, with three quarters having completed vocational training, while nearly 20% are graduates of universities or technical schools (Table III).

The high proportion of women in employment in the GDR has been promoted systematically, including by means of training and a whole range of socio-political measures. The arrangements for women with children are generous and include paid release from work after the birth of a child, shorter working hours and longer holidays for mothers, release from work to care for sick children and an extensive network of creches and day nurseries. Women in the GDR are already very worried about whether they will still be able to cope with family and career after the "turning point".

Centrally controlled planning with all its weaknesses, however, is visible in both the employment structure and the economic structure of the GDR. Security of supply always takes priority. With the restrictions imposed by lack of Western currency and the high level of integration in CMEA with its largely less efficient partners, structural policy intent on autarky was followed from the outset. This led to a large number of what have become antiquated, environmentally damaging and inefficient production centres. There has been far too little structural change. This applies to the broad introduction of modern technologies, the expansion of services and an efficient supply industry.

In 1989, 36% of employees worked in industry, a proportion which has not changed for years. The GDR has not, therefore, experienced the shift from industry to services typical of Western nations. Even the agricultural sector, with around 10% of all employees, still accounts for what is, in international terms, a very high proportion of the volume of work. The whole area of services, on the other hand, is underdeveloped (Table IV). The so-called production-oriented services were largely undertaken by the industrial collectiveness in the manner of do-it-yourself operations, frequently with an unconvincing degree of success. The GDR is now faced with the necessity of catching up on structural changes, shutting down antiquated and inefficient production and developing new production.

Income levels are an important point with regard to present and future competitiveness. The mean gross income per month was around 1,100 Marks in 1988, compared with 3,100 DM in the Federal Republic of Germany. This level of only a third still applies. The gap for net income is smaller, as the burden of taxes and social security contributions is much smaller in the GDR than in the Federal Republic of Germany. Employees in the GDR earned around 940 Marks net a month in 1988, just less than half net incomes in the Federal Republic (2,100 DM). One special feature in the GDR is the comparatively small margin between top and bottom incomes. Master craftsmen and engineers earn little more, and in many cases even less, than workers. Incomes for wage-earners and salaried staff in full-time employment fall between the minimum gross wage of 400 Marks and the salaries of the general managers of large cooperatives of around 3,500 Marks a month. Bonuses were also distributed evenly. Greater output does not pay, with all negative consequences for motivation which that entails.

The incomes of pensioners generally only provide minimum security. The mean pension has been 447 Marks a month since December 1989.

V. *Fixed Assets*

The fixed assets of the East German economy were worth a total of 1,700 billion Marks in 1988 according to statistics, or around 180,000 Marks per employee. These statistics are taken from company records and are based on gross values at 1986 prices. This information is difficult to assess. On the one hand, some licence in the valuation is not out of the question, while, on the other hand, it is questionable how the assets would have to be valued in other currencies. It is certain that many of them are in poor condition. It was often not possible to scrap old plant because replacements had not been approved. More recent information from the

Statistical Office of the GDR also shows the net value of fixed assets and, calculated from those figures, what is called the degree of wear of fixed assets (gross value less net value divided by gross value). This produced the following data for industry under central control in 1988:

	Total fixed assets	*Equipment*
Gross value	662.5 billion M	412.4 billion M
Net value	355.1 billion M	190.5 billion M
Degree of wear	46.4%	53.8%
ditto 1973	41.7%	47.1%

According to the GDR, the degree of wear for equipment internationally – for a similar equipment structure – is about 45%. In 1989, about 20% of all equipment in the productive sector of the East German economy was already completely written off. In 1980, this figure was only 14%. Many industries have to make do with plant which has been in service for more than 20 years and has far exceeded its normal service life. The stock of equipment overall is marked by "polarisation". Old, worn-out equipment stands side by side with new, up-to-date equipment, so the production process is frequently limited by the poorer efficiency of the old machinery.

The cost of maintaining antiquated plant is considerable. It stood at around 38 billion Marks for the national economy in 1988, making it higher than depreciations. Maintenance also ties up a large number of workers. In the area covered by the industry ministries around 280,000 workers, or around 17% of all production workers, were employed on maintenance in 1989.

The infrastructure is also in poor condition. The transport network of the GDR does not satisfy the demands now made on it by the population and the economy. The low investment activity experienced since the beginning of the 1970s in particular has made itself felt in this area. With a density of 12.9 km per 100 km, the railway network roughly corresponds to that in the Federal Republic, but only about one third has two or more tracks and only a quarter is electrified (FRG: a half and more than two fifths). For reasons of energy economy, the railways were declared the absolutely dominant traffic carrier in 1980. The services required, particularly in terms of domestic freight, revealed the poor condition of this traffic carrier: the tracks, points and substructure are in poor condition throughout much of the network, and the load-bearing capacity of many bridges is reduced. More than half the public road network in the GDR displays substantial damage.

The telephone network is a long way behind what the national economy requires in terms of scope and quality of service. Three quarters of local telephone switching technology is more than 30 years old, and virtually everything was installed more than 20 years ago.

VI. *Productivity*

Technological backwardness and antiquation of production plant are good reasons for the great extent to which the GDR lags behind the Federal Republic, for example, in terms of productivity. To this can be added the problems of poor work motivation. In an earlier study by the DIW (Information on the State of the Nation 1987), the disparity in pro ductivity compared with the Federal Republic of Germany was estimated at around 50% in 1983. The gap may well have widened since then. The GDR is now working on the basis of similar ratios. Blame is being apportioned in equal measure to backwardness in the organisation of production processes, backwardness in technology and backwardness in willingness to work. The organisational failings also include the ever desperate state of affairs with regard to supplies which has always prevented a continuous production cycle.

VII. *Competitiveness*

There is currently a great deal of speculation concerning the competitiveness of the GDR after the introduction of currency union. Calculations based on the ratios of productivity and income explained above give an unequivocal result: with a productivity level of 50% and income levels of 30% of those in the Federal Republic of Germany, the East German economy should on average be able to cope with conversion to the D-mark as its currency.

In contrast to these considerations, attention is frequently drawn to the high costs of production in the GDR, with what is called foreign exchange profitability being quoted as an indicator. This indicator specifies the domestic costs which have to be paid in the GDR in order to realise foreign currencies in foreign trade. Foreign exchange profitability has always been calculated in the GDR, but never published. It has now been made public, however. In 1989, in trade with the FRG, it is reported to be 3.70 Mark to realise 1 D-mark. But – facing the high burden of debt with Western banks – the GDR in the last years did not care for rentability but for liquidity in trade with Western countries. Therefore it is doubtful whether the foreign exchange profitability vis-à-vis Western countries is a reliable indicator. The ratio with socialist countries, for example, is much more favourable for the GDR.

Problems caused by costs being too high are also demonstrated by various calculations made by East German firms wanting to ascertain their financial status under the conditions of currency union. They derive their future profits from the fairly identifiable prices for their products in the Federal Republic, while trying to calculate their costs from existing structures.

Calculations of this sort are faced with extraordinary difficulties. The cost structure of East German firms is at present completely distorted for a number of reasons:

1. Prices for raw materials and primary products were laid down by the administration. The price structure of these materials does not agree

with the price structure on the world market. After currency union there should be adjustment to the ratios on the market of the Federal Republic in this respect, with there being price reductions in many cases.

2. Firms were forced to take on countless, mostly unproductive, "out-of-character" product lines in addition to their actual range. This was done under the motto of "own production of rationalisation resources" and "own production of structural supplies", i.e. firms should manufacture some of the investments and primary products they needed themselves. In addition to this, firms manufacturing capital goods were instructed to produce consumer goods (5% of their total production). This led to the proportion of "out-of-character" production generated by the manufacturers of capital goods reaching almost 30%, production that was often totally unprofitable.
3. Cost burdens were also generated by the social tasks to be observed by firms (e.g. day nurseries, holiday homes, sports clubs, employee welfare).
4. Finally, the burden of levies paid into state coffers is a vital point. The productive sector was the most important source of income for the state. The levy burden was made up as follows:

- Production fund levy, a sort of interest paid on capital, with a rate of 6% of gross fixed assets.
- Contribution to social funds, a sort of payroll tax, with a rate of 70% of total wages paid.
- Surrender of net profits with contributions fixed in absolute terms.
- Other different levies from the productive sector.

In 1988, these levies, which came almost exclusively from the productive sector, amounted to more than 200 billion Marks, or 76% of national revenue. Thus, the burden of cost taxation on firms in the GDR is much greater than in the Western countries.

The last point shows that an important step will have to be taken before, or at the same time as, monetary union: transition to another system of taxation. The system of cost-burdening levies used hitherto must be replaced by a system which is linked first and foremost to actual earnings and profits, and, in the case of value added tax, the net product of firms. Only on this basis will it be possible to create cost structures in the GDR which are comparable with those of Western countries.

VIII. *Structural Problems*

The GDR is faced with major structural changes whatever happens. The present employment structure and economic structure are the result of a policy of conservation: a modern structure will have to be developed in the future. With regard to employment, positive effects can be expected in the private sector, with there being more employees than at present in the service sector and trade, while the construction sector is also short-handed at the present time. There will be negative effects on employment in industry and agriculture.

In industry there are three groups of branches:

1. Branches which are competing with other low-wage-countries in the world: light industry, textiles, clothing. Here the competitivity is low and the reduction of labour force will be severe.
2. Branches which are competing with high wage countries: investment goods, machines, heavy machines. They have a big market share in the Soviet Union and some success in the OECD countries. There are some positive signs in these branches but a reduction of employment will be inevitable.
3. Branches producing for the internal markets. With low prices and low income the prospects can be positive.

In agriculture, the level of producers' prices has been very high hitherto; currency union and integration in the market of the Federal Republic and the EC will change that situation. Therefore, the cultivation of low-grade land, for example, will have to be greatly reduced, thereby liberating a large amount of labour.

The final estimate of unemployment depends on the attitude of observers, with present forecasts for the number of unemployment running between 500,000 and 3 million, the equivalent of unemployment rates of between 5 % and 32 %. My own forecast for possible unemployment in the short term is on the more optimistic side (in thousands):

Industry	−1,200
State, etc	−400
Agriculture	−300
Crafts, construction	+300
Trade, services	+600
Balance	−1,000

All observers agree, however, that unemployment in the GDR will only be a short-term problem, with a labour shortage being more likely in the medium-term. Providing adequate opportunities for retraining and obtaining qualifications will be a major task, however.

IX. *Some of the Costs of Restructuring*

The transition to a market economy and the introduction of currency union will entail substantial burdens for the GDR and the Federal Republic. The greatest of these will be the burden on people in the GDR, with a complete changeover to a new system and a high degree of adaptability and flexibility being required of them.

The burdens on the Federal Republic will largely be financial ones. The GDR cannot cope with the changes on its own and will require help from the Federal Republic, mainly in the form of private capital and cooperation projects at company level. Many East German firms will require private capital, together with know-how relating to the market economy and technology, if they are to develop further. It seems that a large number of initiatives have already been prepared in this area.

The starting point for public assistance will be the decision to harmonise the system of taxes and contributions with that of the Federal Republic as postulated above. This will not create a major problem for the social insurance budget. Calculations show that, with the contribution rates of the Federal Republic, it will be possible to finance East German pensions completely from contribution payments. Only the costs of unemployment insurance are difficult to forecast. At a rough estimate, expenditure with one million unemployed will be 8 billion DM, with contributions probably only being able to finance half this amount.

The situation is different for the public budget itself. Once the taxation system of the Federal Republic has been adopted, the public sector revenue in the GDR will quickly melt away. Income tax will not earn high revenues because of the low incomes. The same will apply, in the initial phase at least, to state revenue from corporate income tax and corporation tax. Initially, a large number of firms will scarcely have profits for the state to share. Revenues are only to be expected from value added tax and indirect taxation. The tax yield overall will not be enough to finance the normal state administration budget on a low and economical level. A deficit possibly around 20 billion DM would have to be covered by the Federal Republic.

This leaves the area of infrastructure, that is to say public expenditure on the transport network, environmental protection, education and social welfare, etc. The GDR will not be able to finance the investment required in this area after the changeover. Improvement of the infrastructure, however, is of vital importance to the economy, making support from the Federal Republic indispensable. Estimates of the overall requirements of the GDR run into hundreds of billions, though annual provisions would have to be linked more to the production potential of the GDR. On this basis, an investment budget for the infrastructure of the GDR could be of a size of about 30 billion DM a year, to be covered by the FRG.

X. *Conclusion*

I admit that my forecast for the future of the East German economy is optimistic. The reasons for this are as follows:

- the high level of qualifications among the East Germany population;
- the motivation that will be triggered by currency union;
- a positive evaluation of the competitiveness of the East German economy after the changeover to new cost, price and taxation structures;
- the identifiable interest of West German firms in involvement in the GDR.

Against this background, I consider it to be possible that the GDR will be able to realise high growth rates in terms of production and productivity after the changeover, and that the gap separating it from comparable countries will soon narrow.

The question of income levels is a critical point, however. The growth process in the GDR will require the difference in income levels between the GDR and the Federal Republic to be maintained for some time. Rapid conformation of incomes will eliminate the advantage the GDR has in terms of wage costs and block further development. It is questionable whether the understanding of those involved – employees, unions, government – can be attuned to this problem enough for them to be satisfied with a gradual increase in incomes in line with growth in productivity.

*This paper includes information available up to 30 March 1990.

Table I
Use of GDR National Income at 1985 prices

	Produced national income	Used national income	Including:				
		sector	Net investments in productive sector	Investments in non-productive material	Change in stocks of material	Individual consumption	State consumption
					Mark billions		
1970	121 563	139 928	22 582	11 842	6 205	79 925	19 374
1971	126 956	144 837	21 543	12 206	6 613	83 174	21 301
1972	134 130	153 078	21 751	13 488	6 652	88 106	23 081
1973	141 646	141 646	23 475	15 022	6 826	92 928	24 596
1974	150 807	173 207	23 866	16 450	7 826	98 100	26 965
1975	158 157	177 916	24 618	17 368	5 874	101 342	28 716
1976	163 618	188 991	26 468	18 207	7 590	105 939	30 787
1977	171 884	198 731	27 159	19 490	8 999	110 398	32 685
1978	178 240	200 294	27 065	20 777	4 824	114 088	33 540
1979	185 455	202 332	27 041	20 972	1 862	118 643	33 814
1980	193 644	212 761	26 483	20 538	8 736	123 401	33 603
1981	202 971	214 798	26 283	21 179	6 786	126 214	34 336
1982	208 219	207 405	22 410	20 893	1 573	128 215	34 314
1983	217 836	207 522	21 323	20 686	2 620	129 316	33 577
1984	229 917	214 574	17 729	20 269	7 504	134 636	34 436
1985	241 863	224 940	18 176	21 386	8 670	140 815	35 893
1986	252 220	234 400	20 417	22 006	7 597	146 820	37 560
1987	261 180	244 880	24 360	23 225	5 525	152 010	39 760
1988	268 810	258 020	27 460	23 765	7 983	157 890	40 922
					annual change in per cent		
1971/1975	5,31	5,00	0,69	7,77	2,86	5,00	8,53
1976/1980	4,07	4,03	2,90	4,73	2,88	4,09	4,55
1981/1985	4,31	0,17	-7,35	0,55	-15,47	2,21	0,89
1986/1988	3,80	4,49	14,74	3,68	-10,09	3,95	4,75

Table II
State Subsidies for Private Consumption
Mark millions

	1975	1980	1985	1986	1987	1988
Subsidies for basic needs	11 226,0	16 853,4	40 621,5	47 882,5	49 336,0	49 811,2
including for						
Food	7 178,0	7 847,5	27 561,2	30 859,1	31 419,3	31 947,9
Industrial goods	1 174,0	5 119,2	9 057,0	11 095,2	11 946,6	11 943,2
Fares on public transport, local and long-distance	2 195,0	2 924,4	3 171,1	5 016,3	5 044,0	4 979,1
Drinking water and charges for sewage treatment	) 679,0	702,7	462,2	491,0	455,2	449,6
Repairs and services	)	259,8	370,0	420,9	470,9	491,4
Housing (building repairs on housing stock and expenses for heating, hot-water and power supply, waste disposal. Greening and other economic expenses.)	1 187,0	2 769,6	6 386,8	7 006,0	7 527,4	7 694,0
Total	12 413,0	19 623,0	47 008,3	54 888,5	56 863,5	57 505,2

Source: Statistical Yearbooks of the GDR.

Table III

Population and Labour

1000s - position as at 31.12

	1980	1985	1988
Total population	16 740	16 655	16 676
Population of working age	10 581	10 799	10 831
men	5 324	5 561	5 644
women	5 257	5 238	5 187
Population not of working age	6 159	5 856	5 844
Total in permanent employment	8 890	9 223	9 300
university graduates	501	589	625
technical school graduates	911	1 047	1 095
Permanently employed in productive sector	6 539	6 708	6 710
Permanently employed in non-productive sector	2 351	2 515	2 590

Source: Statistical Yearbooks of the GDR.

Table IV

Proportions of Employees by Economic Sector in the GDR and the Federal Republic of Germany

Economic sectors	Employees	
	GDR 1989	FRG 1987
	in per cent	
Agriculture, forestry	10,3	4,9
Energy and mining	3,3	1,4
Processing industry	35,6	29,5
Construction	6,3	6,4
Trade	8,1	17,7
Transport, posts, telecommunications	7,0	5,6
Services, state organisations	29,3	34,4
Total	100,0	100,0

Hungary: On the Way Towards a Market Economy

Tamás Bauer

Synopsis

This paper analyzes major current trends in the development of the economic system in Hungary. In Section I, past ideas concerning desirable changes in the economic system are described and contrasted with the new conditions that have emerged recently in Eastern Europe. In Section II, the main directions of the current approach to systemic transformation are summed up. In Section III, the present state of the economic system as a point of departure is outlined. In Section IV, some key issues in the forthcoming transformation are characterized.

I. *Market Socialism: The Vision Abandoned*

For more than 20 years now, Hungary has experimented with economic reform. The reformers who drafted the blueprint of the 1968 reform and insisted on its main characteristics for two decades, intended to create an economic system combining social ownership with a competitive market. This has been labelled "market socialism" and has also been advocated by Czechoslovak, Polish, Soviet and, in a different version, by Yugoslav economists and policy makers.

The "market socialist" reform blueprint has not questioned the dominance of social or, more modestly, non-private ownership in the economy. The reformers of the sixties in Czechoslovakia and Hungary, or the reformers of the mid-eighties in the Soviet Union, believed that a market economy may operate on the basis of state and cooperative ownership. The reform blueprints did not imply any substantial increase in the share of the private sector in the economy. It was a central assumption of the reform ideas that, provided institutional and motivational frameworks are appropriately revised, state enterprises will operate similarly to private firms operating in a capitalist market economy. The same way of thinking has characterized most Soviet reformers during the first years of perestroika.

During the early and mid-eighties, the stand of Hungarian reformers has been somewhat different. The inappropriateness of state ownership in respect of small-scale business, particularly in the service sector, in retail trade etc. was admitted, and the development of private initiative in such sectors has been promoted. Thus, the private sector was accepted as an important, indispensable but still subordinate sector in the economy.

The reformers who drafted the reform blueprints of the sixties (or, in the Soviet Union, of perestroika) rejected the counterposing of plan and market. They argued plan and market as control mechanisms are not mutually exclusive but coexistent in most modern economies. Obviously, market coordination coexists with a certain degree of government intervention and even with some government co-ordination in most modern Western economies. Still, the reference to the "new industrial state" was incorrect: that concept includes government control of much more than in any Western market economy. The reform blueprints of the late sixties implied a far-reaching control of investment and of foreign trade by the government. "Control" here means more than influencing macro-variables, like the rate of investment or the trade balance: it means approval of particular investment projects beyond certain value limits by the government, it means a detailed control of foreign trade. It means also that technological change is strongly controlled by government: it has to define the main directions and initiate major innovations. Major innovations and investment projects were to be financed from resources of the government. Obviously, regional economic development was also to be strongly influenced by government authorities.

At the same time, enterprises were to be essentially free in defining the volume and composition of output, in directing sales, in the choice of their suppliers and customers, and in the volume and composition of manpower. A mixed price system was to be created where prices are subject to both market conditions and government priorities, and with some prices set bureaucratically by government authorities and the remainder by trading partners themselves. Thus, in the economic system envisaged, market coordination had to play a substantially greater role than in Soviet-type planned economies while bureaucratic coordination by government authorities had to play a substantially greater role than in Western market economies.

The Soviet-type planning system surpassed national boundaries. Trade between the member countries of the CMEA (and of several Asian planned economies which never joined CMEA) was controlled by means of government agreements involving delivery quotas and settlement in transferable roubles. In this system trade was controlled in a detailed way by government bureaucracies and prices had no influence on the level and composition of deliveries.

In "market socialist" reform blueprints it was assumed that the country preserves her adherence to CMEA which would, however, be reformed. When Czechoslovak and Hungarian economists drafted their reform programmes during the sixties they might have supposed that similar reforms would be undertaken in several other CMEA countries and that trade between them would be reorganized on commercial principles. The two reformist countries made that assumption in their bilateral relations in 1968. In 1971, the Hungarian government suggested substantial changes in the CMEA system which were, however, rejected at that time by the vast majority of the member countries. Still, the idea of reducing the role of inter-state agreements on deliveries and creating more room for enterprise-level decision-making and direct links between enterprises (and an even bigger role for prices, interests and other financial categories) in CMEA trade was preserved and revived during the mid-eighties. During the first years of perestroika, the ideas of direct links between enterprises and joint ventures within the general framework of the traditional CMEA trade system played an important role. Party and government programmes allowed for a general renewal of CMEA on commercial lines. This would suggest that the reformed economy operates within the framework of the economic community of market socialist countries.

The reformers of the sixties in Czechoslovakia and Hungary, and their followers in the Soviet Union in the mid-eighties, connected the economic reform with a certain degree of "democratization" of the political system. In Hungary and in Czechoslovakia in 1966-67 this was particularly limited, with proposals to introduce elements of self-government and pluralism rejected by party leaderships even when these did not involve multi-party democracy. During the Prague Spring in Czechoslovakia, as well as in the Soviet Union under perestroika, the economic reforms have been connected with substantial changes in the political system. Freedom of the press, the appearance of autonomous political organizations and a certain democratization of the communist party itself were characteristic in both cases. Some basic features of the Soviet political system, such as the lack of competing political parties, the presence of the communist party in workplaces and even the principle of nomenklatura was not abandoned.

In Hungary, where the economic reform was not suppressed by foreign intervention, a learning-by-doing process took place during the seventies and early eighties. Without going into the details of Hungarian reform history, let it be just noted that the tensions emerging during the introduction of the reform resulted in a slowdown and even moderate reversal of the reform during the mid-seventies. A second round of the reform was initiated by the government during the early eighties. More room was open from that time on for private initiative, and new forms of business organization were introduced in the state sector. Also the state economic administration was reshaped and the price and financial system was restructured. Still, some basic features of the "market socialist" approach were preserved.

First, though the reformers allowed some room for private initiative, it was still considered as a minority component of the economy. Second, the decisive role of CMEA trade and the established mechanisms of CMEA were not questioned. The role of CMEA in the world economy and the contents of its role for Hungary have substantially changed following the price explosions of 1973 on Western markets and 1975 and later on CMEA "markets", but this had not resulted in a fundamental reconsideration of Hungary's CMEA policy. Third, nothing changed in the political system during these years. Not only was the one-party system not questioned, but such changes as occurred under the Prague Spring in Czechoslovakia or perestroika in the Soviet Union were not initiated or tolerated by the Kádár party leadership.

II. *A New Vision under New Conditions*

The dramatic transformation in the Hungarian political scene that followed the May 1988 party conference resulted in substantially new conditions for economic reforms. True, at the beginning the new party leadership promised democratization in the communist party, emancipation of state and social organizations from control by the communist party, more press freedom and some liberalization of the elections. In 1988 and early 1989 they still insisted on the one-party system, and even when they were forced to give it up, they wanted elections with a Polish-type previous distribution of seats. By mid-1989 the situation had changed. A multi-party system, free elections and guarantees of civil rights were accepted by the communist party. By the end of the year the communist party had to give up its organizations in workplaces, its militia, most of its property and also the claim to have its man elected president at presidential elections before the elections to the parliament. By now, the framework of a Western-type parliamentary democracy have been created in Hungary. In addition to the new framework for state and party politics, the withdrawal of the communist party from workplaces, the abolishment of nomenklatura etc., created new conditions for civil life. Freedom of the press has been more or less guaranteed. More essential for us now, the emancipation of the economy from politics is also likely to be accomplished.

More than one-half of Hungary's foreign trade has, for 40 years, been realized with the CMEA countries. The lion's share of that, one-third of total trade, was with the Soviet Union. This trade has been essential for Hungary, since the Hungarian economy was supplied with most essential raw materials and energy from the CMEA countries, and they were also the biggest market for the Hungarian manufacturing industry. As mentioned above, deliveries to and from CMEA partners were defined by government agreements and payments were settled in transferable roubles, the quasi-money of the CMEA.

By the end of the eighties it turned out that the structure which was characteristic for decades could not be maintained any longer. The easily accessible resources of the Soviet Union have, due to the wasteful growth of production both in the USSR and in the countries of Eastern Europe, been exhausted. The Soviet Union is simply not in a position to expand further, or even maintain the level of, deliveries to Eastern Europe. Though the manufactured products of Eastern Europe continue to be in high demand on Soviet markets, the Soviet Union cannot pay for them with goods in demand in Eastern Europe. Thus, the trade between the Soviet Union and Eastern Europe is likely to decline.

At a time when rational calculation becomes more and more essential everywhere in Eastern Europe, and when mutual trade in manufactures acquires a greater role in trade within the CMEA, the inappropriateness of the traditional trade system becomes more and more obvious. While earlier a gradual commercialization of CMEA trade with strengthening the money functions of the "collective currency" was under consideration, now the whole system of inter-state agreements is to be abandoned and the transferable rouble is likely to disappear as trade between more and more CMEA countries will be settled in hard currencies. Hungary has already agreed on that with the USSR and Czechoslovakia. Obviously, trade with the unified Germany will be settled in hard currency, too. I expect an agreement with Poland and Romania to come soon. This means that the peculiar mechanisms of trade with CMEA countries which have been an important constraint on businesss-like behaviour of Hungarian enterprises will be eliminated.

By now, many Hungarian economists and politicians agree that what Hungary needs is a market economy, essentially identical with the economic system prevailing in Western Europe. The role of the government should be substantially reduced while business firms must enjoy full autonomy and responsibility for their economic results. Prices should, up to some basic communal services, be liberalized. A modern monetary and banking system should be created, including a capital market and stock exhange. Instead of bureaucratic wage controls, a tripartite system of wage agreements should be introduced. A convertible currency is urgently needed, and foreign trade should be controlled primarily by the exchange rate.

The market economy can exist, in Hungary as elsewhere, only on the foundation of private property as the prevailing form of ownership. True, Hungary needs a mixed economy where different forms of ownership coexist, as in all European countries. Still, one has to distinguish between a Polish or Chinese-type mixed economy and a West European mixed economy. While in the first the economy is dominated by an enormous state sector and the behavioural patterns prevailing in the state sector determine the behaviour of all economic agents in the economy, in the latter private firms prevail and public enterprises accommodate their behaviour to that of private ones. To achieve such a state, favourable conditions for the establishment and growth of new private firms are needed. In addition to that, the bulk of the present state sector needs to be privatised. This is to be discussed in Section IV.

Obviously, the Hungarian market economy must be a Soziale Marktwirtschaft: an extensive network of social policy measures is needed, particularly in the forthcoming years of substantial restructuring. The principle of solidarity must dominate the government's policy when it intervenes in the economy.

III. *The Present State of the Economic System*

The objective of moving towards a market economy has been formulated in most East European countries, including recently also Romania. Such developments as the erosion of the Warsaw Pact and the collapse of the CMEA or the abolishment of the power monoply of communist parties also relate to other countries of the region. Still, Hungary's chances to accomplish this task seem better than that of other countries. This results from the different starting point. While in other CMEA member countries the Soviet-type economic system prevailed up to present, in Hungary (and in Poland) the economic system has changed substantially as a result of the economic reforms undertaken since 1968 (in Poland since 1982).

Liberalization of the Hungarian economy had started already in the mid-fifties. When the second wave of collectivization in agriculture brought modest results only, the government made concessions and allowed collective farmers to work independently on their household plots. A growing part of new housing was built by private artisans, mostly unregistered (shadow economy). The same holds true for consumer services. All this meant that businesslike behaviour gained ground. From 1982 on, the government introduced new forms of registered private and semi-private business activities. "Petty cooperatives", "economic partnerships" and other new forms spread over the country very rapidly. In a country where a few hundred big industrial enterprises controlled the vast majority of industrial output, the emergence of 20,000 new small business units constituted a revolutionary innovation. Obviously, they had to survive without any kind of state subsidies, and many of them did.

Substantial changes took place also in the "social sector", that is the state and cooperative sectors. The "New Economic Mechanism" introduced in 1968 and – what is without parallel in Eastern Europe – not withdrawn since then, resulted in genuine changes in the position of state and cooperative enterprises. They obtained a substantial degree of autonomy in decision-making, primarily in respect of current issues but to some extent also in investment. They decided on the level and composition of output and on purchasing and sales policies on their own. Cost and profit calculations became important for the enterprises. They developed independent business and marketing strategies.

Even more has changed in the cooperative sector. The agricultural cooperatives were turned into large organizations of agro-business, with a wide range of independence. They extended their business to more profitable non-agricultural activities. This resulted in an "internal subsidization" of loss-making agriculture by profitable industrial, building and service activities. Thus, they were more independent of the state than collective farms depending exclusively on state assistance. Both in the state and cooperative sectors, prices, costs and profits became main determinants of decision-making. Managers became more strongly oriented towards the market.

From 1966 on, numerous price reforms were implemented. The recalculation of prices related both to producer prices and to consumer prices. As a result, relative price distortions were considerably reduced. Relative prices are much closer to Western ones in Hungary than in most other East European countries. This relates also to consumer prices. Prices were gradually liberalized, and by the end of the eighties the majority of prices are, at least legally, free. This has meant that turnover taxes were unified. While in traditional Soviet-type systems hundreds or thousands of turnover tax rates are in power, in Hungary a system of value added tax was introduced with three rates only.

Even more important for enterprises is the fact that the system of individually defined money transfers from the enterprise to the state budget was replaced by a Western-type corporate tax system, though the operation of the latter has been substantially weakened by numerous exceptions. Credit as a monetary category has also gained ground. Since the single National Bank performing the functions of a central bank and of business banks simultaneously was replaced by a central bank and autonomous business banks competing with each other, bank credit looks more and more like bank credit.

The Hungarian economy under the New Economic Mechanism has been more open to the external world than planned economies usually are. Numerous enterprises were entitled to also trade abroad in the goods they turned out. Those which were not entitled to do so by themselves could commission foreign trade enterprises to trade in their products on their behalf. By the late eighties, all enterprises obtained the right of foreign trade. The state monopoly of foreign trade was first eroded and has finally been abandoned. The domestic economy was linked to the external world by means of the uniform exchange rate. The exchange rate mediated the evaluation of Hungarian economic performance by foreign markets to Hungarian business units. Hungarians became more informed about external market conditions than managers in other planned economies. Hungary has been pioneering in establishing joint ventures with Western firms. This has also been a channel for introducing Western management practices into the Hungarian economy.

Planned economies have traditionally been characterized by serious imbalances. Shortages of food, shortages of raw materials, and inflationary overhang threatening the consumer market endanger economic and social equilibrium currently in the Soviet Union, as an example. The Hungarian situation has been different. Hungarians have forgotten queuing for food for decades, and most manufactured products are also in good supply. The supply of raw materials and intermediate goods for enterprises is also much better than elsewhere in Eastern Europe.

All these improvements against the traditional planned economies have been remarkable but still limited. Private initiative gained ground but was constrained by legal restrictions, and even more by the absence of a favourable economic environment and political climate. The commercialization of state firms was weakened, among others, by the dependence of top managers of firms (and also of the agricultural cooperatives) on state administration and/or party hierarchy. Prices were liberalized formally, while in fact price movements were restricted by an informal price control which resulted in cost-plus pricing. The opening of the economy was offset by anti-import policies enforced by tensions in the current account balance. While domestic markets were more balanced than elsewhere in Eastern Europe, shortages like that of housing, cars and telephone lines disturbed households, and firms were often forced to substitute other kinds of inputs for those which were in short supply.

IV. *On the Way Towards Systemic Transformation*

As indicated in Section II, Hungary is striving currently towards a genuine market economy. This implies a comprehensive reform of ownership, the creation of a competitive market and of a modern monetary system. As in all planned economies, Hungary had an overconcentrated enterprise structure. Most small and medium-scale enterprises were liquidated during the first years of the planned economy. The process of centralization continued during the sixties and seventies. A reverse trend started in the eighties: new small businesses were established. Still, Hungary has fewer small businesses than comparable market economies, and those which exist are economically weak. A vast expansion of small and medium-scale business is required. They will necessarily be private firms. Favourable conditions for the establishment of hundreds of thousands of new small private firms in the next few years must be created. The most important condition is a favourable economic and political climate. Tax allowances are also needed. In my view, however, the most important condition which is still missing is a market infrastructure which helps small enterprises to gain access to imported goods, to modern equipment and to credit. To achieve that, a network of small (essentially private) trade companies (particularly for wholesale and international trade) and small banks is needed.

A desirable structure cannot be achieved merely as a result of an expansion of new private firms: a privatization of state enterprises is necessary also. The experience of Western countries in privatization can, however, not be easily applied to East European countries. In the West, the governments intend to privatize a limited number of companies (not exceeding a few dozen). In Eastern Europe, hundreds of state enterprises need to be privatized within a few years. In the West, state-owned enterprises operate in a market environment, on commercial grounds, and thus they have book-keeping and capital evaluation adequate to a market environment. All this is missing in respect of state enterprises in East European countries. In addition, privatized companies in the West will have to fit in a well established market economy, while in Eastern Europe this market economy is still in the process of birth. All these factors bring a tremendous uncertainty into the privatization process. Abuses and corruption can hardly be fully avoided which, in turn, brings about strong misgivings in the population, widely exploited by all political forces rejecting privatization. Still, privatization is necessary and must be carried out with care and determination. The Hungarian Parliament established a National Property Agency which has to supervise privatization. In my view, a government agency cannot organize privatization itself: initiative must come from the managers of the firms to be privatized. The National Property Agency must supervise the whole process to avoid abuses.

To have a market economy we need competition. Otherwise autonomous enterprises, whether private or public, will not serve the consumer. The first obstacle for competition is the monopolization of the economy inherited from the time of centralized planning. In many sectors there are one or two or three suppliers in Hungary, and even these one or two or three suppliers often divide the market. The most important way to overcome monopolization is to create favourable conditions for entry. This means promoting new small businesses mentioned above. This also means liberalization of imports. And it means, in all cases when an existing large firm makes losses or faces bankruptcy, the disintegration of such firms.

Demonopolization does not only mean to have a second or third or twenty fifth supplier. The crucial point is that the potential competitor must have the chance to appear on more market segments. This has been prevented frequently by the lack of necessary intermediators, agencies, etc., as a consequence of the underdevelopment of market infrastructure in reformed planned economies.

Commerce is a decisive area. Monopolization is very strong in both foreign trade and domestic wholesale and retail trade. All limitations concerning the setting up and expansion of privately owned commercial firms must be abolished. Joint ventures are particularly welcome in this area. Hungarians, and particularly Poles, have demostrated in recent years, notably in the environs of Hungarian, German and even Soviet railway stations how imaginative and innovative in this sector they are. Why not do this legally, with just a little bit more capital and on a much larger scale? Development programmes to promote new firms in wholesale and international trade seem necessary. The same holds for banking. The existing business banks are too much dependent on the state on the one hand and on their customers on the other. New banks should be established with foreign capital, being independent both of Hungarian government and enterprises.

For a small country like Hungary the liberalization of imports is the most important aspect of the creation of a competitive market. Hungary's serious balance of payments problems have hampered the accomplishment of this endeavour. Earlier, during the late sixties and early seventies, import of raw materials and equipment was, in fact, free for state enterprises and cooperatives. The fact that much of the state monopoly of foreign trade was preserved at that time, and that foreign trade companies carried out a certain kind of informal import control, made this relatively easy. Even this had to be suspended during the mid-seventies and particularly during the eighties. Recently, a growing part of import has been liberalized. By now, even the remnants of the state monopoly of foreign trade have been eliminated which limits the possibility of informal import controls. A full and lasting liberalization would require a considerable depreciation of the forint and/or foreign help.

As mentioned above, trade with the present CMEA member countries will be conducted on different lines in the future. Inter-state delivery quotas will be abandoned, and Hungarian firms will obtain full freedom in their decisions concerning imports from and exports to East European countries. Payments for deliveries will be settled in hard currencies. This change does not depend on changes in the domestic economic systems of the partner countries: it only means that Hungarian firms will have the same rights as Western trade partners of CMEA countries. This is the most substantial change in the external environment of the Hungarian economy for many decades. It means that all foreign trade relations will be market relations. The dependence of firms on government authorities, the possibility to rely on government assistance, will be substantially reduced.

Hungary has already reduced the formal control of prices to a degree close to most Western economies. An informal control of prices prevails. This informal control can be removed to the extent that the market is demonopolized and market equilibrium is consolidated. A comprehensive recalculation of prices which seems necessary in countries like Czechoslovakia, Bulgaria or Romania, is, in my view, not necessary in Hungary. Wage controls cannot be fully removed as long as a stable system of tripartite wage negotiations is missing. The main obstacle here is the lack of legitimate trade unions. The existing official trade unions do not enjoy the confidence of workers. As a consequence, while they are capable of mobilizing workers for wage demands, they are incapable of convincing them on the necessity to restrain wage demands. As long as we do not have unions capable of that, we need some kind of bureaucratic wage controls in Hungary.

Polish Economic Reforms: Current Developments, Constraints and Prospects

Marek Grela

I. *Reforming Status Quo*

During recent decades the term "economic reforms" in former Eastern bloc countries has been often abused or misinterpreted. To get things straight one has to differentiate between partial reforms within the existing system and reforms, or rather transformations, changing the system itself.

In the post-war history of Poland serious attempts to reform, or better to improve, the performance of the so-called socialist economy were undertaken at least three or four times. In this period two different approaches prevailed. The more radical economists visualized the reform as encompassing the whole realm of economic activity with the inevitable spill-over effect in the socio-political area (more democracy and economic rationality).

In contrast, the more cautious economists spoke only about "improvements in planning and management", which actually meant that the economy should be moved in the right direction with the use of economic leverage as opposed to crude practices of direct steering by strict planning instructions. It should be made clear that the policy proposals emanating from this group were couched in terms which did not openly challenge the ruling political force's (the party's) supremacy and its all-embracing hold on practically all spheres of life.

In general terms the criticism of economic policy dominated by ideology and distorted by arbitrary decisions was by and large muted by perceptions referred to at the time as "realism", implying incremental change. Accordingly, any plea that the Party should release its grip could be substantiated solely by economic considerations as demands for greater political pluralism and similar heresies would be immediately labelled as "revisionist" and equally swiftly turned down.

Seen in the historical perspective all these reforms were mere palliatives, implemented half-heartedly and never brought to an end. Needless to say they aimed at preserving and strengthening the political system of the country by bolstering up its faltering economy.

The positive results of the reforms were scant and easily reversed. The collapse of the reforms initiated in 1956, and a long period of dogmatic and uninspired economic policy under Gomulka and his orthodox team in the 1960's, culminated in the shattering crisis of 1970. For all that, the significance of 1956 in Poland as a watershed in economic thinking in the Eastern European countries should not be underestimated. The ideas which emerged at that time inspired not only future Polish actions but were also discernible in schemes which evolved in the 1960s in Hungary and Czechoslovakia.

A brave new world began with Edward Gierek who promised to modernize Polish industry and boost the economy as a whole while, at the same time, increasing the living standards of the population. He tried hard and succeeded in making the most of East-West détente and particularly of the low cost credits on international financial markets.

The main thrust of this strategy was to involve Poland more in the international division of labour and to reap the benefits of increasingly competitive exports. However, the "import-led growth" policy was not accompanied by adequate economic reforms which could render the national economy more effective and export-oriented. While changes in economic planning and management remained virtually cosmetic cooperation with the West was visibly upgraded. Easily available foreign credits smoothed all the wrinkles, serving in a way as a handy substitute for badly needed economic and political reforms. Initial, and largely artificial, prosperity terminated in the late 1970s, to be replaced by the deepest economic, political and moral crisis in the post-war history of Poland.

Gierek's policy, while disastrous for the country and its debt-ridden economy, paradoxically accelerated Polish society's drive towards a modern, democratic, market economy state. The economic breakdown of a magnitude unprecedented in Europe since World War II destabilized the system and made the society less governable by traditional methods. The reawakened aspirations to catch up with the world remained a source of even more acute frustrations. It can even be maintained that the whole series of crises of 1956, 1968, 1970 and, lastly, in 1980 forged a new society more aware of its own goals, better organized and resolved to defend its interests.

The crisis which exploded in August 1980, as well as the appearance of the "Solidarity" on the political scene of Poland, proved to be decisive and heightened the demand for economic reform in Poland. An official reform proposal approved by the Party Congress and the Parliament in 1981 envisaged the abolition of command planning without, however, a clear endorsement of the market. Instead the economy was to "operate on the principle of central planning with the utilization of the market mechanism".

The imposition of martial law on 13 December 1981, which entailed traumatic political and social consequences, did not put the brakes on economic reform which was initiated as planned on 1 January 1982. The ruling elites started to introduce a host of market-oriented economic and legislative measures while restoring at the same time, under military umbrella, one party rule.

These reforms — probably the most far-reaching in the history of real socialism in Poland — were designed to decentralize decision-making, improve the price structure, and stiffen the financial discipline of state enterprises. This policy resulted in modest recovery of economic growth, although in 1987 output was still below its 1978 peak. The incomplete and erratic implementation of the reform programme, retarded by conservative policy-makers as well as lack of genuine will to transform the very basic elements of the socialist economy, led to predictable decline: economic growth slowed down, inflation reached the three digit level, foreign debt increased ominously and the widespread labour unrest was renewed (1987-89).

Reform measures in this period undoubtedly created a new "systemic quality" both in the economic and the socio-political areas. They were, however, short of general expectations and blemished from the very beginning with setbacks and inconsistencies. A hybrid system, consolidated with numerous traditional institutions and instruments, gave no chance to overcoming the crisis which in a number of areas began to intensify.

II. *Reversal of the Political Situation*

At the end of the decade there was a broad agreement in Poland that the measures of partial economic liberalization undertaken since 1981 had failed miserably and that sweeping changes were needed to rescue the economy. The dramatic situation of the country, threatened by explosion of new socio-political conflicts, pushed the governing reform-minded elites in 1988 to meet, a year later, the opposition at the Round Table talks. Despite widespread beliefs that seven years – since the imposition of martial law in December 1981 – have been entirely lost, one positive experience of paramount importance cannot be denied. Namely, that the solution to the recurrent crisis could be no longer sought nor found within the existing political system of "real socialism".

This left only two possible options: either to let the internal situation drift uncontrollably toward an explosive and revolutionary situation or to create a framework for a peaceful and evolutionary process oriented toward modern, democratic and pluralistic society. The well known outcome, rightly regarded as a blueprint for national reconciliation, was, despite its fragility, an outstanding political success, paving also the way for similar exercises in some other Eastern European countries.

Originally the Round Table talks were to have chiefly political aims – the division of power and responsibility between the key actors: Party and the opposition led by Solidarity. As the concept evolved economic problems were also placed on the agenda and discussed, even if often overshadowed by ideological and political issues. Despite the general desire for changes a profound disagreement existed on such basic issues as the extent of government control over economic activities, the scope of public ownership and state interventionism, the method and pace of privatization, the role of foreign investment, price and wage policies, etc.

The dramatic reversal of the political situation in Poland after the landslide victory of "Solidarity" in parliamentary elections in June 1989 and creation, in September 1989, of the first non-communist government in this part of Europe, led by Prime Minister Tadeusz Mazowiecki, has opened up the way for Poland's transition towards a market economy. The popular vote, overwhelmingly rejecting the system imposed in Poland by

Stalin some 45 years ago, signalled also the rejection of its economic component which inflicted immense material and moral losses upon the country.

The new government, formed on 12 September 1989, has set about to arrest a rapidly deteriorating situation: investment and output continued to decline; the external current account deficit in convertible currencies has widened sharply, tripling in 1989 to an estimated two billion US dollars (3% of GNP) with some 40 billion US dollars debt overhang. On top of that the provisions of food were scarce and the overall supply situation remained very difficult.

Under these circumstances there was no alternative except to go ahead immediately with the implementation of a radical economic programme, commonly know as the "Balcerowicz programme", after the present Deputy Prime Minister and Minister of Finance.

III. *The Main Aims of the Programme*

The programme initiated on 1 January 1990 has two interdependent aims: first, to stabilize the economy, and second, to transform the economic system in Poland. It should be emphasized that the prime objective is a systemic change. It is not a question of streamlining or modifying but of a switch to Western, market-economy, well tested mechanisms. Putting the economy on an even keel is regarded as indispensable, before its wheels start turning in the opposite direction. On the other hand, the restoration of internal equilibrium, mostly by harsh deflationary measures, would not suffice to ensure the attainment of more ambitious goals.

Without system changes and a highly productive economy, literally "delivering the goods", economic stabilization alone would not be conducive to sustained growth of output, improved living standards and balancing Poland's external position – ultimate goals of the programme.

Such fundamental changes would be impossible if the negative tendencies, such as the hyperinflation estimated for last year at around 650%, were to continue unabated. Given that, the starting point of the entire Balcerowicz programme is a relatively short stabilization phase designed to cut down inflation to an acceptable single-digit level. Attention was focused on the experience of others, which shows that a gradual approach to thwarting a very high inflation would simply not work, particularly in the post-socialist economy with its structural problems and rigidities.

Poland cannot tolerate high inflation for another reason. The determined internal adjustment measures are a well-known prerequisite of any meaningful support from the West. Left to its own devices, without considerable Western assistance, Poland might encounter insurmountable obstacles on its road, called somewhat pathetically, "a return to Europe".

These premises underlie the government programme, referred to by some as a "shock therapy". In fact all kinds of expressions have been used in Poland to describe this programme and the consequences it entails, including "a daring jump" and "zero hour". Put in a nutshell, what happened in Poland on 1 January 1990 was a brisk introduction of a classic market economy, starting with the reduction of the drastic budget deficit, and curtailment or complete elimination of subsidies on prices of goods and services.

As a result, 1 January brought about the following price increases: seven-fold for coal, five-fold for electrical energy, gas and central heating, three to five-fold for railway and bus fares, and two-fold for gasoline. Generally, the prices of food commodities and services soared. Some of the prices, including those for fuels and energy but also the "price" of foreign currencies and the "prices" of work (wages), should remain stable for some time. That is why, at the same time, a sharp curb was put on wages which, according to government forecasts, would result in a 20% drop of real incomes.

This is the bill that has to be footed. In exchange Balcerowicz promises minimum inflation and a normal market already by the middle of the year. A market abundant in goods, without queues or profiteering. And then a gradual improvement in the standard of living.

According to World Bank estimates, after a transitional fall in consumption of about 12% in 1990-1992, the stabilization of the economy and systemic changes should bring about a 14% increase in consumption in 1993-1995.

Prime Minister Tedeusz Mazowiecki stated in the Sejm "we can choose one of two roads. The first is to adopt the attitude: yes to reforms but no to prices we would have to pay. If our behaviour was dominated by this attitude we would all suffer defeat. The second road is to give preference to the common good, the good of the Republic above piecemeal interest, even the most justified".

The bitter pill of a belt-tightening policy is regarded by the majority as an unwanted legacy of totalitarian rule but also as a remedy which has to be administered if the economy is to operate normally at all levels and regain its viability. Despite hardships or even sacrifices involved the society has displayed admirable patience, giving very high support to the Mazowiecki Government and its programme, the main characteristics of which are outlined below.

IV. *Measures to Stabilize the Economy*

On 1st January 1990 the stabilization measures were abruptly put into effect. They include:

1. *Prices.* Restrictions on the setting of almost all prices were eliminated in order to stabilize the market and allow for the efficient allocation of resources. At the same time widespread price subsidies were ended. For the time being hard coal, coke and electricity still have administered prices, but prices for all energy products will continue to move closer to prices on world markets.

2. *Wages.* If wages were allowed to follow the sky-rocketing prices the battle against inflation would be lost. Wages, which for the major part of the last year grew faster than prices, will now be kept under strict surveillance to reverse this trend. Progressive taxation of wages has been

introduced, severely castigating enterprises for overstepping a fixed rate of wage increases. The principles of indexation applied last year have also been changed. The growth of prices is compensated, not by 80% as last year, but by 30% in January and 20% in the following months.

3. *Government spending and fiscal policy.* A strict control of the money supply is the basic canon of the present government policy. The budget, after many years of deficit (of alarming proportions in 1989), is to be balanced in 1990. Government spending will be reduced, primarily owing to radical cuts in subsidies (especially enormous subsidies on the prices of coal and foodstuffs) but also due to the smaller investments and defense expenditures. Greater budgetary revenues will be obtained through sales of a part of the state property and the issuance of treasury bonds. The first bonds were issued last year as a pilot scheme. In 1990 the sale of bonds continues on a larger scale. Of crucial importance will be the modified taxation system. Taxes will be levied strictly and on an across-the-board basis, which constitutes a serious departure from the earlier system with its wide range of reliefs and preferences.

4. *Credit policy.* Poland's, so far, lenient credit policy is becoming a policy of clearly restrictive character. Credit will be expensive and will cease to be a quasi-subsidy to stem the excessive expansion of demand and strengthen the national currency, not only by reducing inflation but also by offering competitive interest rates on zloty deposits. At the same time, higher interest rates (positive in real terms since January 1990) will be an invitation to saving. Generally, in the newly created financial system interest rates set at realistic levels should be the principal means by which credit is allocated among alternative uses. The interest rate as a key variable must, at the same time, offer a sufficiently larger return on zloty deposits in banks than on deposits in foreign currency to make the former more attractive. The interest rates policy is to be instrumental also in improving the efficiency of fixed investment, reducing wasteful stockbuilding and disciplining inter-enterprise credit.

The new banking law establishes the full independence of the National Bank in the realm of credit and currency policies.

5. *Exchange rate policy.* Partial convertibility of the zloty has been introduced. Full convertibility is envisaged.

The main objective of the exchange rate policy in the initial phase of economic stabilization is to create a situation where stability of the new exchange rate provides a firm anchor in the fight against inflation.

The exchange rate system has been liberalized and simplified. Beginning in January 1990 most current transactions in convertible foreign exchange are now channelled through the principal exchange market, in which the exchange rate of the zloty is set at the new level (9,500 zlotys per US dollar compared with rate of 6,000 zlotys per US dollar in December 1989).

During the first three months of 1990 the rate of exchange remained stable and without losses in foreign reserves. Confidence in the sustainability of the rate of exchange has been strengthened by a bridge loan extended to Poland by the BIS and by the availability of a one billion US dollars stabilization fund to which a number of industrial Western countries have contributed.

6. *Foreign trade and foreign investment policy.* A uniform customs tariff has been introduced for commercial and personal imports. From the point of view of GATT principles to which Poland acceded in 1967, the tariff in force fulfils all basic requirements. All quantitative restrictions on imports from the convertible currency area have been eliminated, with very few exceptions (e.g. health reasons). Such imports can now be made, either without a licence or on the basis of liberally-issued general licences.

The export trade regime has also been liberalized, as the range of exports subject to quota is reduced to some basic commodities. Concessions to engage in foreign trade are required in specific cases only.

New opportunities for foreign investors have been created including liberal legal regulations like preferential taxation (foreign investors enjoy three years income tax holidays which in some sectors of investment can be extended to six years). New legislation permits foreign capital participation up to 100% in joint ventures, as well as the setting up of wholly foreign-owned enterprises.

V. *Toward a Market Economy System*

The logic of the government programme is that systemic changes in the economy should not lag behind political changes, seen as mutually supportive in Poland's quest for a democratic and pluralistic state and a sound economy. The second phase of the programme calls for the elimination of remaining administrative controls on prices and of remaining subsidies, the further liberalization of foreign trade and, most important, the privatization of state-owned enterprises. The programme – beginning 1 January 1990 and covering a two year span – consists of a wide range of measures concerning:

1. *Privatization.* There will be profound changes in the ownership structure. Private industry and services will become dominant in the Polish economy (in Polish agriculture 80% of farms are already owned by private persons). At the moment privatization of some services and small businesses is under way according to the existing legal framework. Laws on privatization of state enterprises are almost complete, and once adopted by the Parliament a far-reaching transformation of the ownership of enterprises would begin. The institution representing the Treasury and responsible for privatization is the Agency for Property Transformations.

Privatization will proceed in two stages. First, an enterprise will be transformed into a shareholders company with all shares belonging to the state. The employees' council will be replaced by a supervisory council, made up of managers from within and outside a company. In the second stage the shares will be sold through the banks to all willing to buy them. The former employees could buy up to 5-20% on concessional terms.

The main ownership forms that are envisaged are private joint-stock companies, worker-owned entities, and socialized enterprises. Foreign investors are entitled to purchase stock in Polish companies, become majority share holders, and also set up wholly foreign-owned firms. According to recent polls, a majority of Poles are in favour of privatization of state assets and only some 20% object.

2. *Demonopolization.* The Polish economy is still highly monopolized. This is a legacy of the centrally planned economy. Some extraordinary measures have been undertaken to strengthen anti-monopoly law and to create an environment conducive to competition. Traditionally strong monopolies (among others in food processing and the hard-coal industry) have been broken up. More stringent sanctions on monopolistic practices were introduced and remaining restrictions on setting up new firms were removed. Access of foreign firms, goods and services to the Polish market has been greatly facilitated.

3. *New banking system and other financial institutions.* Poland – like other post-socialist economies – lacks a modern banking system. The modernization and development of the banking system is under way with indispensable foreign assistance. The procedures for establishing new banks, including private banks (a number of which have started to operate) and banks with foreign participation, have been simplified. Improvements have been made in accounting procedures, in putting in place a strong system of bank supervision, in technology of bank data processing, in bank management, etc.

A stock exchange will be established.

4. *New tax system.* Preparations are also underway for a comprehensive reform of the budget and tax system (to be introduced in 1991-92). This reform provides for: replacement of turnover taxes with a value added tax; introduction of a uniform corporate income tax for all economic entities; new regulations on budgetary preparation and control.

5. *Bankruptcy law.* The existing law on bankruptcy (adopted in the early 1980s) has been amended by regulations enabling any creditor whose claims have not been satisfied on time to initiate bankruptcy proceedings. As a result ineffective and financially weak state enterprises will no longer be in a position to operate under an umbrella of ambiguous rules and direct or indirect subsidies.

6. *Labour market.* Bankruptcies as well as recessions create unemployment, which is a rather new social and economic phenomenon in this, so far, planned economy. Administrative regulations (with full employment or rather with hidden unemployment) will be replaced by a real labour market. To cope with a new situation the Labour Code has been updated to make easier the requisite adjustments. At the same time the Labour Fund has been established to provide a protective shield for workers made redundant. The Fund's resources will be used primarily for retraining of laid-off workers, the improvement of labour mobility, the establishment of an efficient labour placement system, and for providing cash benefits to the unemployed.

VI. *Preliminary Results and Economists' Reactions*

It would be premature or even presumptuous to pass any judgements on the programme's implementation. The preliminary results reveal both achievements and difficulties.

The most spectacular success of the first three months of 1990 is the stabilization of the exchange rate for the dollar which, irrespective of the rise in retail prices, remains fixed below 9,500 zlotys. The neck of inflation was broken much faster than expected (with the monthly rate in January some 80%, in February 23% and in March 4%), an accomplishment generally attributed to the fall in real wages and financial resources of the population. The discipline of productive processes has increased and the word "unemployment" has reappeared in the Polish official language.

On the other hand in February the output was smaller (20-30% in comparison with January 1989). Many enterprises halted production for weeks, giving leave to employees. The reason: lack of demand and growing inventories. The agricultural sector has been particularly hard hit as claimed by farmers' organizations. Group lay-offs are in the offing. At the end of March some 250,000 were registered as unemployed.

Understandably enough, the government programme sparked off a very animated discussion among Polish economists. The drive for an open market economy is nearly universally approved, but the argument continues about ways and means to do so.

The most frequent accusation is that a strict adherence to a pure doctrine of new liberalism is divorced from reality and current Western economic practice. For example, one of the most able economists of the younger generation, Professor Grzegorz Kolodko, insists that the orthodox anti-inflation therapy tested with mixed results in Latin America, could, in Poland, involve far greater costs than in the Western Hemisphere. This is because no normal market mechanisms presently function in Poland, threatened by a dangerous mix of hyperinflation, shortages and stagnation.

It is also pointed out that the entire structure of the Balcerowicz programme is based on the assumption that state economic policy, its mechanisms and measures, will promote productivity, enterpreneurship, innovation and savings. But those who are impatient say that these mechanisms and measures are far too weak. The scope of state intervention, which is brought down to a minimum in the programme, is considered by many as too small, and may allegedly involve the danger of market anarchy, at least in the initial period of carrying out this programme. Others claim that the programme is not radical enough. They insist on hastening systemic changes even more, saying that "the critical mass" of radical legislative changes (with regard to privatization and attraction of foreign capital) must be accumulated as soon as possible to initiate true economic recovery.

It goes without saying that the harsh programme has provoked critical reactions of all parties concerned — and concerned are virtually all! Naturally enough, this criticism very often reflects the vested interests of different lobbies, striving for preservation or improvement of their position in changing circumstances.

All in all, Poland has taken the plunge and everyone there holds his breath. Real success depends on the outcome of the second phase of the government programme – that of putting things in motion again. The question remains: did we have any other choice than "fuite en avant"? Weighing all pros and cons, the answer is no.

VII. *Ambitions versus Constraints*

The Poles would like to find themselves soon on the "sunny side of the street". Ultimately, the success of economic reforms in Poland mainly, but not exclusively, depends on the ability of its citizens to face the realities squarely and work well and hard. The human dimension of the ambitious projects is quite conspicuous, as are numerous constraints which have to be taken into account in all future actions.

1. *Economic constraints,* both domestic and external, constitute the most deeply entrenched obstacle on the road toward an efficient economy and affluent society.

Internal constraints are a grim legacy of the past: an obsolete industrial structure, a wide technological gap and low productivity, weak export-oriented sectors, a fragmented agricultural sector, serious ecological problems, underdeveloped public infrastructure, etc. Poland is not able to solve effectively these problems on her own. It lacks capital, modern technology and expertize in many areas needed to put the economy on the right track. Domestic resources are too small to meet even basic ends of industrial restructuring, of improving infrastructure or of solving acute ecological problems. An availability of external resources is thus essential.

If capital inflows are indeed a crucial ingredient in the reform process, then the foreign policy makers are faced with a dilemma, since the relaxation of the external constraint without evident improvement in the economy raises the risk of a more onerous debt burden in the future. Poland's speedy reforms should dispel these doubts. The resolution of the debt issue, however, calls for concerted efforts of involving creditors and international financial institutions.

The huge Polish debt of more than 40 billion dollars is a principal and most distressing external constraint of the reform. The problem is too complex to be discussed in detail in this paper. What should be emphasized is that, despite advantageous terms of the last debt rescheduling agreement with the Paris Club, Poland can no longer stick to the routine strategy "from negotiations to renegotiations" with the foreign debt snowballing beyond any imaginable proportions. A comprehensive solution to Poland's debt problem should be worked out, including resolute debt relief and debt reduction measures. Innovative debt reduction techniques could also be applied, in conformity with the Brady Plan, by commercial banks.

2. *Lack of necessary expertise.* It is quite rightly pointed out that neither a technological gap nor even a management gap, but rather a "Harvard

gap", became the most distressing liability of the Central and East European countries. This fully applies to Poland. After half a century of absence of democratic practices and a market economy we have to learn so much anew, even if it boils down to "rediscovering the wheel". Western "know-how" is thus desperately needed from top to bottom. Starting from the Members of Parliament (MPs), who must learn the art of being MPs, as 80% of them are first time legislators, to many otherwise skilled and experienced company managers who have never experienced the cold showers of free market competition.

3. *Social and psychological constraints* – "economics as if the people mattered". It was sometimes claimed that Polish society, so deeply shaken and divided following the introduction of martial law, would remain passive, meekly accepting the status quo or perhaps resorting to national mysticism to find a justification for the misfortunes befalling it or losing its energy in sporadic and isolated outbursts of protest. To some observers Poland's determined, but sober and even handed, approach came as a surprise. Awareness of a common purpose prevailed over the sharpest antagonisms.

It is in the interest of the country that it be as steadfast as possible. Still, three paradoxes are riveting our attention. Firstly, the conceptual underpinning of the Balcerowicz programme is much more liberal than the existing balance of forces in the Parliament might imply. Secondly, the government is more popular than its policies, which are however also approved of (but by a lesser margin). Thirdly, society at large, savouring the long forbidden fruits of political and civic freedoms, has not fully realized that, like Alice in Wonderland, it has found itself on the other side of the mirror. And here the staircase begins – as the Polish saying goes.

4. *Social fatigue and its political implications.* It would be politically naive to expect, in a country which for half a century had been ruled on the basis of a different political and economic doctrine, that changes would not provoke protests. Market operations, despite their still limited scope, already have differentiated the society, widening the discrepancies between the impoverished and affluent strata of the society. Restructuring of industry, privatization and the accompanying processes, will only deepen this trend. The eternal questions of how to combine efficiency with social justice and what social justice really means for the very society and Solidarity trade union remain open. The slogan that "you cannot make an omelette without breaking eggs" is readily accepted. The problem is that the eggs have become too costly.

It cannot be entirely ruled out that the continued recession, with increasing unemployment, will wither away idealistic motivations, terminate the social peace, and change or diversify the present political map of Poland. The further lowering of living standards for sizable segments of the society is, regardless of good or bad intentions, rather impossible. Against this background the emergence of strong populists forces, social fatigue, internal tensions, chaotic and largely futile actions which constitute a scenario (however improbable at the moment) of rocking the boat.

VIII. *Instead of Conclusions*

In light of dispassionate analysis certain points are, in our view, incontestable:

1. There was no alternative to the Balcerowicz programme from any quarter. The programme elicited various comments, from eulogies to sharp criticism, but none of them made a coherent whole presented as a political challenge to the government.

Since no one ventured to offer a better scheme to weather the economic storms and disengage from real socialism, procrastination made little sense. It was all the more so as fool-proof scenarios of passing from the command economy to the Western-type market economy simply do not exist.

2. The government's policy to introduce systemic change by leaps and bounds was fully consistent with the key assumption that there is no "third way", but only rotten compromises, between the discarded socialist system and the contemporary, effective market economy model based on democracy and a common European heritage.

It is sometimes overlooked that Poland, in the beginning of the last decade, went through the ordeal of the most acute economic crisis which reduced its national income by nearly one quarter. The country, which has never fully recovered from its economic and political plight, was confronted in the late 80's with an only-too-real danger of new economic collapse. Surgical action, then, became evidently necessary because the old motto "what can't be cured must be endured" would not evoke positive reponse in a society known historically for its fierce resistance to the enemy and alien, imposed order.

3. The society was sick and tired, not only of the dogmas and practices of real socialism in its equally disappointing mutations, but it was also fed up with the muddle-through policies and "socialism — with reforms" of the 80's. In addition, political opposition to the failures of socialism has been so deep that the pleasures of burying it, for the moment, is compensation to many for all the discomforts of the incumbent capitalism.

In a certain sense the Poles are just turning back the wheel of history, which in some visions of social development was completely ruled out. Rallying behind the banner of radical systemic change, coupled with tracing our own roots and consolidation of Poland's sovereignty, is apparently for its citizens more appealing than safer prospects of incremental progress. No one can vouch for that, but this is at least the way it has always been, in a country described by the British historian Norman Davies as "the Gods' playground".

Now that the Poles are determined to take again their fate in their own hands this attitudinal momentum should not be lost. Moreover, a hardly definable but nevertheless existing linkage between the pace of political and economic change must be taken into consideration.

4. Sober evolution of the external environment also prompted bold action, taken without delay. There is an evident correlation between the readiness of the West to support the Poles and the measure of their success in assisting themselves.

Poland cannot be pulled out of the muck by its own bootstraps – it is in need of considerable external assistance. Fortunately, this is forthcoming. At the July 1989 Economic Summit of Heads of State in Paris the Commission of the European Communities was given responsibility for co-ordinating assistance rendered by 24 Western countries (Group of 24) to Hungary and Poland. In addition, Poland has obtained access to some new credits (from IMF, World Bank, BIS and individual countries). Other kinds of help have been promised or already rendered.

The external assistance and the speed and radicalism of Polish reforms are clearly interlinked. In many instances, such as training of managers, promoting foreign investments and the like, "the medium is the message", since the absorptive capacity of foreign assistance is augmented by the progressing reforms, which in turn are fuelled by fresh inputs and concepts.

Apart from Western assistance per se, Poland and other post-socialist countries do their best to attract foreign capital and forge new ties of co-operation with Western industrialized countries. In this keen competition only the facts matter. Poland has no time to spare, because doing business with Dr. Jekyll is always easier than with Mr. Hyde.

5. The growing uncertainties as to future developments in the USSR, as well as the breathtaking speed of political change in the other Eastern and Central European countries, were additional reasons to accelerate internal transformations, both political and economic, in order to create certain faits accomplis and thus safeguard Polish national interests.

Changes taking place in Europe, and in particular the prospect of a unified Germany, make Polish efforts to speed up economic recovery and integration with (West) European institutions (including – as an ultimate aim – membership in the EC) a top political priority. At this stage Poland aspires to association with the European Communities, full membership in the Council of Europe and new forms of co-operation with EFTA and – in a broader framework – OECD countries.

6. In the near future there will be no major changes in the present economic policy. The mid-and long-term policies are less clear, since these depend – as indicated above – on a number of domestic and external developments. It is hard to predict precisely when the whole process of economic change will be completed. Nevertheless, the on-going changes are irreversible, as, politically, Poland has evidently reached the point of no return.

Poland's Process of Economic Transformation: How Has the West Helped and What Else Should be Done?[1]

Alberto Chilosi

Synopsis

During Poland's process of economic transformation, the West has helped, and has decided on further help, in the following areas:

– Food help.
– Trade concessions.
– Increasing financial resources in convertible currencies through various forms of short and long-run financing and through debt relief and restructuring.
– Giving technical assistance of various kinds and lessening barriers to technological imports from the West.

What else should be done? A case for further help can be made, but we must avoid repeating the mistakes of the seventies.

Part of future additional aid will probably take the form of debt relief. A close examination of Poland's hard currency balance shows that in fact Poland is utterly unable to satisfy, under any reasonable foreseeable circumstances, its foreign obligations, notwithstanding the remarkable surplus of its current hard currency balance in the recent months.

Finally, the important issues of foreign investments, privatisation and debt-equity swaps are investigated.

I. Poland's Programme of Economic Transformation

Poland has embarked on a serious process of transformation, both political and economic, aiming at introducing a "market system akin to the one found in the industrially developed countries".[2] At the beginning of the year Mazowiecki launched a stabilization policy, agreed with the IMF, which led to a sharp reduction in the purchasing power of the population. In January 1990 real incomes fell by about 24% in relation to December.[3] Even greater has been the fall in living standards, as measured by consumption expenditure at constant prices.[4] However, because of repressed inflation, part of consumption which was foregone was previously misallocated, or allocated at high transaction costs (queues in particular). The loss in living standards therefore is not really as high as the figure for aggregate consumption implies.

Aside from minor disturbances, the population has shown remarkable forbearance, suffering from the Mazowiecki government what it would have certainly not suffered from the previous Communist ones.

The principal short-run objectives of the stabilization programme are twofold: (a) to suppress repressed inflation; (b) to suppress open hyperinflation. In January the first was achieved, but open inflation jumped to 78.6% from the 17.7% monthly rate in December.[5] On the other hand, to suppress repressed inflation you need to increase prices while holding in check the growth of incomes, so as to decrease effective demand. Thus, the price increases needed to abolish repressed inflation did at first contribute to the acceleration of open inflation.

Subsequently, in the months of February and March the persistence of a restrictive stabilization policy (based not only on monetary, but also on budgetary restraint) has in fact led to a sharp reduction in the open inflationary process. In February monthly inflation fell to 23.9%.[6] Forecasts for the month of March are of a monthly rate of inflation of about 5%. Moreover, at mid-March the inflationary process has apparently completely stopped: the reduction of the prices of a number of consumer goods has led to a stationary, or even slightly negative, change in the consumer price level.[7]

There have been complaints about the extent of the deflationary measures: some sectors of Polish public opinion (including some economists) have been complaining about the decrease in production and real incomes and they would have preferred a softer approach. On the other hand the decrease in production, even if large (a 41.6% fall in January and more or less the same in February with respect to the corresponding months of the previous year for the food industry, 28% in January and about 30% in February for light industry, and between 5% and 10% in the other branches,[8] amounting to an overall decrease in production over the two months of 23.5% in relation to the corresponding period in 1989),[9] has been so only on a monthly (or bi-monthly) basis. On a yearly basis the decrease could turn out to be much lower should production pick up in future months, once the results of the stabilization process have been consolidated.

The success of the anti-inflationary battle has been accompanied by the successful implementation of the internal convertibility of the zloty and the remarkably steady zloty-dollar exchange rate, providing for the monetary anchor to which the whole programme has tied the Polish economy. If this anchor were to be swept away by the hyperinflationary tide, an important pillar of the whole programme would have been removed. A reasonably stable rate of exchange has provided the Polish economy with what it missed for so long: a measuring rod of international opportunity cost. Also for the sake of continued stability of the rate of exchange (or at least for keeping its rate of depreciation under control) it is important that the inflationary process not be resumed.

However, important potential seeds of inflation still remain and will not be easy to deal with. In particular the extent of subsidies to the coal industry[10] and the still comparatively low prices of some services, such as railroads, imply the need for possibly inflationary price adjustments in the future. Some problems could arise also from the market readjustment of the price structure of consumer goods, implying possible increases in both the price of necessities and money wages. We shall return to this point later on. Moreover, if forecasts for coming mass unemployment prove to be true, some inflationary pressure towards increased public expenditure could come from the need to pay unemployment subsidies and to finance retraining and redeployment programmes, as provided by the new employment law.[11]

At present there are already signs which point to the fact that the currency may be over-valued: according to exporting firms the present exchange rate is incompatible with export profitability, given the growth of prices from the beginning of the year.[12] However this is usually the stand of exporting firms all over the world. Some of their difficulties could be structural, deriving from necessary cost and production readjustments, rather than from an inappropriate exchange rate. Until very recently the exchange rate has been remarkably stable and no drawing on the $ 1 billion stabilization fund has been needed. Furthermore, in the first two months of the year the Polish payments surplus has amounted to $ 530 million.[13] In January alone the high nominal interest rates (with a monthly prime rate of 40 %), in parallel with a steady exchange rate of the dollar, and severe restrictions on real incomes and demand formation, have led to net purchases by the banking system of convertible currencies from the population of about $ 112 million.[14] The same effect has helped the zloty in February and March, with monthly rates of interest of about 20% and 10% respectively. However the further decrease of the rate of interest, needed both to somewhat relax the deflationary grip on the economy and to adjust the rate of interest to the much lower rate of inflation, may weaken the relative advantage of holding zlotys.

At the same time relaxing monetary constraints will lead to increased imports. Credits totalling $ 1.4 billion are expected to be forthcoming this year, allowing a planned end-of-the-year deficit in the trade balance of $ 800 million.[16]

Even if not actually utilized, the presence of the $ 1 billion stabilization fund provided by Western governments has probably been of essential importance to the success of the convertibility of the zloty. In the longer run modernization of the Polish economy, rationalization of its production structure, and its increased integration in the world economy require sustained assistance from the West of a technical, financial and commercial nature. This represents a more difficult and complex task for the West than the short-run support provided by the stabilization programme. In the course of this paper we shall briefly review the assistance that Poland until now has received, the kind of assistance that has already been decided, and the prospects for further economic cooperation. We shall also consider the issue of what to do with Poland's huge foreign debt in light of the economic results of Poland's 1989 foreign trade balance and present trade prospects. Finally, we shall briefly touch on the issue of foreign direct investments and privatisation.

II. How Has the West Helped and What Further Help Has been Decided to Date ?

Following the development of Gorbachev's reformist programme, and especially since the withdrawal of the Soviet army from Afghanistan, a more positive attitude to East European states and talks of a new Marshall Plan for the East preceded the sudden crumbling of East European Communist régimes. So, when this unexpected event first materialized in Poland, with the electoral defeat of the Communists and eventually, at the end of August 1989, with the launching of the first non-Communist led government of Eastern Europe, Western public opinion was already prepared to help and action has been swift. The first concerted move by the West, the meeting of the Group of 24 under the aegis of the European Commission in July 1989, was just one month following the Polish elections. Assistance to Poland has assumed until now the following forms:[17]

Food aid

The total amount of food aid pledged by the Group of 24 (the European Community providing the greatest share) has been over 500 million Ecu. According to Polish sources (*Gazeta Bankowa* no. 12, 18.3-24.3, 1990) the value of total food aid received by the end of 1989 amounted to $88 million, and in the first two months of this year $71 million.[18] The countervalue of a part of food aid (about 200 billion zloty) has been placed in the Polish/EC jointly managed European Fund for the Development of Polish Agriculture, which has also been provided with $20 million for financing imported equipment from the West.[19]

Trade concessions

A more durable and far reaching form of help has assumed the form of trade concessions, which hopefully will help Poles to help themselves, earning precious hard currency on Western markets. These concessions appear generous, even if it is too early to assess their real impact on Poland's trade balance. However they may help explain February's rapid growth in exports of light industry and especially agricultural products to the West (respectively 33% and 82% in comparison with February 1989).[20]

The EEC in particular has abolished quantitative restrictions on Polish exports from 1 January 1990 (five years ahead of schedule in relation to the original date contained in the commercial treaty with the EEC). Still, quantitative restrictions remain in the areas of the multifibre agreement, of certain agricultural products and of coal and steel. Talks on the multifibre agreement are presently under way. Upon renewal, an undertaking by the EEC towards abolishing quantitative restrictions against Poland and Hungary will become operative. The GSP (General System of Preferences, non-reciprocal concession of free-of-duty import quotas, originally extended to underdeveloped countries) has been applied to Poland and Hungary from 1 January 1990, entailing sizeable reductions in customs duties and, for some agricultural products, the possibility to actually penetrate the EEC customs barrier.

As at the end of January 1990 trade concessions by Western governments were as follows: (a) GSP had been granted by Australia, Austria, EEC, Japan, Canada, New Zealand and the USA; (b) most favoured nation (MFN) treatment had been given by the above countries plus Finland, Norway, Switzerland and Sweden.[21]

Increasing financial resources in convertible currencies through various forms of financing and through debt relief and restructuring
Short-term resources include a standby $1 billion stabilization loan, granted to Poland to support convertibility of the zloty. Also in February the IMF granted Poland a short-run standby credit of $723 million.

In February Poland's 17 principal creditor countries agreed to grant Poland favourable rescheduling terms on their share of Polish debt, amounting to about $10 billion (of a total Polish foreign debt in hard currencies totalling about $41 billion). The agreement allows for rescheduling over 14 years, with an initial grace period of 8 years.[22] The rescheduling relates to arrears due until the end of December 1989 ($6 billion) plus everything (interest and capital repayments) due until March 1991. These terms were considered by commentators in the press as very favourable. If the same approach is applied to rescheduling of private credits, Poland will be free of any payment on debt servicing in the first crucial year of stabilization and economic transformation.[23]

Restructuring of debt has avoided earmarking scarce convertible resources for debt servicing, at least in the immediate future. But Poland is still not really in a position to raise substantial new resources on the international capital markets. Somebody else has to do it on Poland's behalf. The influx must first of all come from multilateral organizations. This kind of help will be provided through the following schemes:

i) Technical assistance and channelling of financial resources to develop a private market economy through a specially created European Bank for Reconstruction and Development, which should become operative in the course of the year with a planned capital of around $10 billion.[24] The aim of this bank is to channel resources into East European economies for aiding the development of private enterprise (the American view) and also for financing reconstruction of public infrastructure (the European view). A case could be made for extending the support of the Bank to public works projects, aiming at employment creation, in order to soothe the social consequences of the sectoral readjustment problem and to absorb unemployment created by structural readjustment and the phasing out of subsidies and tightening of budget constraints. The different viewpoints on the scope of the Bank have been recently overcome in a compromise according to which 60% of available finance is going to be directed to private investment and 40% to investment in public infrastructures.

ii) The World Bank is planning "to lend up to $ 2.5 billion to Poland over the next three years."[25]

iii) Poland, as well as Hungary, has been made eligible by the EC Council

of Ministers for financing of projects by the European Investment Bank and for some financing by the European Coal and Steel Community.[26]
iv) A European-Polish investment Bank has also been proposed.

For the time being, while ad hoc multilateral financial institutions are being developed, a number of Western governments have decided to grant long-term credits and credit guarantees. A document discussed at the Polish Central Planning Office[27] put those credits, by the end of January, at $4,938 million. Adding $341 million specifically dedicated to the development of the Polish private sector and $360 million already decided by the World Bank, one arrives at a total of long-term development aid, already agreed, of $5,639 million. Financial assistance towards tackling environmental problems has been offered by a number of countries (in particular Scandinavian ones).

COCOM has recently decided to reduce its restrictions on exports to Eastern Europe and to redraw the list of embargoed products before the end of May, liberalizing previously forbidden exports in the area of computers, machine tools and telecommunications.

A number of schemes for the training of personnel needed for the new market economy institutions and for technical assistance for all of Eastern Europe are presently being organized by the different governments and by the European Community.

III. *What Else Should be Done ?*

Should the West do more? Comparisons have been made with the size of the Marshall Plan, under which the East (Poland included) would have received much more in aid than what is envisaged at present. Taking into consideration that "during the $3\frac{1}{2}$ year authorisation period of the Marshall Plan, the US granted 1.3% of its gross national product", the *Financial Times* concludes that "on a comparable basis, the European Community alone could now consider a total fund of $200 billion for assistance to Eastern Europe and, ultimately, the Soviet Union." Then, "if such a programme were ultimately to be split 60:40 between Eastern Europe and the Soviet Union and Poland's share were to be according to population, it should receive roughly $40 billion",[28] which, curiously enough, corresponds to the total amount of Poland's foreign convertible debt. However, the Marshall Plan took many months to become operative. As we have seen, a number of measures have already been undertaken, and we are only at the beginning: more could be done in the future.

But the case for a much bigger influx of resources is not clear-cut. It is true that the Polish economy is in bad shape, but still it has not been ravaged by war. Neither do people really starve, unlike the case in many third world countries. Politically, though, the stakes are very high. For the first time the Communist party has been defeated in free (albeit not a priori too fair, as to the original rules) elections, and the first non-communist led government in the whole of the Soviet bloc has been installed. Poland has shown by the force of a successful experiment that the Brezhnev doctrine is really dead, so long at least as Gorbachev is in power, and everybody in Eastern Europe has drawn the consequences. But, because of that, Poland is no longer a special case. If Poland deserves aid, so do the rest of Eastern Europe, with which Poland must share available resources. It could be argued that Gorbachev deserves aid too, for what he has allowed to happen and for the possible dire consequences of his downfall.

The point in this, as in other policy matters, is that the real consequences of decisions are often much different from what they are first envisaged to be. The huge influx of foreign resources into the Polish economy during the seventies, which in the short to medium term provided the Polish communist rulers with a way to avoid much needed fundamental reforms, in the long-run has contributed to the crisis of the eighties and to the eventual downfall of the Communist regimes. Contrary to what even very senior officials (such as the late Franz Josef Strauss) thought at the time, it was very bad business, economically, both for the giving and for the receiving end, but in political terms it has provided enormous long-run returns. The risk always exists that help can become a way for the receiving end to avoid putting its house in order. This is taken care of at present by making help conditional on IMF monitoring, and financing of projects on assessment by Western lending agencies. The risk of uncoordinated excessive lending should somehow be taken care of by the coordinating function of the EEC in the group of 24.

What the West should absolutely not do this time is to repeat the scheme of the seventies: to give easy credit and then to raise trade barriers to prevent Poland (and other East European countries) from exporting what is needed to repay the debt. Trade concessions and help to develop Poland's export potential should be (and in fact have been) privileged, so that Poland may earn the foreign currency it needs to modernize its economy and to repay at least part of the debt.

However, if Poland (and the other East European countries) are going to increase their export potential and become integrated into the European and world economy, low labour costs of a reasonably well-educated labour force will be the basis of comparative advantage, and this is going to hurt somebody. It should be considered that at present the average monthly Polish wage, at the current exchange rate of the zloty, is below US $ 100.[29] This does not correspond to the real wage in comparable purchasing power terms because of the much lower price of basic foodstuffs and services. Traditionally, a relatively much lower price of necessities was the outcome of the old practice of keeping the internal foodstuff price low and insulating the internal from the international price structure through state monopoly of foreign trade and quantitative limitations on foodstuff exports. At the moment the direct export capabilities of Polish farmers have yet to be developed. Moreover, a number of export limitations directed at maintaining internal supplies of a number of agricultural products, as well as to satisfy agreed international quantitative limitations on Polish exports, have been in force.[30] However, the phasing out of subsidies on most agricultural commodities[31] and the change in foreign trade institutions, together with the greater openness of Western (and in particular

European Community) markets to Polish foodstuff exports, will in due time be fully reflected in their impact on the internal price structure. This will presumably lead to internal prices of basic foodstuffs more in line with the international opportunity cost, which also will contribute to the objective of giving a sustainable stable set-up to Polish agriculture.[32] This development, together with the inevitable increase in energy prices tied to the liberalization of the price of coal (which according to some proposals could be for the first of July[33]) and the readjustment of the prices of some services (such as railroads), notwithstanding an expected downward readjustment in the relative price of consumer durables, will eventually lead to an increase in the foreign exchange cost of Polish labour, if the purchasing power of Polish wages in terms of necessities is going to be maintained.

In other words, in part the present low cost of Polish labour is achieved at the expense of farmers and of the state budget, as well as of foreign donors of agricultural products. The costs of these subsidies to the national economy are paid through disincentives to increased agricultural production and investment and through the overall weight of taxation.

However, one can expect that, even when a suitable readjustment of Polish consumer prices takes place, the wage costs will probably remain much lower than elsewhere in Europe, so long as the government is able to maintain trade union support and to avoid populist policies. Thus, the relatively low labour costs will probably continue to be, for some time to come, a fundamental characteristic of Polish opportunities in the international division of labour.

Then the danger arises that, once the enthusiasm for what is happening in the East is over, the threat that East European exports represent for a number of labour intensive or technologically intermediate Western product groups (such as agricultural production for north-central European countries or textile and leather products for southern European ones) could weigh more heavily than the diffused interests of the consumers of these products or overall political considerations. But at present the far-reaching trade concessions that the West has made to Poland are really a good start, and because of the above considerations, this was the right moment to make them. In future social expenditures directed to help restructuring industries in the West which have lost comparative advantage could usefully substitute for part of the aid given to former socialist countries, as well as to underdeveloped ones.

At the same time the opportunities for trade are going to be presumably enhanced by systemic change. In due course a more stable organization and better institutional guarantees and availability of supplies to Polish private agriculture could be the basis for its expansion and for the expansion of its export capability. Reduction of energy and raw material intensity of production will also presumably both enhance export capabilities of raw materials and put their imports to better use.[34] Likewise, in the long-run, the improvement in the quality of manufactured goods brought about by the market and competition, both internal and international, and by the influx of foreign capital and know-how, may increase export capabilities.

The latter will be obviously enhanced by a further demolition of the barriers to trade. But this will need time to develop. In the meantime East European countries, Poland among them, need further short-run and medium term assistance to overcome the present critical economic situation and to undertake restructuring of their economies.

IV. *Poland's Balance of Payments and the Debt Issue*

But is Poland really capable of absorbing huge amounts of aid without dissipating resources and falling back into the irresponsible atmosphere of the mid-seventies? This doubt does not obviously apply to the option of freeing Poland from the crushing weight of the existing hard currency debt. The magnitude of the latter is much larger than the influx of resources until now considered either by would-be new lenders or donors. As we have seen above, according to recent calculations by the Polish Central Planning Office, the value of the influx of resources to develop the Polish economy (excluding food help, resources devoted to the environment, technical help, purely financial support — such as the stabilization fund — and short-term credits) following decisions taken before 31 January 1990, amounts to $5.7 billion for the next 3-4 years,[35] a figure still lower than the debt service due for 1989 alone. Moreover "the bulk of financial arrangements are debt-creating"[36] and so they may turn out eventually to increase the debt problem in the future.

Before the February rescheduling agreement with the Paris Club, debt had reached the amount of $41,4 billion (as of end of 1989), of which about 1/4 was held by foreign commercial banks and the rest was official debt. This represents more than 5 times the revenues from hard currency exports, which in 1989 amounted to $8.113 billion (the highest coefficient among the CMEA countries) and more than 3 times the overall revenues of the current account balance of $13.171 billion. The hard currency trade balance amounted to a mere $126 million (down from the $941 million level of 1988), mostly as a consequence of greater fuel imports from the hard currency area due to reduced consignments by the USSR. To this must be added a negative service balance of $211 million and a positive transfer balance of $1,232 million to arrive at a current balance, net of interest payments and receipts, of $1,147 million. This represents a mere 37% of outstanding net interest payments of $3,069 million (of which only $1,075 million were actually paid, up from $950 million in 1988). To this should be added $3,096 million of repayments due for long and medium term debts (of which only $497 million were actually honoured, down from the $636 million of 1988), to arrive at an overall amount of debt service of $6,165 million. This sum is close to 50% of all current account receipts and 76% of Poland's hard currency exports. The payments actually made in 1989 for servicing the debt amounted to 19.4% of export revenues, down from 29.2% in 1986, 26.5% in 1987, and 21.3% in 1988.

The debt situation is due to get worse in terms of the overall outstanding debt during 1990, since the trade balance is planned in the red by

$800 million as a consequence of a planned 6.4% increase of imports (up to $8.5 million) and a planned 5.1% decrease of exports (down to $7.7 million). The plan was agreed with the IMF in order to ease market tensions and to facilitate the successful execution of the adjustment programme. Interest due next year is forecast at $3.6 billion on the basis of a dollar interest rate of 8.8%. Only a small part is probably going to be paid, and therefore the overall amount of debt is correspondingly going to increase. Another factor pointing in the same direction is the forecast of an influx of long-and medium capital funds of $1,450 billion (different from the previous years when the influx was minimal). Moreover, of the $2.8 billion capital reimbursements falling due in 1990 only $0.3 billion are going to be repaid, the rest going to increase the size of the debt. Also repayment is planned of $200 million of short run capital funds, borrowed the previous year for financing urgent import needs. In conclusion, the extent of the Polish debt in convertible currencies is foreseen, at the end of 1990, to amount to $43.3 billion. The real figure will depend in the end on, among other factors, the changes in the exchange rate of the US $.

On the other hand the final outcome of the foreign trade balance will depend on effective Polish capabilities to import and to export. As to the latter, internal excess supply has spilled over into free exports for convertible currencies which, in the month of February, increased (in comparison with February 1989) at the respectable yearly rate of 20%. Exports to the West in the framework of barter or countertrade are gradually decreasing, conforming to a policy decision taken at the start of the year.[38] For the moment the export drive works mostly in such sectors as agricultural products and light industry, which have been the highest hit by reduction in internal demand and which can more readily shift their sales to foreign markets. Other sectors may soon follow suit, however. Not surprisingly, imports from the West have gone down a few percentage points with respect to the previous February. Consequently the balance of trade with the West in February showed a surplus of $243 million.[39]

With respect to the CMEA countries Poland is also in debt. However, Poland's transferable rouble (trb) indebtedness of 5.8 billion (mostly with the USSR) at the end of 1989[41] represents much less of a problem than the indebtedness in convertible currencies. First of all, its size is much smaller, both translated into dollar equivalent at the current official exchange rate of 2,100 zloty for the rouble and 9,500 zloty for the dollar (amounting in this way to $1.20 billion[42]), and as compared to the 11.320 billion trb 1989 exports to the CMEA area. Moreover, Poland's problem is not that it doesn't know either how to repay or to service the debt, but on the contrary that the current surplus in trb is much higher than planned (in 1989 it was 978 million trb vs. 300 million trb planned surplus, twice as much as in 1988, and a surplus of 1,104 billion trb in the overall current balance, again three times as much as planned and twice as much as in 1988). This arises from, first of all, the Soviet Union not honouring its export commitments to Poland, especially of fuels and energy, and thus running a 2 billion trb deficit. Notwithstanding Poland's intentions of halving its current surplus with the Soviet Union, the trend has continued in the first months of this year. On the one hand Polish firms facing a falling demand on the internal market and finding it difficult to shift exports to more remunerative Western markets are all too eager to keep up their exports to the Soviet Union, on the other the Soviet Union is unable to keep up its export commitments to Poland. In February, for instance, imports from CMEA countries are down by more than 20% and exports to them up by 5% in relation to February 1989. Consequently in February the CMEA trade surplus has amounted to 351 billion trb.[43] As a result Polish debt to the Soviet Union continues to fall, embarrassing Poles who prefer to renegotiate their debt rather than to repay it. The Polish stand on the issue is, in fact, that indebtedness results from undervalued compulsory participation in CMEA investment projects, such as the Yamburg gas-pipeline, and should therefore be cancelled. In the recent Polish-Soviet negotiations on the issue the Soviet side requested that, "since the Polish debt ... has arisen as a consequence of conjunctural changes on the world market, the debt should be converted into a dollar one".[44] Eventually it was agreed that Poland would run a 200 million trb trade surplus this year.[45] Moreover, 10-15% of trade is going to be on world prices on the basis of dollar clearing.[46]

While the CMEA debt problem of Poland, notwithstanding all recent wrangling on the issue, is obviously not by any means an intractable one, the same cannot be said of the Western debt, towards which Poland has been openly and hopelessly insolvent.

It is obvious that there are three possible approaches open to creditors towards a country (such as Poland) which is insolvent. The first is sanctions, the second debt remission, the third rescheduling. Since nobody in his right mind is willing, under present circumstances, to consider the first approach (and the Poles know it) this automatically limits the possible choices open to foreign credits to two main approaches:

a) to settle once for all the debt issue by reducing the debt to proportions which are comfortably manageable for the Polish economy to service; or

b) to roll-over the debt, hoping for a future improvement in Polish capabilities to pay.

In general, the advantage (from the creditor countries' point of view) of rolling over debts, instead of outright remission, lies (aside from the hope of getting some future payments) in the continuous leverage that this allows over the debtor's policies (there is always the possibility that the next rescheduling will be less benevolent, and the debtor knows it). Once remission is granted leverage is gone. Leverage can be exerted both for conditioning internal economic policies, in particular through IMF supervision, or for deterring adverse political developments. In the case in point, in the event (however unlikely at present) of an authoritarian shift in the Polish political course, due to internal or international events, the hazard of having to face a non-conciliatory rescheduling procedure could exert some moderating influence towards preserving Western interests and values.

It seems inevitable however that, sooner or later, some substantial amount of debt relief must be granted to Poland. So long as Poland is not even in a position to pay interest on the debt, the latter is tendentially increasing at the same rate as the rate of interest for the part on which interest remains unpaid.[47] Presently the rate of interest is certainly not lower than the prospective rate of growth of the Polish economy, nor of some reasonable estimate of its sustainable potential hard currency exports. So, short of outright debt relief (either in the form of concessional interest rates or of reduction in the amount outstanding, in one form or another), or of a dramatic reduction in world interest rates, the debt burden is not going to diminish. Neither is Poland going to become solvent. However, what amount of debt would be compatible with Poland's solvency is very difficult at present to estimate. We are at the start of a long and painful process of economic reconstruction, and only the future can tell us the impact on the Polish external position of recent trade concessions and various measures of international assistance. At the same time a substantial decrease in the rate of interest on US $ loans, following a tighter fiscal policy in the USA and a drastic reduction in USA budget deficit, cannot be ruled out. This would be in fact a suitable way to use the "peace dividend" deriving from reduction in military expenditures following lessening in international tensions.[48] Therefore times are not ripe for assessing the extent of sustainable Polish debt nor for a definitive solution to the Polish debt problem. The latter should also be seen in the framework of the overall world debt problem. A straightforward remission of Polish debt would be much more costly than the debt remission itself, since it would create a precedent for the other most indebted countries of the world. At present, the most (as well as the least) that Poland could hope for would be a season of rescheduling-cum debt relief of the menu-type approach, as in the framework of the Brady plan.

Ultimately the Polish debt issue may find its solution in the framework of an overall solution to the debt problem of the most indebted countries of the world. As, in the last few years, the overall financial flows facing the most indebted countries continue to be negative, lower penalties are associated to debt repudiation and better terms may be reached in debt rescheduling negotiations.[49] With time, indebted countries get better rescheduling conditions as their debt problem becomes more and more intractable and previous concessional boundaries are broken, while bank reserves for irretrievable debts are increased, leading ultimately to write-offs.

This could be the future solution for the Polish debt problem, too. In the meantime officially granted credits and officially insured direct investments could be the substitute for the access to private credit markets and uninsured investments that the persistence of the debt problems makes difficult to obtain.

V. *Foreign Investments*

Once a suitable environment is created, foreign direct investment could do quite a lot of good to help to develop those sectors and initiatives where there are positive returns and to draw in foreign technology and management. So long as the debt issue is present, however, in order to improve opportunities for direct investments some guarantee, as to the political risk and availability of foreign exchange, for foreign direct investment should be (and is currently being) given by Western governments.

Foreign investment could also actively participate in the privatisation process. Moreover, exchange of real assets for financial ones could be in future a way to reduce the outstanding debt and at the same time to carry on privatisation.

Privatisation through sale to foreigners of State firms has some advantages to the ordinary Polish citizen, in comparison to the process of nomenklatura privatisation which has taken place for some time: [50] i) net influx of convertible currencies (so long as at least profits don't start to be repatriated); ii) influx of technology and technical and managerial capabilities; iii) avoidance of the inegalitarian consequences on the distribution of wealth among Poles of private appropriation of State firms by those who are in a privileged position to do so.

In the Polish case (as in the case of other former socialist countries) privatisation through the sale of productive assets to foreign investors is facilitated by the very low proportion of foreign direct investments in overall capital. This implies that, in contrast with some other heavily indebted countries, even a sustained process of transfer to foreign investors of national assets (for instance in a far-reaching debt-equity swap process) would leave Poland with a still relatively low proportion of national capital under foreign ownership. At the same time, in Poland, as in other former socialist countries, the debt-equity swap option theoretically offers great opportunities, owing to the extent of public ownership of economic activities.

However, at present the market for Polish firms is thin, and the risks to foreign investors are high. First, there is a problem of evaluation, which is rendered more difficult than in other heavily indebted countries, by the absence of a real stock exchange. In the end the value of a firm will depend on its expected profit flow. But the profit flow of a firm is strictly dependent on the economic and institutional environment and on the established rules of the game. So long as the latter are still very uncertain, having yet to be established, so, too, is the value of a Polish firm to foreign investors. So long as the foreign investor discounts the possibility of unfavourable future institutional arrangements, the evaluation of a firm is going to be lower than with the favourable institutional set-up that the government could in future establish for private enterprises, foreign or national. (And that Poland is going to do just this is for many the whole purpose of the foreign aid exercise.) The present difficulties of evaluating Polish firms and the different expectations of foreign investors, Polish authorities and Polish workers is exemplified by the emblematic case of the former Lenin shipyards and of the would-be American-Polish buyer, Ms. Barbara Johnson, with the estimate ranging from the $200 million of the original joint venture proposal down to $0.5 million (the lowest estimate by

Arthur Anderson).[51] The cold turkey policy pursued by Mazowiecki under IMF supervision has at least the merit of showing determination in building up a viable market economy, and so it could reduce the perceived risks to foreign investors. But probably, before much help can be forthcoming in this way, stabilization has to be accompanied by the establishment of a new coherent institutional set-up which should eliminate, or at least reduce, the risk element which was considered before. And the nature of the eventual institutional set-up, in part, is dependent on the outcome of the current privatisation debate.

Notes

1. Documentation on this research was completed on 23 March 1990.
2. Statement of intentions by the Polish government, quoted in *Financial Times*, 28 December 1989, p.10.
3. *Gazeta Bankowa*, n. 11 (11/3-17/3/1990), p. 9. The measure of this fall results from a growth in the official consumer price index of 78.6% and a growth in money incomes of the population of 35.8%. It should be noted that the exact formula to be used for calculating the proportional rate of change of a real variable in the time unit, r, is as follows: r=(y-p)/(1+p), where y is the proportional rate of growth of the corresponding money variable in the time unit, and p is the proportional growth rate in the price index. The approximate measure y-p can be taken only if p is small relative to 1, which is not the case here.
4. About 35% in relation to December according to *Gazeta Bankowa*, no. 10 (5/3-11/3/1990), p. 2. See ibidem for further information on monetary indicators. The greater decrease in consumption expenditures than in real incomes can be explained as being the product on the one hand of the wealth effect, following the reduction in the real value of money assets, and the need to reconstruct real money balances for transactional purposes, and on the other of the very high nominal interest rate *in the presence of a fixed exchange rate and convertibility of the zloty.* The latter factor led in particular to a reduction of 3.2% in January in the amount of bank credit (and a 40% reduction in new credits) and an increase of 18.8% in bank deposits, notwithstanding the very high inflation rate and a highly negative real interest rate in *zloty terms.*
5. Official GUS figures for the monthly rates of growth of consumer prices. The monthly rate of inflation of producer prices in State industry was much higher in January: 109.8%, but only 7% in February (*Rzeczpospopolita*, 23/3/1990, p. 7).
6. GUS figure of the growth rate of average consumer prices (*Gazeta Wyborcza*, 17/3/1990, p. 1). Population incomes increased only by 3.2%, and expenditures decreased by 10% in comparison to January (*Gazeta Bankowa*, no. 12, 18/3-24/3/1990, p. 2). In the first two months of the year the State budget was running a considerable surplus (for the relevant budgetary data see "Statystyka Polski-Informacje Glownego Urzedu Statystycznego", *Rzeczpospopolita*, 23/3/1990, p. 8).
7. According to GUS, the consumer price index was 0.8% lower in the second week of March as compared with the first (*Gazeta Wyborcza*, 17/3/1990, p. 1). Sporadic price reductions were already coming about at the end of January (*Gazeta Bankowa*, no. 10, 5/3-11/3/1990, p. 2).

8. *Gazeta Bankowa*, no. 10 (5/3-11/3/1990), p. 9.
9. *Zycie Warszawy*, 15/3/1990, p. 2.
10. These are expected to amount to 9,600 billion zloty (about $1 billion at the present rate of exchange) in 1990. Still they will not be enough to avoid closure of coal mines and unemployment in the course of the year (*Gazeta Wyborcza*, 23/3/1990, p. 2).
11. At the end of February registered unemployed were 152,200, still a very modest percentage of a labour force of about 18 million (17.8 million in 1988, according to the 1989 *Rocznik Statistyczny*). On the other hand unemployment is increasing fast: from the end of January to the end of February the increase has been of 96,400 units. The expenditure for unemployment benefits in February was a mere 4 billion zloty (about US $420,000), but this is bound to increase more or less as fast as unemployment does. (Data taken from "Statystyka Polski-Informacje Glownego Urzedu Statystycznego", *Rzeczpospopolita*, 23/3/1990, p. 7).
12. *Gazeta Bankowa*, no. 11 (11/3-17/3/1990), p. 2.
13. *Gazeta Bankowa*, no. 11 (11/3-17/3/1990), p. 2.
14. *Gazeta Bankowa*, no. 10 (5/3-11/3/1990), p.2.
15. *Gazeta Bankowa*, no. 11 (11/3-17/3/1990), p. 9.
16. *Gazeta Bankowa*, no. 11 (11/3-17/3/1990), p. 2.
17. The following list purports by no means to be exhaustive, but to give merely an overall idea of the various measures and areas of intervention.
18. "Statystyka Polski-Informacje Glownego Urzedu Statystycznego", *Rzeczpospopolita*, 23/3/1990, p. 8.
19. *East European Markets*, 26 January 1990, p. 12.
20. *Gazeta Bankowa*, no. 12 (18/3-24/3/1990), p. 2.
21. Source: *Kierunki wykorzystania kreditow gwarantowanych oferowanych Polsce przez rzady panstw zachodnich i instytucje miedzynarodowe*, Warsaw, March 1990, mimeo.
22. *Sole 24Ore*, 17/2/1990, p. 1.
23. According to press reports, private creditors, however, are not terribly happy at the kind of debt rescheduling which has taken place, since it has included interest arrears and interest payments coming due.
24. *La Repubblica* 17 February, 1990.
25. *East European Markets*, vol. 10, no. 2, 26 January 1990, p. 2. Recently an agreement was signed on lending to Poland $150 million for modernizing Poland's transport system (and in particular railways). (*Rzeczpospolita*, 21/3/1990, p. 2).
26. *East European Markets*, vol. 10, no. 2, 26 January 1990, p. 9.
27. *Kierunki wykorzystania kreditow gwarantowanych oferowanych Polsce przeez rzady panstw zachodnich i instytucje miedzynarodowe.* Warsaw, March 1990, mimeo.
28. *Financial Times*, 28 December 1989, p. 10.
29. In February the average monthly wage in State industry was 800,000 zloty, US $84 at the present exchange rate. ("Statystyka Polski-Informacje Glownego Urzedu Statystycznego", *Rzeczpospopolita*, 23/3/1990, p. 7).
30. A decision of gradually phasing out export quotas of agricultural products has been recently taken by the Polish Council of Ministers. Only export limits on wheat, sugar, and pork, arising from international agreements on export restraints, are going to be maintained. (*Gazeta Wyborcza*, 20/3/1990, p. 1; *Rzeczpospolita*, 21/3/1990, p. 1).
31. Subsidies remain on milk as well as on some agricultural inputs such as fertili-

zers and pesticides. It was decided recently to increase nominal subsidies on the latter, as well as on the price of milk (*Rzeczpospolita*, 21/3/1990, pp. 1-2).

32. The latter has been in the past starved of supplies. Limited availability of hard currency to import animal feedstuffs from the West has led in recent times to the slaughter of livestock. The same process seems to be underway at present, as Polish farmers are squeezed between decreasing demand and higher production costs.
33. *Rzeczpospolita*, 23/3/1990, p. 2.
34. A bleak note is provided, however, by the much greater environmental consciousness, which renders much Polish coal, because of its high sulphur content, unsuitable for export to the West.
35. The above estimate may be compared with that by the United Nations Economic Commission for Europe of $5 billion for the various aid commitments to Hungary and Poland by the group of 24 before the end of 1989 (*Economic Bulletin for Europe*, vol. 41, 1990, p. 54). The latter figure does not include $1 billion credit facilities granted by IMF and World Bank, nor debt relief for 1990. "According to calculations by W. Trzeciakowski, Western help for Poland, either conceded, or only declared, did have at the end of January a value of above $8.7 billion". (*Gazeta Bankowa*, no. 10, 5/3-11/3/1990, p. 2). The different estimates depend on the different ranges of inclusiveness as to the type of help considered.
36. *Economic Bulletin for Europe*, vol. 41, 1990, p. 55.
37. The data reported in the present and the following section are mostly taken from Bronislaw Sulimierski, "Bilans platniczy '89 — II obszar walutowy", *Gazeta Bankowa*, no. 12, 18/3-24/3/1990, pp. 1, 7.
38. *Gazeta Bankowa*, no. 12 (18/3-24/3/1990), p. 2.
39. Ibidem.
40. Final data on Poland's 1989 foreign trade balance with the CMEA area are taken from Bronislaw Sulimierski, "Bilans platniczy '89 — I obszar walutowy", *Gazeta Bankowa*, no. 11 (11/3-17/3/1990), p. 3.
41. At the time of signature of the new Soviet-Polish trade protocol for 1990 (19/3/1990), the size of the debt in transferable roubles is reported at about 5 billion (*Rzeczpospolita* 21/3/1990, p. 2).
42. It would amount to about a third if the market exchange rate for transferable roubles were taken into account.
43. *Gazeta Bankowa*, no. 12 (18/3-24/3/1990), p. 2.
44. *Zycie Warszawy*, 19/3/1990, p. 2.
45. *Gazeta Wyborcza*, 20/3/1990, p. 1.
46. *Rzeczpospolita*, 21/3/1990, p. 2.
47. In 1989, for instance, the capitalization on unpaid interests contributed $2.4 billion to the increase in convertible foreign debt (*Gazeta Bankowa*, no. 12, 18/3-24/3/1990, p. 3).
48. It is worth recalling that the onset of the world debt crisis in general, and of the peculiar difficulties with the Polish debt, in particular, have been precipitated by "a rise of 20 percentage points in real interest rates on floating-rate debt from 1980 to 1981". (Barry Eichergreen and Richard Portes, *The Anatomy of Financial Crises*, mimeographed conference paper, December 1986, p. 53).
49. For the importance that circumstances of this type may have on the terms of rescheduling negotiations, up to the point of allowing rescheduling to lead to the formation of a cartel extracting consumer surplus from the indebted country through exertion of monopolistic power, see Sule Özler, "On the

Relation Between Reschedulings and Bank Value", *American Economic Review*, December 1989, pp. 1117-1131.

50. An idea of the extent to which the Polish economy has been privatised to date can be obtained by considering that in one year (from February 1989 to February 1990) employment in the 5 principal branches of the State economy has decreased by 8.5% (*Rzeczpospopolita*, 23/3/1990, p. 7). An interesting light on the practical legal aspects of privatisation is shed by a query addressed from the Ministry of Justice to the Supreme Court on the validity of "a contract to establish a limited liability company or a joint stock company, stipulated by a State company and a physical person, in case the latter acts both on his own account and as director (official) of the State firm." Whatever the answer of the court, the practical prospect of invalidating those, of the recently established more than 30,000 companies which were constituted in the way hinted at by the query to the Court (probably the greatest part of them), seems rather unlikely. (See *Gazeta Bankowa*, no. 10, 5/3-11/3/1990, P. 10).
51. See *East European Markets*, 9/2/1990, vol. 10, no. 3, p. 8.

The Romanian Economy: Policy and Prospects for the 1990 s

Alan H. Smith

Synopsis

"Two generations of peace and clean government might make Roumania an earthly paradise." R. W. Seton-Watson. A history of the Roumanians, 1934.

"Nicolae destroyed the economy and Elena destroyed the culture." Silviu Brucan, Adevarul, 28 February 1990.

Romanian economic prospects for the 1990s will continue to be seriously affected by the legacy of the executed President Ceausescu. The circumstances facing the Romanian economy in the 1990s differ substantially from those confronting the central East European economies. One positive effect of Ceausescu's policy of debt repayment is that Romania does not have a debt burden and the authorities could reduce net hard currency exports by $2.5-3.0 billion per annum in the 1990s without incurring any further external debt. This advantage, however, will be far outweighed by the damage caused to economic and social infrastructure by cutbacks in productive investment during the 1980s, by restrictions on imports of machinery and equipment from the West and by the squandering of available resources on grandiose investment projects with little or no return. The continued pursuit of heavy industrial priorities combined with vastly overoptimistic projections of domestic energy production has placed additional strain on Romania's primary energy supplies and has resulted in overrapid depletion of crude oil and natural gas. Energy and power generation in particular will be major constraints to economic growth.

Economic recovery, however, will depend critically on long term political stability. The prospects are not good. While the population is demoralised by years of drastically repressed living standards, Ceausescu's political legacy is one of widespread distrust. Virtually all industrial and administrative personnel with the skills required for economic recovery have been forced into some form of compromise with the Ceausescu régime, however small. Support for the Front for National Salvation, which assumed power after the popular revolution which overthrew the Ceausescu régime, appears to be largely confined to urban areas. Economic policy for the 1990s will depend critically on the form of government that emerges after the elections. The prospects of a more broadly based coalition appear to be evaporating as intellectuals have withdrawn their support for the Front. The Front's leaders are largely drawn from former party members who fell foul of Ceausescu, but did not have the courage to oppose him openly. The few details that have emerged about their economic platform indicate a very conservative approach, with only a limited role for private enterprise and foreign capital.

I. *Introduction*

Professor Seton-Watson's hypothesis has not been tested over the last 50 years, but it still gives a good indication of the minimum necessary conditions and the possible time scale for Romanian economic recovery. The government that takes power after the elections scheduled for 20 May, whatever its nature and legitimacy, will be faced with the urgent task of restoring social and political stability against a background of economic collapse.

This will not be easy. The pervasiveness of Ceausescu's security police (Securitate) and the repression of any alternative form of expression ran far deeper in Romania than in any other country in Eastern Europe and totally prevented the creation of even a rudimentary form of civil society. Romania's isolation from the outside world and from outside ideas has also been far more substantial than elsewhere. There are far fewer indications that there are relatively free thinking individuals in academic institutions who have managed to maintain contact with outside ideas than is the case in Czechoslovakia, Poland, Hungary, East Germany and, to a lesser extent, Bulgaria. The depth of this isolation is reflected in Silviu Brucan's claim in Adevarul (28 February) that there is not a single Romanian student enrolled at a foreign university or college. The community of younger emigrees who have managed to maintain contacts with the country could be a source of expertise, and could assist in the provision of education and training and exposure to outside ideas, but it is also significantly smaller than in the case of Poland, Hungary or Czechoslovakia.

A new government will therefore have to be formed which contains people who have either served in posts under communist (including Ceausescu-led) governments or will have to rely on personnel with very limited experience of even the theory of government and administration. Probably more seriously, it will be difficult, if not impossible, to fill posts in the government and economic administration with personnel who are not in some way compromised by their participation or even collaboration with the Ceausescu régime. Virtually every banker, financial official, accountant, statistician, foreign trade official and factory manager has been forced to make some accommodation with the former régime. Even if there is to be a major programme of privatisation of industry some of these officials will be needed to exercise some of the remaining functions of central economic administration, while the newly privatised industries will also need to utilise what expertise exists in the major task of reconstruction.

II. *The Import-Led Growth Strategy*

The current problems facing the Romanian economy result primarily from the failure of the import-led growth strategy which Romania embarked on in 1967 and pursued throughout the 1970s, until the debt crisis at the end of 1981 and the subsequent policy of debt elimination in the 1980s. A brief analysis of the reasons for the failure of the import-led growth policy is essential for understanding the contemporary economic problems in Romania and the prospects for their solution.

The strategy of import-led growth was in part a deliberate attempt to reduce Romanian economic dependence on the CMEA countries, and the USSR in particular, and to redirect trade flows in order to benefit from technology transfer from the industrialised West. The strategy combined elements of pre-war Romanian nationalism, in that it rejected an agrarian form of economic development in favour of accelerated industrialisation, and elements of conventional Stalinism in that it gave priority to investment in heavy industry, in particular steel and mechanical engineering, although the country had only limited deposits of iron ore and coking coal. Similarly in the second half of the 1970s Romania expanded its oil refining and petrochemical industries although domestic crude oil output had fallen below the requirements of domestic consumption since 1977.

This policy suffered from a number of inherent flaws which culminated in an inability to sustain a level of hard currency exports sufficient to both service debt and maintain imports of machinery, equipment and components. First, the policy was directed at import-substitution, rather than export-generation. As a result investment was not primarily directed at those sectors where Romania had a traditional comparative advantage and consistent export potential. This refers not just to agriculture, but to other areas such as textiles, clothing, footwear and furniture, which could have permitted a higher level of value added if production had been directed towards emerging specialist markets. Second, investment was concentrated on a wide-range of industrial production (a "many-sided industrialisation"), including areas in which Romania had little or no experience such as aerospace and cars.

Finally, the policy was a conscious attempt to imitate the "product-cycle" model of multinational investment, which had proved to be a vehicle of technology transfer to Western Europe in the 1960s, without relinquishing control over either ownership of the plant (in the form of majority equity participation) or over the minutiae of plant operation, including such details as manning levels, wage rates and quality control. The strategy attempted to acquire Western technology by a number of measures including licence purchase, co-production agreements and, finally, joint-ventures involving minority Western equity participation. The detailed control exercised over foreign investment meant that Romania offered Western multinationals a less flexible, lower-quality and higher-labour cost base for production than the newly industrialising economies of South-East Asia in particular. As a result Romania was less successful than the NIEs in attracting inward investment and had to place greater reliance on straight purchases of machinery and equipment, using hard currency credits.

The Romanians planned to repay loans from the proceeds of increased hard currency exports that were expected to materialise later in the decade. However the unwillingness to permit full or majority foreign equity participation in the economy and the reliance on purchases of equipment meant that Romanian enterprises were not integrated into the production-to-market cycle of Western multinationals who had no reason either to provide continuous modernisation of technology or to find markets for the products. Consequently Romania was confronted with major difficulties in marketing exports to the West.

The inability to move to a stage of self-generating technical progress meant that, by the late 1970s, Romania was faced with continued demand for imported technology, both to sustain the import-led growth policy and for industrial components to maintain existing output. The impact on the balance of trade and payments was aggravated by growing demands for imported raw materials (including iron ore, coking coal and crude oil) which, mainly as a result of Romania's break with the CMEA, had to be imported from hard currency sources. In addition the failure to encourage agricultural development meant that by 1981 Romania had even become a substantial net importer of foodstuffs from non-socialist countries (although remaining a net exporter of foodstuffs to socialist countries and in toto). Ironically, in view of what followed in the 1980s, the level of hard currency food imports in 1981 played a major contribution to the inability to meet scheduled debt repayments that year.

These problems were exacerbated by "exogenous factors", including the earthquake in March 1977, which accelerated the falling trend in crude oil output, by the increase in world crude oil prices in 1979 which reduced the profit margin on refining, and critically, by the increase in the level of interest rates.

III. *The Debt Repayment Programme*

Romania alone among the East European countries succeeded in eliminating its convertible currency debt by maintaining balance of trade surpluses throughout the 1980s. This has, however, been achieved at an enormous human and economic cost which will have a major impact on the prospects for Romanian economic recovery in the 1990s.

Prime Minister Petre Roman announced on 4 January 1990 that Romanian foreign debt was at "a highly acceptable level, with only half a billion dollars outstanding". Roman was presumably referring to gross debt, as BIS data show that by the middle of June 1989 Romania was a net creditor with BIS banks, with assets of $1,063 million against liabilities of only $334 million. In addition a report by Rompres, the new Romanian press agency, published on 5 January 1990, stated that Romania's external credits amounted to just under $3 billion. The report stated that trade credits amounted to $1,267 million at the end of October 1989 but that over 74% of this sum "could not be paid owing to the debtor's financial difficulties". One unnamed country was said to owe Romania over $1.6 billion, of which $0.6 billion comprised overdue payments. It is not clear whether the $3 billion figure includes assets with BIS banks or refers only to country to country loans.

Although the existence of some external debt at the end of 1990 conflicts with Ceausescu's claim that Romanian debt had been paid "in its entirety" by the end of March 1989, it confirms that Romanian net debt was indeed very low at that period.

Table I
Major Aggregates of Romanian Debt
($ million)

	1981	1982	1983	1984	1985	1986	1987	1988
Debt stocks								
Total	10477	10003	9128	7758	7008	6983	6662	2790
Long term	8071	7797	7585	6255	5805	5653	5425	1946
of which								
Official	2747	2604	2813	2552	2737	2948	3257	1496
Private	5324	5193	4772	3702	3068	2705	2168	450
Short term	1786	1344	596	566	543	617	730	700
IMF Credit	590	862	947	937	660	714	507	144
Total Debt flows								
Repayments	1236	2148	1214	1484	1414	1318	1425	3726
Interest	822	762	660	632	673	662	604	509
Debt Service	2057	2910	1874	2116	2087	1981	2028	4234
Disbursements	2521	3227	1542	403	509	819	592	94
Net Transfers	464	317	-333	-1713	-1578	-1161	-1436	-4141

Source: World Debt Tables 1980-90. External Debt of Developing Countries Volume 2. The World Bank.

The major aggregates relating to Romanian debt stocks and flows, according to World Bank data, are shown in Table I. They show that Romania has succeeded in reducing its net debt from an end-year high of $10.5 billion at the end of 1981 to $2.8 billion at the end of 1988. This was further reduced to an estimated level of approximately $0.5 billion at the time of the revolution at the end of 1989. World Bank data show that repayments of principal amounted to $14.0 billion between the end of 1981 and the end of 1988, with interest payments of an estimated $5.3 billion and total capital inflows of $9.7 billion over the period. Hence, net transfers between the end of 1981 and 1988 amounted to $9.6 billion. The pace of debt reduction in 1988 is surprisingly high and may reflect unrecorded cash inflows from developing countries.

The reduction in debt was principally achieved by running consistently high trade surpluses in convertible currency trade. Table II shows that this was achieved by compressing imports, which were cut by over 40% (measured in current dollars) between 1980 and 1983 (the fall in the value of both exports and imports from 1986 onwards is affected by the collapse of world oil prices in 1986). In the first half of 1987 Romania had a hard currency trade surplus of $1,068 million and a current account surplus of $980 million.

Unfortunately Romania has not provided any data on trade and payments to either the IMF or Western banks since the middle of 1987, and this data had not been supplied by the new government at the time of writing. Similarly the Annual Statistical Yearbook has not provided any data on the direction of trade since 1985. Estimates based on trade partners' data indicate that Romania substantially increased its trade surpluses with the OECD from 1987 onwards by further compressing imports and boosting the value of exports to over $4 billion, despite the fall in the price of refined oil products, a major component of Romanian exports to the West. This was partly achieved by increasing the volume of exports of refined oil products, assisted by increased imports of crude oil from the Soviet Union.

Table II
Romanian Trade in Convertible Currencies 1981-88
($ million)

	1980	1981	1982	1983	1984	1985	1986	1987	1988
Romanian Exports	6503	7216	6235	6246	6892	6280	5960	na	na
Romanian Imports	8037	7012	4710	4558	4706	4835	4043	na	na
Balance	-1534	204	1525	1688	2186	1445	1917		
Current account balance	-2399	-818	655	922	1536	915	1408		
Trade with OECD									
OECD exports	3905	3201	1704	1308	1392	1428	1644	1296	1284
OECD imports	3408	3549	2604	2700	3708	3456	3588	4044	4056
Romanian surplus	-497	328	900	1329	2316	2011	1671	2748	2772
Adjusted surplus	-675	175	775	1255	2130	1855	1765	2550	2575

Sources: Rows 1-4 from IMF International Financial Statistics
Rows 5-6 OECD Monthly Bulletin of Statistics
Adjusted surplus takes account of the cif evaluation of imports for EC data provided to the OECD.

IV. *The Costs of Debt Repayment on the Domestic Economy*

The debt repayment programme has placed a major strain on the economy by reducing the availability of resources for distribution between consumption and investment in the domestic economy. The estimation of the costs of the Romanian debt repayment programme is unusually complicated by the unreliability of Romanian data, which appears to be far greater than that of other East European countries. Romanian official statistics on domestic economic performance have always been of doubtful value, but both the quantity and quality of Romanian official data has deteriorated sharply since 1985. Romanian TV reports earlier this year even suggest that Ceausescu personally falsified statistical data in addition to the routine falsification of reports submitted by economic sub-units which were faced with sanctions for failure to fulfil overambitious production targets. As a result it is very difficult to arrive at credible estimates for macroeconomic indicators such as GNP, consumption, investment, industrial and agricultural performance. Any estimates can only be of a very approximate ball-park nature.

Two alternative methods can be used to estimate the proportion of GNP dedicated to debt repayment in the 1980s. The first is to compare the level of net exports measured in domestic prices with GNP in domestic prices. The second is to compare the dollar value of net exports with an estimate of the dollar value of GNP.

The Romanian authorities provided national income measured in domestic current prices to the IMF until 1986. These data are shown in Table III. The use of these data is complicated by the fact that it is virtually impossible to reconcile them with other data published in either the annual statistical handbook or communiques on plan fulfilment. They may, however, serve as a first approximation to the proportion of GNP dedicated to debt repayment. The data initially suggest that a relatively small, but not insignificant, proportion of GNP was dedicated to net exports. In 1984 net exports are given as 51 billion lei, equivalent to 6.0% of GNP (or 6.7% of national income). This proportion fell to 3.5% of GNP in 1986 (or 3.9% of national income). This figure appears to be a significant underestimate. First, it excludes the item "addition to stocks", some or all of which represents stocks of commodities for export but which have not actually been exported. Second, there is a growing unexplained statistical discrepancy. These have been aggregated in Table III to provide an estimate of the proportion of GNP that has not been allocated to either gross investment or consumption in the domestic economy. If the increase in stocks and the statistical discrepancy are arbitrarily allocated to net exports they indicate that the proportion of GNP allocated to net exports varied from 5.8% in 1982 to 11.2% in 1986.

Even this figure appears to be an underestimate compared with estimates linking the value of net hard currency exports, measured in dollars, to estimates of GNP, measured in dollars. Unfortunately the unreliability of Romanian statistics means that Western estimates of Romanian GNP show a substantially wider spread than those for any East European country, ranging from a low of $722 per capita for 1988, estimated by Credit Suisse First Boston (CFSB), to $5,490 per capita by the CIA. The latter figure, in particular, appears unrealistically high. These estimates are very susceptible to the exchange rate used for converting estimated domestic GNP into dollars. The CSFB estimate has been obtained by dividing the Romanian official data for GNP in 1988 (at 1985 prices) of 1001 billion lei by 75% of the black market exchange rate for the lei (given as 80 lei to the dollar) in 1989. CSFB themselves prefer an arbitrary estimate of $1,000 per capita. This methodology has been extended in Table IV. First, official data for GNP in constant prices have been revalued at the new official exchange rate. This provides an estimate of net exports of the region of just over 5% of GNP for most years. Second, an arbitrary exchange rate of 40 lei to the dollar has been supplied. This indicates a net export to GNP ratio varying from 7.9% in 1985 to 11.2% in 1988. It is probable that this is an underestimate in view of the upward bias of GNP data.

Table III
Romanian National Income Data: Official Statistics.
(lei billions- current prices)

	1980	1981	1982	1983	1984	1985	1986
GNP	620	642	747	786	843	874	918
Depreciation	60	65	71	75	82	88	91
National Income (NNP)	560	577	676	711	761	786	827
NMP		531	629	655	709	751	772
Private Consumption	360	381	443	440	456	491	510
Government consumption	37	43	45	50	53	54	56
Gross fixed capital formation	212	209	216	231	245	256	249
Total	609	633	704	721	754	801	815
Net exports	-18	3	28	32	51	32	32
Increase in Stocks	23	8	20	34	21	17	24
Discrepancy	+6	-2	-5	-1	17	+24	+47
Total	11	9	43	65	90	73	103
% GNP	1.8	1.4	5.8	8.3	10.6	8.4	11.2

Source: IMF International Financial Statistics except NMP which are taken from plan fulfilment data. Net export to GNP ratio varying from 7,9% in 1985 to 11.2% in 1988. It is probable that this is an underestimate in view of the upward bias of GNP data.

Table IV

	1982	1983	1984	1985	1986	1987	1988
Official GNP							
i) lei bn 1985 prices	741	772	828	874	927	969	1001
ii) $ bn at official rate	35.2	36.8	39.4	41.6	44.1	46.1	47.7
iii) $ bn arbitrary rate	18.5	19.3	20.7	21.9	23.2	24.2	25.0
Hard currency net exports ($ bn)	1.8	1.9	2.3	1.7	2.0	2.7	2.8
Net hard currency net exports to GNP							
i) official estimate	5.2	5.1	5.9	4.2	4.4	6.0	5.9
ii) own estimate	9.8	9.7	11.2	7.9	8.4	11.1	11.2

Sources and notes: GNP in 1985 dollars from IMF International statistics. Net hard currency exports estimated from tables 2 and 3.

V. *The Legacy of Debt Repayment for Economic Recovery*

Western media attention to Romania, both before and after the revolution, has quite naturally concentrated on the human suffering that has been generated by the policy of rapid debt repayment. This has involved draconian restrictions on household energy consumption and food supplies which have reduced urban living conditions to possibly the lowest levels experienced in the country since the Second World War and to the lowest currently in Europe (with the possible exception of Albania). Since the revolution the effect of the neglect of investment in health facilities, including the spread of Aids amongst infants and the suffering endured by the chronically ill and the mentally retarded, has been revealed. In addition investment in safety equipment in enterprises and environmental protection has been negligible or non-existent, resulting in an abnormally high incidence of industrial thromboses and cancers.

Ten years of severely depressed living standards combined with coercion, and in some sectors, military discipline, have left a demoralised labour force that will be exceedingly difficult to motivate. In addition, however, much of the burden of import cuts has been borne by investment in machinery and equipment. Imports of machinery and equipment from non-socialist countries has fallen from $1.3 billion per annum in the late 1970s to $0.3 billion in the 1980s. At the same time exports of machinery and equipment to socialist and developing countries grew from $2.6 billion in 1979 to $4.0 in 1984 according to data presented to Western banks.

This has contributed to a neglect of investment in industrial modernisation, the effects of which have been exacerbated by squandering resources in a series of prestige investment projects with little or no return in the form of productive capacity (e.g. the Danube-Black Sea Canal, the Presidential Palace and the Avenue of Victory).

Prime Minister Petre Roman claimed that the majority of industrial plants are using obsolete technology, which in many cases dated back to the early 1950s, and that little or no industrial modernisation had been undertaken during the 10 years of the debt repayment programme. Silviu Brucan described Ceausescu's policy in Adevarul as a "strategy of underdevelopment", in which modern high technology industries were neglected in order to maintain priority for more traditional heavy industry. As a result, Brucan argued, Romanian industry now lagged 15-20 years behind the technological levels of the West. It must be admitted that the Front for National Salvation (or any alternative government) has an incentive to overstate the problems inherited from the Ceausescu régime in order to minimise their own unpopularity resulting from the unpleasant decisions that economic regeneration will necessitate. However, there are indications that these claims are not grossly exaggerated, and they coincide with the analysis, made before the revolution, of Western specialists on the scale of the problems that a post-Ceausescu government would inherit.

Energy production and power generation in particular will be major bottlenecks to industrial development. The power supply system is inadequate to meet the country's needs. The chronic supply shortages to the household sector experienced in the 1980s have, in part, been alleviated in January 1990 by reducing supplies to industry and, in part, by increased imports (which accounted for 12% of total consumption). Household electricity consumption doubled from 6% to 12% of total output in January (1,000 MW daily), but it is accepted that this level of production and household consumption is insufficient to meet industrial demand (Adevarul 27 January). There is little prospect of a major increase in domestic power generation, currently 7,900 MW a day, before the Cernavoda nuclear power plant is commissioned. Crude oil output has fallen consistently since 1977 to reach only 9.4 million tons in 1988, while natural gas reserves have been depleted excessively in order to boost primary energy production. Figures for coal production are badly distorted by the aggregation of low quality brown coal and lignite with higher quality coal production in official statistics.

Investment in infrastructure and in telecommunications in particular has been badly neglected. Brucan argued that Ceausescu had deliberately destroyed the Institute of Mathematics which, he claimed, ranked third in the world in the early 1970s, and the Institute of Information Technology, which was the most advanced in Eastern Europe. It was announced in February that investment in telecommunications is to be increased from an initial target of 900 million lei to 2 billion lei in 1990, including the construction of four telephone exchanges in Bucharest. Similarly the petrochemical industry is in urgent need of modernisation.

VI. *Scenarios for Economic Recovery*

It is too early to attempt to estimate the cost of the investment that will be required to repair and modernise the Romanian economy. It is becoming increasingly apparent, however, that merely diverting net exports to domestic consumption will not be sufficient to satisfy the competing demands for the growth of investment and consumption. This can only be achieved with foreign investment and new borrowing. Immediate priority is to be given to improving living standards, with a planned increase in food imports of 15% per month until June 1990 and restrictions on energy exports, which it is expected will result in a virtual elimination of trade surpluses during 1990. But what prospects are there that foreign investment on anything like the desired scale can be achieved?

First, a new round of commercial credits is both highly unlikely and undesirable under current circumstances. The failure of the import-led growth strategy in the 1970s has clearly indicated the drawbacks of sovereign lending to unreformed centralised economies and Western commercial banks are still extremely cautious in their appraisal of the political risk of lending to Romania. Economic recovery will therefore require major input of Western investment which should take the form of equity participation under far more favourable terms than were offered to Western firms in the 1970s. Furthermore Romania will find itself in a far more competitive environment, in relation to other East European countries, if it wishes to attract Western capital in the 1990s compared with the 1970s.

One method of analysing Romanian prospects for economic recovery is to examine the requirements for, and dangers of, the process of transition from a centrally planned economy to a market economy and determine how these might affect Romania. A spectrum of scenarios can be proposed for the economic prospects for the reforming economies of Eastern Europe in the 1990s. At one extreme the most optimistic scenario proposes that some or all of the East European economies will succeed in restoring the "lost" economic potential that has been submerged by 40 years of central planning and the imposition of Stalinist heavy industrial priorities. This implies that after an initially very difficult transition period, involving the restructuring of industry, the East European economies will achieve relatively rapid and sustained economic growth in the second half of the 1990s. It is argued that the minimum necessary conditions for the realisation of this optimistic scenario are:

i) The introduction of market-oriented reforms involving unregulated wholesale and retail markets that permit substantial gains in economic efficiency. This may ultimately include the privatisation of much large-scale, as well as small-scale, industry and handicrafts and the development of a capital market.

ii) The decollectivisation of agriculture and assistance to promote the development of private agriculture.

iii) The restructuring of industry away from the traditional smokestack industries towards an industrial structure based on modern technology with a higher degree of value added.

iv) The redirection of trade links away from the safe Soviet market for low quality manufactured goods towards the more competitive conditions experienced in Western markets.

v) Large scale investment in infrastructure.

vi) Investment in education and training, particularly in management skills.

vii) Measures to attract a substantial volume of inward equity investment.

The optimistic scenario is largely based on the experience of the successful newly industralising economies which were capable of attracting inward investment, principally by multinationals seeking lower cost production bases for re-export to the industralised West. It is argued that the East European economies can repeat this experience by offering Western multinationals an industrial labour force that is relatively well trained in basic engineering skills and relatively close to what is expected to be an expanding EC market.

Unfortunately Romania is not well placed to fulfil this scenario. Although the majority of political parties contesting the election agree on the need for a greatly increased role for market forces, for the decollectivisation of agriculture, and the extension of privatisation and other measures to attract foreign capital, there are major differences of opinion on both the scale of market measures and the speed with which they should be implemented. The Front for National Salvation favours the gradual implementation of market reforms.

At the other end of the spectrum, the most pessimistic scenario envisages that, even with substantial Western assistance, the transition process will prove to be too difficult for many of the East European economies and will act as a barrier to economic take-off. It is argued that the relaxation of central controls on prices, which is essential for the development of market forces, will release inflationary overhang which will result in hyper-inflationary pressures. These will only be overcome by strict controls on the money supply, which will in turn require the elimination of budget subsidies to losing enterprises and an accelerated rate of enterprise bankruptcies. Although this may be necessary on grounds of long term economic efficiency the resulting combination of rapid inflation and widespread unemployment will lead to major social tensions. This could result in a relaxation of monetary controls, fuelling further inflation and the collapse of reform or, at worst, it could even stimulate ethnic tensions and unrest. The prospect of political instability will, inter alia, make it exceedingly difficult to attract equity investment.

Unfortunately at the time of writing, which is less than three months after the revolution which resulted in the overthrow and execution of Ceausescu, it is difficult to be optimistic about Romania's prospects. Although all or the majority of the parties contesting the May elections support the introduction of market reforms, decollectivisation and support for mechanisation of private agriculture, the extension of the private sector and measures to attract foreign investment, there are major differences between them on the scale of marketisation and the speed with which market oriented reforms should be introduced. These policy differences are exacerbated by long standing personal antagonisms and emerging nationalist conflicts. Furthermore the scale of the internal problems that must be overcome in Romania is far greater than in central Europe.

In the longer term there is no realistic alternative to the closure of a large number of obsolete, energy-intensive, highly polluting enterprises. This will inevitably result in extensive unemployment, the social effects of which will be aggravated by the virtual absence of a state welfare system and the dependence on a single large enterprise as the major source of employment in a number of provincial towns and localities. This is likely to strengthen local demands for a gradual approach to the introduction of market measures and for maintaining output and employment in obsolete factories. This may well spill over into resentment against those who benefit from market reforms, which will carry political and economic dangers to the reform process. First, it will strengthen support for the local bureaucracy, many of whom are former members of the party and even the Securitate, who will be best placed to bargain for relief from the centre from the effects of harsh policies. Second, it implies a far slower rate of economic recovery with a slower rate of growth of consumption and the continued production of energy consuming and polluting enterprises. This will in turn threaten the success of market reforms in industry and agriculture. Will a backward agricultural sector invest in mechanisation unless the supply of consumer goods on offer in rural areas is radically improved?

In summary, it will require considerable political wisdom to overcome the economic problems confronting Romania in the 1990s.

East-West Trade: Current State and Prospects

Norman Scott

Synopsis

The principal "traditional" determinants of the level and development of East-West trade have to be re-assessed in the light of the nature and extent of the changes introduced in the economic institutions and policies of the Eastern European countries and the scale of support for these changes offered by their Western trading partners. The growth of import demand in the markets of the latter may be expected to continue to be a key determinant, qualified by changes in commercial policies providing improved market access for Eastern imports. At the same time, it is necessary to assess the prospects for arresting the declining competitiveness (and market shares) of Eastern exports in relation to the probable deterioration, at least in the short term, of supply conditions in the Eastern European economies during the transition to more market-oriented and decentralized decision-making.

This, in turn, calls for an attempt to evaluate the East-West trade effects of a continuing contraction of inter-CMEA trade, a probable increase in foreign direct investment flows into the Eastern European economies, privatization, and progress towards limited convertibility. Other factors which have to be taken into account in assessing East-West trade prospects include the possible incidence of domestic economic reforms (and Western assistance, where applicable) on the commodity structure of Eastern exports, the conversion of military industries to civilian production, and the admission of Eastern countries to membership of an increasing number of international economic organizations.

I. *Introduction*

"Time present and time past
Are both perhaps present in time future"

T.S. Eliot - The Four Quartets

Applied to the extraordinary turmoil of political and economic change and debate unleashed in Eastern Europe over the past few months for a multitude of reasons, some of which still inscrutable, the aptness of the above quotation may be questioned. Some observers may be tempted to prefer Keats who, on first reading Chapman's translation of Homer "then felt .... like some watcher of the skies when a new planet swims into his ken". Nonetheless, Eliot's "time future and time past" remains, in my view, apposite. A great sea-change has begun, but it will be long before it runs its course. During the transition to a modern, market-oriented economy, which will be slowest in the largest single actor in East-West economic relations – the Soviet Union – many of the well-known features of the landscape of central administration of the economy will continue to loom large, and to cast a long shadow over attempts at reform. In this paper, the continuing presence of some of these landmarks of central planning are recalled as a basis for assessing future prospects.

East-West economic relations have always in the past attracted a degree of attention disproportionate to their share in the world economy. This was primarily due to the interest taken in the influence of the political climate on the volume, composition and development of East-West exchanges. Assessments on both sides of the optimal level of these exchanges were strongly coloured by non-economic considerations ranging from ideological dogmas about the competition of the two systems to defence concerns about the tolerable degree of dependence (or implicit vulnerability) of one set of trade partners on the other, or the type and amount of technology transferred from one to the other.

Now, just over the threshold of the new decade, political concerns are again uppermost in the minds of policy makers. But with a few conspicuous exceptions (the mysterious Mr. "Z" writing in DAEDALUS, or Madame Marie-France Garaud in her recent open letter to President Bush) these political concerns are of a different nature. They relate to the prospects for stability in the Eastern European countries following the abrupt political upheavals of the past few months and the possibly disruptive consequences of the transition from centrally administered to decentralized systems of economic organization.

Of course, outside the political sphere, the subject of East-West trade has always been of interest in academic circles, where the questions discussed have related to the criteria for deciding the optimal level of foreign trade in a centrally-planned economy, the most effective use of imported resources, the relationship between foreign and domestic prices and – last but not least – the search for explanations (and remedies) for the small share of the state-trading countries in world trade.

In this brief presentation it will obviously not be possible to treat more than a few of these issues. What I propose to do is to consider, first, the main features of East-West trade and payments as they developed during the past year, against the background of the trends discernible in the earlier years of the decade. I will then go on to consider the partial reforms attempted in some of the Eastern countries up to the end of last year (liberalization, decentralization and the acceptance of joint ventures) and, finally, to review some of the lessons of that experience in the context of the new factors which have to be taken into account in assessing prospects for East-West economic relations in the 1990s.

II. *The Situation of East-West Trade at the End of 1989*

(a) *Overall developments*

The rush of political and systemic change in Eastern Europe from mid-1989 until the beginning of this year took place in the context of a deepening economic crisis which in itself was the culmination of deteriorating economic performance in the region during most of the earlier years of the decade. The interaction of political and economic factors in provoking the historic changes experienced by most countries of the region has been complex even within individual countries. Generalisations are therefore more than usually hazardous. It seems fairly certain, however, that the disruption of supplies in the Soviet Union caused largely by strikes and civil strife in regions such as Armenia and Azerbaijan led to interruptions in exports and to an upsurge of emergency imports as the year progressed. This in turn produced symptoms of a near-breakdown in the intra-CMEA trading system which was already weakened by the diversion of exportables from intra-CMEA to convertible-currency markets. Difficulties of domestic and external imbalance in the smaller European CMEA countries were thus compounded by the vulnerability of their economies to external shocks emanating from their principal CMEA trading partner. This, in turn, generated a further downward push to the already faltering rates of growth of NMP throughout Eastern Europe.

The aggregate NMP of the European CMEA countries rose by less than 2% in 1989 (data for the first three quarters) and, having slowed down throughout the year may have declined in most of these countries in the last quarter. Industrial output stagnated in the smaller countries and rose by less than 2% in the Soviet Union, and agricultural production increased by less than 1%. The development of external trade to some extent cushioned the effects of this poor performance – possibly the worst year since postwar reconstruction – on supplies to domestic destinations. Thus, the volume of Eastern European exports decreased by 3% while imports rose by 0.2%. For the Soviet Union, there was no change in the volume of exports but imports rose by an estimated 9% resulting – when magnified by a slight deterioration in the terms of trade – in a reversal of the earlier Soviet trade surplus of $3.5 billion in 1988 to a trade deficit of $5.5 billion in 1989.

Within this sombre overall trade picture, the development of East-West trade in 1989 offered little by way of consolation, being characterized by weakening export growth and surging imports – particularly towards the end of the year. Exports from the CMEA 6 to the West expanded by 3% during the first nine months and probably by less than that for the year as a whole, when the effects of political disruptions in the last quarter reduced export deliveries. Imports from the West into the CMEA 6 rose in volume by 13%, largely boosted by the strong import expansion into Poland and Hungary (possibly in consequence of the liberalization of trade régimes in these countries). As a result, the trade surplus of the CMEA 6 with the West dwindled to the vanishing point. This, taken together with a sharp increase in their deficit on invisibles pushed the balance on current account in convertible currencies of the CMEA 6 into a deficit estimated at $2 billion.

The Soviet Union's export and import performance on Western markets was similar to that of the CMEA 6 – that is, a volume growth of exports at 3%, with a decelerating tendency in the course of the year as fuel and transport supply difficulties aggravated. The upsurge of imports already referred to showed up in a 22% volume expansion, propelled – especially towards the end of the year – by emergency imports of consumers' manufactured goods. The outcome of the widening gap between the growth of exports and imports was an enlarged Soviet trade deficit with the West which worsened from about $3 billion in 1988 to some $6.5 billion (on the basis of Soviet data) for the full year. Owing to the adverse development of the services account, the Soviet deficit on current account deteriorated still more with a resultant increase in Soviet net indebtedness estimated by the ECE secretariat at $10 billion in nominal terms, from $26.5 billion to $36.5 billion.

(b) *Terms of trade and commodity composition*

The main relevant development in 1989 was the recovery of fuel prices, led by petroleum products and crude oil which rose by 16% and 12% respectively in the first nine months of the year. Because of the large share of fuels in Soviet exports the result was a 5% increase in Soviet export prices over the same period. In consequence, the long-lasting and steep decline in Soviet terms of trade during most of the 1980s was reversed, import prices having remained largely unchanged.

Improved fuel prices also brought some benefit to exports from the CMEA 6, but this was more than offset by a reduction in their deliveries to Western markets. There was, however, a somewhat surprising improvement in the sales of engineering goods to Western markets where – thanks to the buoyancy of demand (an overall increase of 7% in the first three quarters) – there was stronger export growth than for several years and a slight resultant improvement in commodity composition. It is possible that the overall export performance of Hungary and Poland, which have been in the vanguard of economic reform – has been stronger in the past few years than that of any of the other Eastern European countries owing precisely to the additional export incentives provided by the reforms. Chief amongst these have been convertible-currency retention accounts, but active exchange rate policies and the grant of foreign trading rights to a greatly increased number of enterprises have presumably also contributed to their relative success in boosting exports. IMF conditionality as applied to the Hungarian current account probably also provided a powerful incentive to the authorities to engage in an export drive.

Some of these factors – notably the grant of foreign trading rights to enterprises (some 13,000 permits are reported to have been issued) – should also have been at work in the Soviet Union. If so, they have not yet surfaced in the trade returns on the export side. According to Western commodity trade statistics, a significant part of the 3% increase in the volume of Soviet exports in the first nine months of 1989 consisted in primary goods, mainly non-ferrous metals, ores and minerals. Soviet sales of semi-manufactures (mainly, iron and steel) and some consumer goods rose rapidly; but the volume of sales of crude oil and of engineering goods declined. On the other hand, Soviet deliveries of natural gas to the EC shot up by 15% in the first half of the year – much faster than the total expansion of import demand (2.5%) in that major market.

Given the predominant share of oil and oil products in Soviet exports, the reduction in availabilities in 1989 must be (yet another) source of serious concern to the Soviet authorities. The reduced volume of exports in 1989 has been attributed to a shortfall in domestic production, compounded by a reduction in Soviet re-exports of Middle Eastern crude. Domestic shortages are said to have been caused by scarcities of oil-field equipment and transport bottlenecks. Export potential may also have been curtailed by strains in the overall energy balance caused by a 32 million ton fall in coal output and a slow-down in the commissioning of nuclear power-generating plant.

Turning to the geographical and commodity pattern of the upsurge in imports, the expansion amongst the CMEA 6 was led by the GDR, Hungary and Poland. In the others there was virtually no growth in imports into Bulgaria and Czechoslovakia and a further deep cut-back in Romania until the last quarter. The import boom, in those countries where it occurred, consisted largely of engineering goods into Hungary, the GDR and Poland (the same leaders in this sector as in 1988) and to higher purchases of foodstuffs by all of this group of countries other than Romania. As on the export side, it is likely that the part of the upsurge of imports into the "early-reforming" countries – most conspicuously, in Hungary – was due to the decentralization and liberalization of the trade régime and showed up in above-plan imports from the convertible-currency area of machinery and equipment and semi-manufactures.

Despite the strong growth of 13% in the volume of Soviet imports from the West in 1989, the 1988 level was still not reached. The main commodity groups affected by this expansion were foodstuffs, followed by engineering goods – mainly machinery and office and telecommunications equipment. Consumer goods' imports did not progress until the latter part of the year.

(c) Trade balances, current account developments and indebtedness

As already mentioned, the European CMEA countries as a group moved from a current account surplus in convertible currencies of over $3 billion in 1988 to a deficit of $6 billion in 1989 – the largest deficit recorded since 1980. Trade balances generally deteriorated and most countries had to cope with higher net interest payments owing to rising levels of indebtedness and higher interest rates. The Soviet Union posted a record trade deficit with the market economies as a whole of nearly $3 billion – and of $6.2 billion with the developed market economies alone. However, the Soviet Union remained in surplus in its trade with developing countries, although much of its deliveries to these countries are supplied on long-term credit terms which do not generate cash flows which can be set against deficits incurred in other trade flows.

According to the data shown in Table VI the combined gross indebtedness of Eastern Europe and the Soviet Union increased from $137 billion in 1988 to nearly $145 billion in 1989 and net debt by an equal increment to nearly $112 billion. (Incomplete official data show higher levels of gross debt amounting to $157 billion in 1989.)

In 1989 most countries borrowed for balance of payments support, thereby raising their liabilities (with the exception of Romania and possibly Czechoslovakia). The net liabilities of the Soviet Union are estimated by the ECE secretariat to have risen by over $7 billion, on an exchange-rate adjusted basis, following an increase of nearly $4 billion in 1988. There are indications that a change has occurred in Soviet policy towards borrowing from the West. In earlier years when the external balance came under pressure rapid measures of adjustment were taken to boost exports and cut back on imports. Thus, in the two years following the collapse of oil prices in 1986 exports were pushed and imports from the West reduced by 28%. At the same time, to support these measures, gold sales were increased to around $8 billion.

Developments in 1988-1989 no longer followed this pattern. The sharp deterioration in Soviet terms-of-trade in 1980 evoked further gold sales of roughly $3.7 billion, and an increase of borrowing leading to additional net indebtedness (on an exchange-rate adjusted basis) of nearly $3 billion – in contrast to an increase of less than $1 billion on the earlier occasion. Nor have there been any signs of trade adjustment measures to narrow the widening trade deficit with the West. On the contrary, as noted earlier (see also Table I) imports were allowed to climb at an accelerating rate while exports remained sluggish.

Nonetheless, the overall level of indebtedness of the Soviet Union remains moderate in comparison with that of the smaller Eastern European countries (other than Romania). The interest-payments ratios of all of them (again, with the exception of Romania) increased as they faced higher interest rates on – in many cases – a rising stock of debt. These countries also experienced higher net-debt to export ratios which reached nearly 470% in Poland, 342% in Hungary and 325% in Bulgaria. These deteriorating financial indicators, compounded by uncertainties regarding domestic stability during the transition, led Western lenders to apply stiffer terms for credits, the average margin (base points over LIBOR) paid by Eastern countries doubling from 24 points to 1987 to 52 points in 1989.

To sum up, the external trade and payments position of East Europe worsened significantly in 1989, partly as a result of deteriorating domestic economic performance (and uncertainties surrounding the beginning or acceleration of the reform process), partly as a symptom of the underlying weakening of their role in the international economy over almost two decades. It may be useful to recall, at this juncture, the indications during the earlier years of the 1980s that the unreformed system was not capable of remedying or reversing these adverse tendencies.

III. *The State of East-West Trade on the Threshold of the 1990s*

In summary, the position of the Eastern countries in the international economic system before the abrupt political upheaval which occurred in the last quarter of 1989 could be characterized as follows:

- Their share in world trade has continued to shrink (to about 4% separately for the Soviet Union and Eastern Europe).
- Intra-CMEA trade appeared likely to grow only very slowly, if at all, without far-reaching reforms in member countries and in the organization itself.
- The outlook for a strong, sustained growth in Eastern exports to the West was unpromising. Although the level of demand in Western markets is a major determinant, and shows few signs of weakening, the unfavourable commodity structure of Eastern exports and the poor competitiveness of their manufacturers do not hold out much hope for an improvement in the Eastern countries' trading performance or market shares.
- Import growth into several Eastern countries would not exceed that of exports since they have approached the limits of indebtedness (unless there was a stronger inflow of foreign direct investment).
- Supply constraints in Eastern countries, notably on oil in the Soviet Union, may be expected to further limit export growth (unless there is another big increase in oil prices).
- The competitiveness of all Eastern countries' manufactures has continued to fall, with a resultant decline in their share of Western markets since the mid-1970s.
- The high concentration of Eastern Europe's trade on intra-CMEA exchanges has perpetuated technological backwardness in the quality of the goods traded on account of the absence of competition. In these circumstances, deflection of such exports to Western markets would not be feasible – although attempts to increase the amount of such goods offered as counterdeliveries in countertrade could be expected.
- The commodity composition of exports to the West, heavily weighted with fuels and primary materials, continues to prevent the Eastern countries from benefiting from the rapid expansion of world demand for manufactures (although the Soviet Union has enjoyed windfall gains from the oil-price rises).
- Although manufactures occupy a large share in Eastern imports, convertible currency scarcities have dictated import restraint so that in recent years the volume of imports of machinery and equipment has not risen above that of the 1970s.
- Traditional features of economic management in the CPEs explain their comparatively unfavourable position in international trade and may set limits (unless the reforms succeed) on the scope for using international trade to stimulate economic growth.

IV. *Some Lessons from Earlier Attempts at Reform*

Several of the measures of reform introduced in Eastern European countries before the radical changes envisaged at the end of 1989 were precipitated by external imbalances. The limited – and disappointing – results which they yielded provide some pointers to the nature and scope of the structural and policy changes which will be required in the 1990s.

Hungary, the most open and outward-looking of the European CMEA countries, has the longest and richest experience of attempts to reform the traditional system of central planning. In some respects, the results of these reforms were positive. For example, by 1988 the share of exports to the West in NMP produced had risen to 21% (from only 14% in 1980) and a considerable inflow of foreign direct investment had been obtained – estimated at about $1.1 billion (consisting of $600 million of FDI in joint ventures and wholly-owned subsidiaries, and Western equipment worth $500 million acquired through leasing agreements). Imports of consumer goods from the West were higher in per capita terms than in any other of the East European CMEA countries with the exception of the GDR, having increased at an annual average rate (in real terms) of 10% between 1965 and 1986.

On the other side of the balance sheet, growth was very sluggish – only 1.3 per annum over the past 10 years and the heavy concentration of exports on CMEA markets provided easy outlets for Hungarian enterprises sheltered from competitive pressures and quality requirements with a consequent lack of stimulus to technological innovation. As a result, exports to convertible currency markets were not adequately developed. Moreover, the country's gross hard-currency debt surged between 1970 and 1989 from $1 billion to $21 billion, much of which went to creating new capacities to serve CMEA markets.

The cumulative effect of the policy measures which the successive waves of reform embodied has been to endow the Hungarian economy with some features of the foreign trade system which should ease to some extent the transition to a market economy system.

In *Poland,* where a series of stop-go attempts at reform also date back several decades, the need to achieve a higher degree of international specialization and benefit from comparative advantages in international trade were frequently recognized. The dismal story of the misuse of borrowed resources in the 1970s is by now well-known and need not be rehearsed here. (As in Hungary, the move away from comprehensive quantitative planning to a system of greater enterprise autonomy and economic regulation using fewer control indications was accompanied by industrial concentration and the creation of larger economic organizations/production units.)

In the sphere of foreign trade, the main changes introduced at the beginning of the 1980s concerned trade in convertible currencies. Besides the removal of centrally-planned directives, organizational changes permitted a rapid increase in the number of economic agents authorized to engage independently in foreign trade from 245 in 1982 to 905 in 1988. At the same time small foreign firms – the so-called "Polonia" enterprises – were allowed to be established under a law passed in July 1982 and joint ventures with foreign investors were authorized by a law enacted in April 1986. By the beginning of March 1990, some 1,000 joint ventures had been registered in Poland.

From 1982 onwards a policy of flexible adjustments in the rate of exchange of the zloty was adopted, with the aim of achieving the profitability of 75-85% of the value of exports to both convertible and non-convertible currency areas. As a result, an increasing proportion of contractual prices was determined under the influence of prices paid or received in foreign currencies at current exchange rates. Retention quotas of foreign exchange (to finance intermediate imports and capital goods) and foreign currency auctions both helped to stimulate export-oriented production.

But by 1987 the main objectives of the reform had not been achieved. Internal and external imbalances persisted. The existence of adverse external constraints was part of the explanation – the mounting debt-servicing burden, lack of new Western credits, deteriorating terms of trade and limited import availabilities from the USSR and other CMEA countries.

Nonetheless, strict control over imports made it possible for Poland to achieve a trade surplus of approximately $1 billion in every year from 1983 up to 1989 when it disappeared altogether as import growth surged.

Reforms of the foreign trade system in the *Soviet Union* came much later than in Hungary or Poland, although in view of the predominant share of the USSR they are potentially much more significant for the development of East-West trade. It has to be recognized, of course, that the Soviet economy has never been as "open" to international trade as its smaller Eastern European neighbours because, as the most richly endowed country with natural resources in the world, foreign trade plays, in comparative terms, a secondary role in the economy.

Nonetheless, changes in the organization of foreign trade were influenced in the Soviet Union before any of the other major elements of Gorbachev's perestroika, the first announcement being as early as March 1986 during the 27th Party Congress. The stated aim was to enable branch ministries and many enterprises to engage directly in international trade with a view to improving the commodity composition of exports by raising the share of manufactures while at the same time encouraging producers to raise their levels of productivity, technical progress and competitiveness.

The most striking feature of the Decree of August 1986 on this "perfectioning of the management of foreign economic relations" was the dismantling of the monopoly power of the Ministry of Foreign Trade and its amalgamation, with the State Committee on Foreign Economic Relations, in a new Ministry for Foreign Economic Relations supervised by a State Foreign Economic Commission. At the same time, as a first measure of decentralization, 21 branch ministries and 67 large associations were granted foreign trading rights. These rights were subsequently extended to the Republics, to more ministries and – by the end of 1989 – to 13,000 enterprises. Nevertheless, in that year 35% of total Soviet imports were still handled by the FTOs of the MFER.[2] Incentives to enterprises to make effective use of these rights were provided in the form of retention quotas entitling them to retain 30-50% of export earnings – much of which was in unusable transferable roubles.

In fact, the effectiveness of these reform measures was limited by at least three factors. One was the tendency for branch ministries to take over control of the trading operations of enterprises. Another was the system of currency coefficients (of which there were 11,000 by the end of 1988) used to calculate the domestic rouble value of each product internationally traded. Thirdly, the management of enterprises acquiring foreign trade rights as a rule had no prior experience of international marketing.

Lack of visible benefits from the first set of measures, compounded by confusion amongst foreign businessmen and Soviet enterprises about the true location of decision-making power as regards foreign trade, prompted various corrective actions. Notable amongst these was the adoption by the Council of Ministers in March 1989 of Resolution 203, giving the Ministry of Foreign Economic Relations, other ministries and Republics, the right to license exports and imports. This was justified by examples of inexperienced Soviet enterprises selling goods at undervalued prices and buying at overvalued prices.

The resulting confusion attendant on what appears to be a "stop-go" approach to the reform of foreign trade and the lack of a coherant policy of reform in this sector has provoked criticism from unexpected quarters. Thus, Ivan Ivanov, the Deputy Chairman of the State Foreign Economic Commission, has roundly challenged the government approach, stating that "everything is removed from export and priority is given to imports – as a result, the indebtedness of the country increased. There is no opportunity, in the absence of a ban on collateral and real estate, to build an active credit system. There are no (favourable) conditions for foreign investments" (*Sotsialisticheskaya Industriya,* 30 November 1989). Similarly, Academician Georgiy Arbatov had harsh words at the Congress of People's Deputies for Prime Minister Ryzhkov's report on "Measures for Economic Recovery, Stages of Economic Reform and Fundamental Approaches to the Elaboration of the 13th Five Year Plan" (approved by the Congress on 21 December 1989). He said "the foreign business world is showing interest in us today .... yet, we have to ask ourselves, are we ready for this new era .... Alas, no .... neither in the juridical, nor the financial, nor the organizational, nor the economic, nor the personnel plan".

If a wind of change were not now sweeping through Central and Western Europe, the economic results recorded by the countries of the region in 1989, coming after almost two decades of deteriorating economic performance, both domestically and in international economic relations, would have pointed in the direction of continuing decline, intractable imbalances domestically and externally, and the relegation of these countries to the rank of minor actors in the world economic stage. Indeed, it is probably a realistic perception of this ineluctably bleak prospect which inspired Mr. Gorbachev to launch perestroika and to allow the CMEA 6 to cut themselves adrift from the sinking old tramp steamer of central planning and the unreformed CMEA.

But the wind of change has already blown away not only many dogmas and illusions but also many of the economic and political institutions through which they were articulated. The daunting task for observers and analysts is now to try to assess how the new mechanisms and policies announced or being introduced at varying pace in East Europe, and in intra-CMEA relations, will affect the future of East-West economic relations. To be complete, such an assessment would have to take account of the following elements of change:

– The potential impact of Western foreign direct investment and joint ventures on the domestic economic performance and external trade of the European CMEA countries.
– Progress towards full convertibility of the CMEA currencies.
– The future shape of trade relationships within the CMEA and, indeed, the very future of that organization.
– The nature and scale of Western (G24) support for the reforms (and the resultant effects on levels of indebtedness).
– The incidence of disarmament in those economies and the scale of conversion of resources devoted to military purposes to civilian uses.
– The speed and extent of privatization.
– The degree of openness of Western markets.
– The relaxation of COCOM restrictions on exports of Western high technology to the East.
– And, in general, the smoothness (or degree of disruption) with which the transition from centralized planning to a significantly more decentralized, market-oriented economy takes place in Central and East Europe.

V. *Foreign Direct Investment and Joint Ventures*

Despite the high priority (and large share of national income) traditionally accorded by central planning to investment in fixed assets, the European CMEA countries did not until recent years admit foreign direct investment from non-socialist sources. They thus deprived themselves, for essentially ideological reasons, of an important *potential* source of financing their industrialization. The qualification "potential" has to be stressed, since it may be doubted whether foreign investors would have obtained rates of return on their capital in the unrestructured Centrally Planned Economies (CPEs) comparable to those obtainable elsewhere. The alien operating environment of a Stalinist-type command economy characterized by scarcities, artificial and often meaningless price-relatives, irregular domestic and imported supplies, highly circumscribed contacts with producers and transporters, and inconvertibility would all have militated against a significant inflow of Foreign Direct Investment (FDI) even had the enabling legislation been in place – which it was not until enacted in Yugoslavia (1968), Romania (1971) and Hungary (1972).

Indeed, little more than a trickle of foreign capital ventured into these three countries until liberalization of the joint venture regulations in Yugoslavia (not further considered here) and Hungary in the mid-1980s.

The faint interest shown by Western investors was essentially due to the range of constraints on their operations mentioned above. Romania's experience of joint ventures exemplifies this point: of the nine joint ventures set up in that country (all in the 1970s) only four were still in operation at the end of 1989 (and not very profitably at that).

In short, by an act of self-denial without any economic rationale, the CPEs deprived themselves of the FDI which could have raised the levels of technology, management productivity and export-performance of their extractive, manufacturing and service industries. The two countries which experimented with joint ventures failed to offer conditions for FDI compatible in attractiveness to those obtainable elsewhere and as a result had little to show for their innovativeness.

A powerful stimulus for liberalization of joint venture regulations, and for other European CMEA countries to follow suit, was provided by China's early success in attracting FDI on a large scale. As part of its "open-door" policy announced in 1978, China authorized foreign direct investment on its territory in 1979 and by the end of 1986 had already obtained investment commitments on the order of $8,215 million. This was viewed by European CMEA Governments as proof that foreign capital could find an acceptable *modus vivendi* in the context of a centrally planned economy and acted as a spur to Poland (1986), the USSR (1987), Czechoslovakia (1987) and Bulgaria (1987) to allow joint ventures on their territories. Within little more than a year all of these countries (as well as Hungary and Yugoslavia) had revised or augmented the initial regulations in the direction of liberalization – by authorizing, for example, foreign firms to hold majority share-holdings and even wholly-owned subsidiaries in Bulgaria, Hungary and Poland. Additional tax incentives were offered, investment guarantees were provided (or negotiated), and certain relaxation of the rules governing the repatriation of profits were introduced.

These more attractive conditions for FDI evoked a positive response from foreign investors, as shown by the upsurge in the number of joint ventures registered in the European CMEA countries. The total rose from only 165 at the beginning of 1988 to 3,495 on 1 March 1990. Their distribution by host countries is shown below.[3]

NUMBER OF JOINT VENTURE REGISTRATIONS IN CMEA COUNTRIES AND YUGOSLAVIA

	1.01.88	1.01.89	1.07.89	1.08.89	15.10.89	1.01.90	1.03.90
Soviet Union	23	191	700	770	1000	1274	1400
Hungary	102	270	420	450	600	800	1000
Poland	13	55	190	308	400	900	1000
Czechoslovakia	7	16	28	35	50	60	60
Bulgaria	15	25	25	25	25	30	30
Romania	5	5	5	5	5	5	5
SUBTOTAL	**165**	**562**	**1368**	**1593**	**2080**	**3069**	**3495**
Yougoslavia		368		568	670	750	820
TOTAL	**400**	**930**		**2161**	**2750**	**3819**	**4315**

Judged by the criteria of their effectiveness in promoting the aims of the economic reforms or restructuring, the most relevant questions are: how much foreign capital is now being invested in the European CMEA countries, in which branches of their economies and with what effects on the domestic economy or export competitiveness?

To the first question, the answer is not particularly encouraging. The cumulative foreign capital invested in joint ventures in the Soviet Union amounted to $1,620.8 million by the beginning of October 1989, and is estimated to have risen to $1.9 billion by the beginning of March 1990. This gives an average foreign investment (which includes the capitalized value of the foreign partner's technology and know-how) of only $1.5 million (down appreciably from an average of $3.9 million for joint ventures registered in 1987). In short, the scalc of capital inflow is not impressively large, is on a much smaller scale than in China, and is rather thinly dispersed over a large number of undertakings. This feature of FDI has led the Soviet authorities to consider introducing a minimum foreign investment requirement for joint ventures, as has been done in Poland. At the same time it should be noted that the average foreign share in the capitalization of JVs has tended to rise, from 34.9% in those registered in 1987 to 43.3% for JVs registered in 1989.

After the raising in December 1988 of the ceiling on the share of foreign investors in the statutory capital of JVs in the Soviet Union, when foreign partners were allowed to hold majority shares, 65 JVs were registered (up to the beginning of October 1989) in which the foreign partner held more than 50% of the statutory capital. In 19 JVs their share exceeded 60%, and in six cases it was over 70%, but there were no cases registered of foreign partners holding more than 90%.

The industrial distribution of foreign capital shows 60% invested in manufacturing, within which about 30% is in engineering. Hotels and restaurants account for over 8% and business services for slightly less (7.87%), although in the latter branch of activity there are many small-scale joint ventures (56) providing computer-related services but with low capitalization (amounting to only 2.5% of total FDI).

Unfortunately, there are too few data yet available on the operating results of joint ventures to allow even an approximate assessment of their effects on domestic economic activity or export perfomance. Indeed, when reviewing any of the statistics provided above it has to be borne in mind that only about 10% of the JVs registered in the Soviet Union are actually operational. This is true, in particular, of JVs in the manufacturing sector, where there are inevitably longer lead-times between registration and start-up. Nevertheless, it is precisely in manufacturing that the difficulties of the interface between the operation of the joint venture and the domestic supply network are likely to be most acute.

Western investors complain of the poor quality of imports provided from domestic sources, irregular deliveries, complex and obscure local legislation – especially as regards taxation and ownership (lack of protection guarantees), accounting rules, and procedures for repatriating assets in the event of bankruptcy. Above all, criticism is directed at the requirement that the foreign partner's profits must be obtained from the joint venture's earnings in convertible currencies. This means, in the manufacturing sector, that the joint venture must be capable of producing goods of a price and quality which are competitive on Western markets. In the view of these critics, this approach ignores the fact that part of the JVs production is substituting for imports and should therefore be permitted to share in the resultant foreign exchange savings.

The limitation on the repatriation of profits also obliges the joint ventures to try to acquire Soviet products with their rouble profits and then find purchasers for them on Western markets. Ways round this difficulty have been found by United States and French consortia (or "currency pool") arrangements. For these reasons the USSR and Czechoslovakia are now preparing revisions of their joint venture regulations to make it easier for companies to repatriate profits and to sell on domestic markets. There has also been much discussion in the USSR of the possible advantages of creating Special Economic Zones with limited convertibility for non-residents.

In this connection, it is of interest to compare the pattern of foreign investment, and the operating experience of joint ventures, in Hungary where the business environment is less centrally constrained.

In Hungary, the cumulative investment of foreign capital in both joint ventures and wholly-owned subsidiaries – of which there were some 420 at the end of the first quarter of 1989 – amounted to $263 million. Again the small-scale of the foreign investment is striking – only $1.5 million on average, remarkably closer to the corresponding value of foreign investments in Soviet-based joint ventures. There are also strong similarities in the distribution of JVs by industrial branches between Hungary and the Soviet Union. In the former country 35% of the foreign investment is in manufacturing industry, followed by financial services and hotels, accounting respectively for 30% and 18% of FDI.

VI. *The Options of Countertrade and Leasing*

The decision of the CMEA ministerial meeting held in Sofia in January 1990 to switch to pricing and settlements in convertible currencies from the beginning of 1991 is bound to have major consequences not only for the external payments position of these countries but also for East-West trends and payments. It should be recalled that several of the small Eastern European countries run large surpluses in their non-convertible currency trade with the Soviet Union. Hungary, for example, earned a surplus of about one billion roubles in its trade with its CMEA partners in 1981 alone. The comparable figure for Poland is roughly the same order of magnitude. In the GDR the surplus in intra-CMEA trade has been put by the Minister of Economics at between DM3 and DM4 billion.

As these countries attempt to divert exports previously destined for the CMEA to Western markets, where in the short to medium term they will not be competitive, a large proportion will probably be offered as counter-trade productions which Western suppliers of machinery and equipment will be required to accept in payment for their deliveries.

A more attractive prospect for Western exports would be increased recourse to leasing of industrial equipment. This is a technique which permits investment in machinery and equipment while separating economic use from legal ownership in financial leasing, or "full pay-out" as it is often called; the Western supplier arranges to finance the lease which is often paid in annual installments by the return flow of its products until the equipment has been amortised. At that point ownership is transferred from the lessor to the lessee. It is worth stressing that the Western supplier not only retains ownership during the lease but also full control over the project (installation and operation of the machinery etc.) thus ensuring the flow of lease-payments.

VII. *Some General Lessons from the Reforms Attempted before 1990*

The experience of the reforms enacted, if not fully implemented, in a number of Eastern European countries over the past decade raise some questions relevant to the options available to the new governments of these countries in the decade of the 1990s. The answers to these questions may also throw some light on the prospects for success of the new reform programmes – our interest being focussed, of course, on their possible consequences for East-West economic relations.

The most pertinent questions would seem to be the following:

(a) Did the earlier reforms yield any improvement in the external trade and payments position of the Eastern countries? If yes, should they be taken farther? If not, what went wrong? The concept or the implementation?

(b) What was the inter-linkage between attempts to correct external and internal imbalances and to achieve other aims of the reforms such as stimulating productivity growth and competitiveness?

(c) Do the new reform programmes suggest that the lessons of earlier experience have been learned and incorporated in the new approach?

To the first question, the answer is a qualified negative. Some reforming countries (Hungary, Poland) recorded some successes in boosting exports to the West, sufficient to reduce trade deficits but not enough to cut back indebtedness significantly. But these modest – and often short-lived – improvements in trade balances were more the product of central administrative actions than of a stronger spontaneous export orientation of producing enterprises or newly created trading companies. Romania is a case in point, where exports to the West were forced by administrative means by deflecting supplies from the domestic market and in the absence of any significant reforms of the centrally planned system.

The reasons for the failure are to be found both in the concept and in the limited implementation of the reforms. Insufficient stimulus was provided through the regulated prices and exchange-rate mechanism to encourage enterprises to innovate and attain higher levels of competitiveness. By maintaining earlier investment priorities and related supply allocations, the central authorities – for example, in Hungary – ensured that production of "soft" goods for the CMEA markets was an easier option for enterprises than trying to break into, or enlarge their share of, Western markets. In short, the incentives offered to enterprises to develop their exports to convertible-currency markets were weak, and tended to be further weakened in practice by the surviving power of the ministerial bureaucracy to influence contractual prices, to allocate supplies and to determine investment priorities.

As regards the inter-action between external and domestic objectives of reform, government policies were not sufficiently coherent or assured to prevent the emergence of conditions or practices which frustrated some of their other policy aims. Thus, there was a lack of control of the state budget deficit, of inflationary pressures and of administrative methods which allowed "exceptional" regulations to become the rule.

Put differently, a realistic approach to the twin goals of "opening up" to, or improved integration in, the world economy, on the one hand, and "marketization" of the domestic economy on the other requires them to be viewed as two sides of the same coin. Unless price signals and market incentives from abroad are allowed to influence domestic structural adjustments these will take place haltingly and be guided by administrative intervention. The allocation of resources in the domestic economy will still be insulated from market forces and the resultant imbalances, scarcities and waste will frustrate attempts to raise productivity and competitiveness to levels at which a stronger export-orientation will be achievable.

Turning to prospects, the approach to reform still differs so much from country to country that generalization is fraught with hazards. Poland and Hungary have, to use an Americanism, "bitten the bullet" and set their compass for full-fledged marketization with the aim of replicating OECD-type economic organizations and institutions and a concomitant sharp reduction in the economic role of government. In the Soviet Union, the Deputy Prime Minister in charge of the economy, Abalkin, has put forward plans which point in the same direction - although the plan adopted by the Supreme Soviet is far less bold than his public proposals.

Notes

1. For a more detailed analysis of the development of East-West trade in 1989-1990, see the United Nations *Economic Survey of Europe in 1989-1990*, United Nations publications, Sales No.: E.90.II.E.1; ISBN 92-1-1164-69-9.
2. Many Soviet enterprises have also grouped together into "independent associations" to replace Ministries or to compete with those that strive for foreign business.
3. By 1 July 1990 the members of registered joint ventures had risen to 5,070 in the five CMEA countries listed (excluding the GDR) and to 1,800 in the Soviet Union. For further detail, see the UN/ECE quarterly newsletter *East-West Joint Ventures News*.

TABLE I

East-West Trade: Value, Volumes, Prices, and Terms of Trade, 1985-1989

(Percentage change over the same period of previous year)

	Eastern exports					*Eastern imports*				
From/To:	*1985*	*1986*	*1987*	*1988*	*1989 QI-III*	*1985*	*1986*	*1987*	*1988*	*1989 QI-III*
					Values (in US dollars)					
Eastern Europe and the Soviet Union	-8	-1	12	5	7	2	6	4	12	12
of which:										
Eastern Europe	-2	10	13	7	5	8	18	13	6	11
Soviet Union	-11	-10	10	2	9	-1	-3	-3	18	13
					Volumes					
Eastern Europe and the Soviet Union	-4	10	3	8	3	3	-13	-4	5	13
of which:										
Eastern Europe	-1	1	-	6	3	7	-1	2	-	13
Soviet Union	-7	21	7	9	3	-	-20	-9	9	13
					Prices (in US dollards)					
Eastern Europe and the Soviet Union	-4	-11	7	-1	3	-1	20	9	8	-1
of which:										
Eastern Europe	-2	9	13	2	1	1	20	11	7	-1
Soviet Union	-5	-26	2	-6	5	-2	20	7	8	-
					Values and volumes					
Memorandum item:										
Total western imports/ exports										
Eastern Europe	4	12	19	13	8	4	16	18	14	8
Volumes	6	8	7	7	9	4	2	6	8	7

Eastern terms of trade (1975 = 100)

	1983	*1984*	*1985*	*1986*	*1987*	*1988*	*1989 QI-III*
Eastern Europe and Soviet Union	152	153	146	109	108	98	102
of which:							
Eastern Europe	115	114	111	101	103	98	100
Soviet Union	190	198	191	117	112	97	102

Sources: United Nations commodity trade data base (COMTRADE); OECD, *Statistics on Foreign Trade,* Series A, Paris; IMF, *Directions of Trade* and *International Financial Statistics,* Washington, D.C.; Statistisches Bundesamt, *Warenverkehr mit der Deutschen Demokratischen Republik und Berlin (Ost),* Reihe 6, Wiesbaden; United Nations, *Monthly Bulletin of Statistics* (volume indices of total western exports to and imports from the world); national statistics.

Note: Price and volume indices: for the methodology and derivation, see United Nations Economic Commission for Europe, *Economic Bulletin for Europe,* vol. 31, No. 1, New York, 1979.

These data reflect the trade of 23 western reporting countries (Appendix table C.6 contains a list of the countries included). The same data are used in chart. 4.2.1.

Source: UN-ECE *Economic Survey of Europe in 1989-1990* (for this and the following tables).

TABLE II
East-West Trade: Value and Volume, by Eastern Country 1985-1989
(Percentage change)

From/To:	Eastern exports					Eastern imports				
	1985	*1986*	*1987*	*1988*	*1989*[a]	*1985*	*1986*	*1987*	*1988*	*1989*[a]
					Value change (in US dollars)					
Bulgaria	-2	3	3	4	10	26	17	7	1	-4
Czechoslovakia	-5	15	10	6	6	8	19	18	7	1
German Democratic Republic	-3	14	11	5	-	1	27	23	4	7
Hungary	2	13	21	11	13	11	21	11	1	19
Poland	1	7	16	15	10	7	7	16	21	32
Romania	-7	5	12	1	-4	4	17	-24	-7	-11
Eastern Europe	-2	10	13	7	5	8	18	13	6	11
Soviet Union	-12	-10	10	2	9	-2	-3	-3	18	13
Eastern Europe and the Soviet Union	-8	-1	12	5	7	2	6	4	12	12
Memorandum item:										
Total Western imports/ exports	4	12	19	13	8	4	16	18	14	8
					Volume change					
Bulgaria	-1	-7	-9	4	9	25	-4	-4	-3	-3
Czechoslovakia	-4	1	-2	3	5	7	-3	6	1	3
German Democratic Republic	-1	6	-3	4	-1	-	8	10	-1	8
Hungary	5	-1	7	7	13	8	1	-1	-5	21
Poland	1	-6	8	9	8	10	-12	8	12	33
Romania	-3	7	-5	5	-8	5	2	-30	-12	-11
Eastern Europe	-1	1	-	6	3	7	-1	2	-	13
Soviet Union	-7	21	7	9	3	-	-20	-9	9	13
Eastern Europe and the Soviet Union	-4	10	3	8	3	3	-13	-4	5	13
Memorandum item:										
Total Western imports/ exports	6	8	7	8	9	4	2	6	8	7

Source: As for Table I.
a January-September.

TABLE III
East-West Trade: Value, by Country Group, 1985-1989
(Percentage change of value in US dollars)

	Eastern exports					Eastern imports				
	1985	*1986*	*1987*	*1988*	*1989*[a]	*1985*	*1986*	*1987*	*1988*	*1989*[a]
Eastern Europe and Soviet Union with:										
Developed market economies	-8	-1	12	5	7	2	6	4	12	12
Western Europe	-7	-2	11	3	7	7	10	7	7	12
of which:										
EC	-8	-1	13	4	7	5	13	13	7	14
EFTA	-4	-9	13	-1	4	8	14	8	8	8
North America	-10	-1	5	21	-	-24	-32	-5	63	31
Japan	-10	22	31	30	4	10	16	-14	19	-9
Eastern Europe with:										
Developed market economies	-2	10	13	7	5	8	18	13	6	11
Western Europe	-1	12	14	6	6	9	19	14	6	13
of which:										
EC	-	15	16	6	7	14	23	15	5	15
EFTA	1	4	14	9	2	4	20	22	7	8
North America	-5	-2	4	11	-14	-15	1	-11	20	13
Japan	-28	12	47	43	2	15	21	5	8	-24
Soviet Union With:										
Developed market economies	-11	-10	10	2	9	-1	-3	-3	18	13
Western Europe	-11	-13	9	-1	8	4	2	-	9	11
of which:										
EC	-14	-13	9	2	7	-3	2	10	10	11
EFTA	-7	-16	11	-9	5	10	11	-1	9	8
North America	-26	2	6	58	43	-26	-41	-2	82	37
Japan	-4	24	28	26	5	9	15	-19	22	-5

Source: As for Table I.
Note: Appendix tables C.6 and C.7 contain similar data for all Western countries.
a January-September.

TABLE IV
East-West Trade Balances, East with Western Country Groups, 1984-1989
(Billion US dollars, f.o.b. - f.o.b.)

	1984	*1985*	*1986*	*1987*	*1988*	*1988 Jan.-Sept.*	*1989 Jan.-Sept.*	*1989*[a]
			(A) Western data					
Eastern Europe and the Soviet Union with:								
Developed market economies	6.4	2.0	-0.8	2.1	-0.9	0.6	-1.3	-2.5
Western Europe	11.4	6.2	2.1	3.7	2.1	2.6	1.4	1.2
of which:								
EC	10.1	6.7	3.9	4.2	3.7	3.4	2.4	2.4
EFTA	1.8	0.9	-0.7	-0.4	-1.2	-0.6	-0.9	-1.2
North America	-3.6	-2.4	-0.9	-0.7	-2.1	-1.5	-2.6	-3.1
Japan	-1.4	-1.9	-2.1	-0.9	-0.9	-0.5	-0.1	-0.5
Eastern Europe with:								
Developed market economies	3.8	2.1	1.0	1.2	1.6	1.7	0.6	0.6
Western Europe	3.2	1.6	0.6	0.6	0.8	1.1	0.2	-0.1
of which:								
EC	2.5	1.2	0.5	0.6	0.9	1.2	0.3	-
EFTA	0.5	0.4	-	-0.2	-0.2	-0.1	-0.3	-0.4
North America	0.7	0.8	0.8	0.9	1.0	0.7	0.4	0.6
Japan	-0.1	-0.3	-0.4	-0.3	-0.1	0.1	0.1	0.1
Soviet Union with:								
Developed market economies	2.5	-0.2	-1.8	0.9	-2,5	-1.1	-2.0	-3.0
Western Europe	8.2	4.6	1.5	3.2	1.3	1.5	1.2	1.3
of which:								
EC	7.6	5.6	3.4	3.7	2.8	2.2	2.1	2.4
EFTA	1.4	0.6	-0.7	-0.1	-1.0	-0.5	-0.6	-1.8
North America	-4.3	-3.2	-1.7	-1.6	-3.0	-2.2	-3.0	-3.7
Japan	-1.3	-1.6	-1.7	-0.7	-0.8	-0.4	-0.2	-0.6
			(B) Eastern data					
Eastern Europe and the Soviet Union with:								
Developed market economies	7.8	1.8	-3.7	2.4	-2.2	0.2	-3.6	-5.0[b]
of which:								
Eastern Europe	4.6	2.7	0.7	1.4	0.5	2.3	1.5	1.4[b]
Soviet Union	3.2	-0.9	-4.4	1.0	-2.7	-2.1	-5.1	-6.4[b]

Source: As for Table I.
Note: Section A is based on Western data which have been adjusted to an f.o.b. - f.o.b. basis by the ECE secretariat; section B is based on Eastern national sources.
a Extrapolated on the basis of January-September data for exports and imports. b Full year data.

TABLE V

East-West Trade Balances, by Eastern Country, 1984-1989

(Billion US dollars, f.o.b. - f.o.b.)

	1984	*1985*	*1986*	*1987*	*1988*	*1988* Jan.-Sept.	*1989* Jan.-Sept.	*1989*[a]
Bulgaria	-0.8	-1.2	-1.5	-1.6	-1.7	-1.3	-1.2	-1.5
Czechoslovakia	0.8	0.4	0.4	0.1	0.1	0.3	0.5	0.4
German Democratic Republic	0.9	0.7	0.2	-0.5	-0.4	-0.1	-0.5	-0.6
Hungary	-0.1	-0.3	-0.6	-0.3	0.1	-	-0.2	-0.2
Poland	0.8	0.6	0.7	0.8	0.7	0.6	-0.1	-0.3
Romania	2.2	1.9	1.9	2.7	2.8	2.2	2.1	2.8
Eastern Europe	3.9	2.1	1.0	1.2	1.6	1.7	0.6	0.6
Soviet Union	2.5	-0.2	-1.8	0.9	-2.5	-1.2	-2.0	-3.0
Eastern Europe and the Soviet Union	6.4	2.0	-0.8	2.1	-0.9	0.6	-1.3	-2.5

Source: As for Table I. ECE secretariat estimates based upon Western data.
a Extrapolated on the basis of January-September data for exports and imports.

TABLE VI

Eastern Europe and the Soviet Union: Estimated Convertible Currency Debt, 1983-1989 [a]

(Billion US dollars, end-of-year)

	1983	*1984*	*1985*	*1986*	*1987*	*1988*	*1989*[a]
Gross debt							
Bulgaria	2.4	2.1	3.5	4.9	6.2	7.7	9.0
Czechoslovakia	3.5	3.1	3.3	3.9	5.1	5.2[b]	5.1
German Democratic Republic	12.1	11.6	13.6	16.1	19.1	20.2	20.6
Hungary[b]	10.7	11.0	14.0	16.9	19.6	19.6	20.6
Poland	26.3	26.9	29.7	33.5	39.2	39.2	39.9
Romania	8.9	7.2	6.6	6.4	5.7*	3.1	1.4
Eastern Europe	63.9	61.9	70.7	81.7	94.9	95.0	96.5
Soviet Union and CMEA Banks	26.9	25.6	31.4	37.4	40.3	41.7	50.6
Eastern Europe and the Soviet Union	90.8	87.5	102.1	119.0	135.1	136.8	147.1
Net debt[c]							
Bulgaria	1.2	0.7	1.4	3.5	5.1	5.9	7.7
Czechoslovakia	2.6	2.1	2.3	2.7	3.5	3.5	3.1
German Democratic Republic	8.7	7.1	7.1	8.6	10.1	10.7	11.0
Hungary[b]	9.4	9.4	11.7	14.8	18.1	18.2	19.5
Poland	25.1	25.4	28.1	31.8	36.2	35.6	36.5
Romania	8.4	6.6	6.3	5.8	4.3	2.3	-0.1
Eastern Europe	55.5	51.2	56.4	67.1	77.3	76.3	77.7
Soviet Union and CMEA Banks	16.0	14.2	18.3	22.5	26.1	26.5	36.4
Eastern Europe and the Soviet Union	71.4	65.4	74.7	89.7	103.4	102.7	114.1

Sources: As for Table I. National data for Hungary, Poland, until 1986, and Romania; BIS/OECD, *Statistics on External Indebtedness, Bank and Trade-Related Non-Bank External Claims on Individual Borrowing Countries and Territories,* various issues, Paris and Basle: for Bulgaria, Czechoslovakia, German Democratic Republic (adjusted here to include claims of the Federal Republic of Germany arising from clearing exchanges), Soviet Union (including CMEA banks). These data exclude any indebtedess to countries outside the BIS/OECD reporting area (e.g., all developing market economies).

a Preliminary estimates except for Hungary, the German Democratic Republic and Poland.
b Revised series.
c Gross debt less Eastern assets with BIS reporting banks only.

East-West Financial Issues

Piero Zaino

I would like to touch on three main points in this presentation: first, Finance and Debt in East-West Relations; second, the Financial System (the case of Hungary); and third, Currency and the Possible Roles of the Transferable Rouble and the ECU in the Reform of Monetary Relations between CMEA Countries. For the latter, I am grateful for the contribution of Mr. Alfonso Iozzo, who was unable to present his paper in person.

I. *Finance and Debt in East-West Relations*

The accumulation of debts in hard currency at the end of 1988 is estimated to be approximately $150 billion ($120 billion if we deduct deposits at Western Banks). This represents about one-third of the total debt of the developing countries. During the 1981-88 period, three of the countries were forced to reschedule: Poland in 1981, Romania in 1982 and Yugoslavia in 1983. Poland has been unable to generate sufficient foreign exchange to service the interest on its debt, and as a result its total debt has risen from $25 billion to $38 billion. The maturities of East European debts have been extended during the last three years to provide for later debt expiry. Loan conditions, in terms of interest rates paid by Eastern banks, have been quite favourable, at least until 1987, with a spread on the libor on average of about 0.25%. Nevertheless, since 1988 the attitude of Western banks towards the most indebted Eastern countries has changed and conditions have become more favourable for the granting banks.

With regard to the issues of bonds, they had been very small up until 1987 and had been effected only by Hungary, Poland and Czechoslovakia. In 1988 the USSR also entered the market, with two issues in Swiss Francs and Deutchmarks for a total of $600 million. This instrument (bonds) is expected to be more and more important in the future as a way to find financial resources on international markets for Eastern borrowers. The subscribing countries will accept higher financial margins in order to make the subscription more attractive and to prevent the bonds' excessive depreciation on the secondary market during the period following issuance.

The perspective situation of the debt of some Eastern countries (mainly the USSR and Czechoslovakia) which still have the possibility of finding new funds on the international market appears to be towards increases, as their own financial reputation on the market is still considered good. For the more indebted group of Eastern countries (which includes Poland, Hungary, Bulgaria and Yugoslavia) the changed attitude of lenders and the elevated loan conditions could make finding new funds appear problematic, and the situation will become even more difficult with increases of international interest rates which are still in course. In this context, East Germany (GDR) is in a unique position, as its political and monetary problems are closely linked to special conditions due to relations with West Germany and pending reunification.

If we consider the financial help of Western countries on a short term basis, we can say that these might relieve the problem. But all these efforts will be useless if the East European countries do not succeed, in a relatively short time, to improve their competitivity on international markets. Otherwise, new credits would only worsen the financial situation of these countries, rather than helping to solve their problems. Unfortunately, the increase of debts of East European countries has not produced a higher potential for export, and therefore the most significant debt ratios have worsened.

The global cost of financing, which is understood as the ratio between the net debt of a country and the income in hard currency coming from the export of goods and services during the period of one year, has reached an average of one and one half years for the repayment. Therefore, at present the debt-costs are approximately 50% higher than five years ago. In the opinion of the economic experts the countries showing a relation between debt and income in hard currency longer then two years are likely to stop repayments. Probably the COMECON-countries could stand an even higher debt "burden", because the supply of raw material is effected by a clearing system within the COMECON without payment in hard currency. Anyway the situation of individual countries ranges from the most indebted, Poland, up to "debt-free" Romania, and we all know very well how Romania succeeded in repaying its foreign debt.

The forecast for the future foresees an increase of the Eastern countries' debts. Experiences with other, non-European countries, where new credits served more to back up the existing structure rather than to change it, should persuade one to be careful. This is especially true if we consider that in addition to the country risk (as the borrower normally was the country itself or the National Bank), we now have to also consider the entrepreneur risk. Therefore, the following two main factors will play significant roles in influencing future bank strategies in lending to the East: (1) the perception of worsening credit risk due to political upheavals in the area, and (2) an increasingly active role of Western governments in trade and financial relations with the East.

Even though political structures have changed radically in many countries, the economic systems remain largely unchanged, unreformed and, unfortunately for the moment, not more efficient. In my opinion, these countries should try to raise their own financial resources, both through the establishment of private industry and by selling "public properties". In addition, I would recommend that the most indebted countries try to reduce their debt by applying selected "debt to equity swaps".

In the absence of a properly functioning capital market and banking system, which hinders the efficient internal allocation of investment and financial resources, countries in Eastern Europe must be aware of the importance of restructuring the banking and financial sectors in the economic reform process. Any delay in achieving this objective could reduce the effects of general economic reforms. Economic reform cannot succeed without a well functioning, fully operational banking system.

While most of these countries are still going through the first phases of reform, Hungary, with its three year old, two-level banking system and with a growing financial market which is rapidly setting forth on the way to internationalization, should represent a "bridge-head" towards the West, and a reference point for both the East and the West in the process of mutual approach. Hungary features itself as the country which has diversified its recourse to international financial markets most and has proved significantly responsive to financial innovation. It is interesting to recall that Hungary has been officially quoting the ECU for a long time and that it was the first (and the only one until now) among the East European countries to launch an international bond issue denominated in ECU. Apart from the possible role that the use of the ECU could have in the gradual process leading to florint convertibility, it should be mentioned that the ECU represents an innovative financial instrument in itself and a vehicle for financial innovation in the area.

But what characterizes the Hungarian experience most is its openness to foreign banks. The move depends on precise conditions: a liberal approach to these banks can make a major contribution to a healthy competitive environment. They also provide expertise in the functioning of banking activities with respect to technological infrastructures, know-how and personnel training. More specifically, the presence of joint venture banks with foreign participation could:

- give impetus to new financial activities coming from abroad, by attracting foreign economic entities and investors as well;
- introduce both traditional financial instruments — such as medium/long-term financings, consumer credits, mutual funds, etc. — on a widespread basis, and new financial tools deriving from Western experience.

Taking into consideration that the Hungarian banking system (which was started on 1 January 1987) has inspired changes in the banking field of almost all the Eastern countries, I believe it useful to make some remarks on the subject.

II. *The Financial System (The Case of Hungary)*

Despite the heavy debt position and the growing rate of domestic inflation (a rise in consumer prices of 17% in 1989, which is expected to grow even further), Hungary is the most advanced country of the region with respect to both economic and financial reform. The deficit on current account position rose from $600 million in 1988 to $1.4 billion in 1989. The country has also experienced difficulties on the side of internal growth, which has been stagnant for nearly two years, and on the control of aggregate demand. The budget deficit, after having been reduced to 0.5% of GDP in 1988, has shifted up to an estimated 1.7% in 1989.

Nevertheless Hungary has proved successful in attracting foreign direct investment and in maintaining access to international financial markets. The main reasons for this success are the advanced degree of economic reform, with a legislative framework quite favourable to business (as is shown by the legislation on foreign joint ventures, the most liberal of the region), the setting up of a modern banking system on the pattern of those operating in market economies, the beginning of a financial market, and the recourse to international bond issuing.

The banking reform started on 1 January 1987 with the introduction of the two-tier banking system, and it has been further implemented with more relaxing of rules concerning the activity of commercial banks. The National Bank of Hungary (NBH), which operates under the supervision of the Council of Ministers, performs the following traditional central bank functions:

- issues banknotes and coins and controls the money supply,
- formulates proposals on monetary and credit policy,
- exercises supervision over the activity of commercial and savings banks and other specialized financial institutions,
- manages reserves of gold and foreign exchanges,
- determines exchange rate policy,
- controls foreign exchange operations,
- co-ordinates relations of Hungary with international financial institutions.

The NBH accomplishes its task of control over monetary and credit policy through conventional instruments such as refinancing, interest rate policy, reserve requirements and open market operations (in 1988 it started issuing treasury bills).

The second level of the present Hungarian banking system consists of commercial banks, savings banks and cooperatives and specialized financial institutions. The commercial banks are set up as profit oriented joint stock companies, with the Ministry of Finance as majority shareholder. At the beginning of the reform five commercial banks were set up, deriving from specialized branches of the NBH or from the merging of the former specialized banks. Nowadays other commercial banks have been instituted, even if the first five banks are perceived as far stronger on the market, with respect to their capital, dimension and diffusion in the country.

The main aim of the reform was the introduction of a competitive banking system which, forced to practice credit discrimination, is expected to exercise a far more positive influence on enterprises' efficiency. Thus commercial banks have national jurisdiction, with no geographical or competence limits, and they are entitled to deal with all banking transactions mentioned as such by the financial law, i.e. granting credits, collecting savings and providing financial services.

A further step on the path of decentralization was achieved on 1 July 1987, when companies, formerly channelled to banks according to NBH regulations, were allowed to choose freely the bank which would keep their accounts. They can choose no more than one bank for this purpose, even if companies can deal with all other banks as far as deposits and loans are concerned.

Starting from 1 January 1989, any remaining areas of competence between commercial and savings banks were abolished, and now they can openly deal both with corporate companies and with private individuals. In spite of this, anyway, it is reckoned that a steady percentage of population savings is still kept by the savings cooperatives (whose number amounted to 260 in 1987). The transfer of trade-related foreign exchange operations to commercial banks in 1989 is a major feature of the decentralization process, even if so far the system has not been very responsive to this innovation and the 80% of foreign exchange trade-related transactions is still managed by the NBH, which keeps a monopoly on hard currency credits and foreign debt management. The remaining 20% is largely managed by the banks with foreign participation which are operating in the country. In 1989 ten specialized financial institutions were operating in Hungary. Set up as joint stock companies, they are controlled by the commercial banks. Their task is the provision of long-term financing for development projects and the provision of financial services. In this respect, it is remarkable that, through the activity of these institutions, modern financial instruments have been introduced in the country.

The state development institution has been set up to strengthen financial activities connected to state development policies. It is involved in formulating financial strategies related to specific projects, in long-term financing and in implementing the range of financial tools. The settlement of other long-term financing institutions, which are bound to play a crucial role in the further development of the country, is under study.

A peculiar feature of the Hungarian banking system is the presence of five banks with foreign participation, one of which, the Central European International Bank, has been operating as an off-shore financial entity for 11 years, representing a unique experience in the CMEA area.

In 1988 the CIB founded the Central European Creditbank, aimed at the domestic market. Other banks with foreign participation fully operating in the Hungarian banking system are:

- The Citibank Budapest Ltd.
- The Unicbank.
- The Inter Europa Bank RT.

A further increase in the number of foreign banking joint ventures in Hungary is foreseeable in the future, according to the growing interest of Western bank and financial institutions towards the country.

At the moment the only Hungarian banks abroad are two:

- The Central Wechsel Und Creditbank, AG, set up in Vienna and fully owned by the NBH.
- The Hungarian International Bank Ltd, founded in London in 1973.

During the first three years since its establishment, the reformed banking system has faced several obstacles impeding its smooth functioning.

These can be summarized as follows:

- Political resistance to change and to abandoning centralization, at least prior to the political uprising which took place last autumn.
- The Commercial Banks, being undercapitalized and dependent on the NBH for their refinancing, are not as autonomous in credit allocation as they were expected to be. Thus the hoped for incentive effect on enterprises' efficiency is actually weakened.
- The rising interest rates, determined by the anti-inflationary tight monetary policy adopted in recent years, and the heavy engagement of the NBH in the budget deficit financing have slackened the development of a lively banking sector.

Nevertheless, the reform has proved quite successful in giving Hungary the most advanced banking system in the region, thus making the country ready to play a leading role in establishing relations with Western financial institutions and in promoting the financial integration of the area.

Further reasons for optimism in the future of the Hungarian banking system are the creation of an interbanking market, needed to manage the liquidity existing within the system, the introduction of new financial instruments and the development of a financial market. The latter is expected to play a basic role in mobilizing savings and allocating investment funds, replacing the state in this function, thus overcoming difficulties represented by the strong preference for liquidity shown by savers and by the inflationary pressures which are under way.

Besides the official reopening of the Budapest stock exchange on 1 January 1990, reasons for optimism about the future of the Hungarian financial market are to be found in the inflows of foreign capital as direct investment in the country and the entrance of foreigners on the financial market. This could restore confidence in it and accelerate its internationalization. Financial dynamism is also confirmed by the hard currency bond issuance on international markets, with the first bond issue denominated in ECU in September 1989, and by the creation of foreign mutual funds investing in Hungarian securities.

III. *A Possible Role for the Private ECU in Reforming Monetary Relations Between some CMEA Countries*

The radical changes that have occurred in the East European countries after Gorbachev's perestroika couldn't fail to deeply affect the economic relations among those countries, with particular reference to the CMEA. The Central European countries, which are turning from centralized economies to the market, surely wish to strengthen their economic ties with the international market as much as possible, particularly with the European Community. The economic reform process in those countries will take a long time, and the possibility of joining the Community — a much-felt aspiration of people at the present time — is to be seen as a medium-term objective, not to be achieved immediately. The protective walls which for so many decades isolated socialist economies from foreign competition weakened them from the economic point of view. Only their gradual demolition will allow those countries to fully participate in the world economy.

Founded in 1949, the Council of Mutual Economic Assistance (CMEA) reproduced the Soviet centralized planning system for all Eastern European countries. During the first two decades it played a comparatively effective role in making the economic mechanisms homogeneous and in helping the development of heavy industry within the area. However, the CMEA never represented a "common market" but rather a "managed" trade area. As a matter of fact it lacked three essential elements: demand, currency and prices.

In the CMEA countries, demand is regulated by the planning system. Foreign trade is conducted by Foreign Trade Organisations and primarily to obtain essential imports. This implies that exports are a way to finance the necessary imports and not an end in themselves or a way to increase aggregate demand and therefore to decrease unemployment. Trade is thus controlled by import and export quotas. This state monopoly has negative effects, because enterprises which produce or need traded goods have no direct contacts with each other. This situation has brought about other major consequences:

- a very low level of trade in the whole CMEA area, in comparison with the level of national income of the member nations;
- a very low quality and technological sophistication level of CMEA commodities as compared with Western standards.

The absence of real demand has produced a price system in the CMEA which is not a measure of the relative shortages, and therefore prices are not consistent with world market prices. The way of fixing prices, deducing them from the average world market prices of each good over the previous five years, proved to be quite rigid, especially when sudden and strong upward or downward fluctuations occurred, as was the case during the seventies for oil prices. Similar considerations on price irrationality can be extended to the most important relative price, which is the exchange rate, with the consequence that national currencies are inconvertible. Currency inconvertibility is strictly connected with bilateralism in trade. In such a situation, in fact, no nation wishes to hold balances in national currencies, so that annual and long-term trade and payment agreements are based on keeping trade between two countries in balance in physical terms.

As a matter of fact, the CMEA tried to introduce a collective currency — the Transferable Rouble (TR) — in 1964 to make steps towards better economic and monetary integration. The TR and the IBEC (International Bank for Economic Cooperation) themselves were created in response to the specific need to replace the bilateral clearing system and its unit of account — the so called Rouble clearing — which had been in use since 1945 and had caused several problems. Unfortunately the process of multilateralization has proceeded very slowly so far, and as a means of payment the TR is imperfect in many respects. A currency ought to represent a generalized purchasing power. That is its power should be closely linked to the freedom with which the currency can be spent. The fact that the Transferable Rouble is not "substantially convertible" — i.e. the possessor of a financial surplus is not free to use it to purchase goods and services in one of the countries of the area — is perhaps the main obstacle which the socialist countries have to overcome if they wish to improve their monetary cooperation. This type of inconvertibility — known as commodity inconvertibility — largely depends on the planning system, which, by forbidding those purchases and sales that are not regulated by the plan, impedes a widespread use of the Transferable Rouble in transactions with third countries and prevents the proper operation of the mechanisms set in motion by the creation of the system.

The CMEA Summit held in Sofia last January was successful insofar as it helped all those topics to emerge and to be debated, spurred by the desire to achieve economic renewal that characterises all the socialist countries today. In particular, the need to overcome the artificial mechanisms currently regulating intra-CMEA relations, and consequently the desire to gradually come closer to market rules, emerged. Therefore the emotional reactions which would lead to the breaking off of all relations with former CMEA partners are to be rejected. It is in the Eastern countries' interest to carry on — and if possible to extend — their trade within the old bloc, provided that the CMEA undergoes radical changes.[1] In this respect Poland, Hungary and Czechoslovakia can represent an "economic workshop" — as the Polish Prime Minister called it — in which to experiment together on a common approach to the market.

The choice of starting a profound reform in the CMEA is extremely important for the future of international trade, and for EEC-CMEA trade in particular. The EEC itself is objectively interested in a possible evolution of the CMEA and in its taking part in the world market. In fact, should the CMEA break up, the EEC would not be able to completely replace the old economic relations. Nor could it bear the burden of possible profound economic crises in Central Europe, which would be difficult to keep under control also from the political point of view. Therefore, the gradual transition from a situation of commodity inconvertibility and bilateralism to commodity covertibility and multilateralism appears to be the fundamental approach for the economic growth of East European countries and for their opening to the market.

The CMEA shall have to proceed in parallel in two directions:

i) commercial, ii) financial. In fact, a reform of the payment mechanisms towards foreign countries is clearly significant only if measures of commercial liberalization are jointly taken.

i) On the commercial side

CMEA countries need first of all to reverse their attitude towards foreign trade: from an import-oriented view to one in which export becomes the objective. The CMEA countries should modify, initially at least, the minimum set of tradable goods, with non-residents allowed to buy these products freely. Firms should therefore be permitted to have resort to the external market and, more or less freely, to make use of a part of the export profits for the purchase of products and services abroad. Domestically, the principle of the client-supplier relation could be replaced with a system of direct relations between firms. Simultaneously the domestic price system should be reformed in order to keep prices for the freely tradable commodities consistent with world market prices. Obviously, removal of direct controls should be accompanied by the introduction of indirect instruments, such as taxation, credit and investment controls and a new revenue policy. A sudden liberalisation of foreign trade could, in fact, bring undesired effects, such as a remarkable increase in consumer goods imports.

ii) On the monetary side

Instead of the Transferable Rouble a more suitable "monetary standard" should be adopted, one more in line with the current evolution and able to help the price system fulfil its duty of allocating resources, an aim that the old Five-Year Plans failed to achieve. In this respect, in Sofia the Soviet Prime Minister proposed the use of convertible currencies for trade inside CMEA, starting in 1991. Though there is general consensus from all CMEA countries on this kind of evolution, almost all the other countries asked for a longer transition period. In fact, many are the problems that hamper a short-term transition, the hardest being the fact that it will be the Soviet Union, in particular, to benefit from the process. Because it has internationally valuable energy exports, the East European economies, with their substandard goods to export,[2] will be harmed. In this respect Czechoslovakia, Hungary and Poland have been most determined that some mechanism is found which allows them a transition period between CMEA trading and the rigours of the free market. When enlarging and multilateralizing exchanges inside the CMEA as a growth factor for the economies themselves, for world trade and for the strengthening of commercial relations with the EEC, what must be avoided is a situation in which those countries that are currently experimenting with new market forms find themselves bound to withdraw "trade quotas" from other countries of the area and divert them outside in order to obtain the hard currency necessary to re-equilibrate their financial positions. In this sense the "monetary standard" of reference must be anchored in some way to the international market in order to guarantee that the intra-CMEA relations are not penalized with respect to possible trade with the world market.[3]

IV. *The ECU as a Monetary Standard*

The need for a "monetary standard", with an international anchor, to denominate trade within the area gives rise to the problem of deciding which currency will be able to play that role. In principle it doesn't matter which freely convertible Western currency is selected, but the ECU seems to enjoy three clear advantages over all other countries. First, the political advantage. The ECU is not a national currency but an international unit, not managed by a particular country. This "neutrality" makes its acceptability more attractive. Second, the economic advantage. Being a basket, the value of the ECU is an average resulting from the performances of 12

European countries. Among those countries there are the major trading and investment partners of East European countries. Besides, there is a strong analogy between the composition of the ECU and the currencies used in trade between the two areas. Third, choosing the ECU is crucial in the light of the creation of the Economic and Monetary Union, following the decisions taken by the European Council at meetings held in Madrid and Strasbourg. Many East European countries might one day become members of the EEC. Adoption of the ECU as a reference currency at this initial stage could represent some sort of "association" to the EMS, one that could both reinforce the possibility of realizing economic reforms in a stable monetary environment — internally and externally — and pave the way for later full membership in the Economic and Monetary Union.

V. *A Possible Intervention by Commercial Banks to Foster the "Economic Workshop" of Hungary, Czechoslovakia and Poland*

While possible new monetary systems for the CMEA are being studied in various places, and the establishment of institutions which from Western Europe can contribute to channel that flow of financings necessary to the development of Eastern countries is being effected, both Eastern and Western market forces should act in order to give a decisive impulse to the necessary reforms. While the institutional aspect is essential to the achievement of the pre-established objectives in the long run, market operators can undoubtedly play a role that is equally important in the short run. The idea of an "economic workshop" outlined by the three Central European countries is in one sense a recall to these market forces. It is not yet clear which kind of experiments will be carried out: for instance, a sort of cooperation like that of the Benelux agreement in Western Europe could be tried within these countries, similar in size, structure and orientation. In consequence of that, the Western banking system could also act and give its positive contribution to the aforesaid "experiments". This would correspond to the interest of the banks themselves, whose customers are looking with ever increasing interest for spaces and opportunities in those countries. Some West European banks, in order to favour that trend, have recently intensified their direct presence in the area, establishing new banks or taking a participation in the capital of existing ones. As mentioned before, the closest tie for Hungary, Poland and Czechoslovakia is represented by their financial situation, and the establishment of hard-currency reserves is a way of reducing their financial dependence on foreign countries. Therefore home trade, at present denominated in non-convertible TR, is an obstacle to the achievement of that objective and runs the risk of affecting adversely the economies of those countries. This problem has already partly emerged in Hungary, where in January, after the Sofia and Prague meetings, a measure to suspend all export licences denominated in Transferable Roubles was taken, in order to divert CMEA exports towards those countries which regulate imports in hard currency. Nevertheless, the problems of a drastic non-convertible trade balance reduction clash with the structure of foreign trade. As far as Hungary is concerned, about 2/3 of exports towards CMEA are represented by the engineering industry and a timely placement of that production on Western markets is rather difficult. It is, therefore, necessary to find solutions with a certain timeliness.

First of all the three countries should authorize the use of the ECU as a monetary standard for commercial transactions effected inside the area. Thanks to the aforesaid characteristics (stability and neutrality), this could represent the best link to the international market. In particular the ECU could initially perform two of the three functions of a currency:

- "unit of account", in order to define the trade contracts;
- "store of value", in order to guarantee that the credit value to the exporting country persists until the settlement of the transaction.

As far as the function of "means of settlement" is concerned, the contracts might provide that the debtor country engages itself to supply goods — obviously at international market prices — without binding itself to pay its debt by making use of hard currency reserves. A sort of Transferable ECU could then be used as a substitute for the old Transferable Rouble.

But it is necessary that a small group of West European banks participate in the realisation of this project, by creating a sort of "clearing" for the Transferable ECU. In the case of trade between two countries, this sort of "clearing" could concretely happen if the bank placed at the disposal of country A — which is the Transferable ECU creditor towards the debtor B — the relevant amount in ECU. So the bank would replace as a creditor the country A, which would acquire hard currency from exports within the CMEA area, while B would obtain a credit and that transaction would enable it not to draw on its hard currency reserves in order to settle its debt towards A. The transaction would close with an opposite sign operation towards the bank: B would then settle its debt towards the bank thanks to the proceeds of an export towards A, from which the necessary Transferable ECU would be obtained. After the transaction is completed, there is neither utilization of hard currency reserves by the involved countries, nor an increase of hard currency reserves in absolute terms,[4] and the bank will have performed its function to transfer money in time and to finance the temporal lag which separates the two opposite sign transactions. In this way the bank favours the performance of the market forces, which would be set in motion by a true incentive to export, unlike the present situation where these are governed by rigid Five-Year Plans. Of course this system, which plays an active role by matching demand and offer and which can involve banks from both EC and CMEA member countries, may be extended to a wider number of countries and therefore lay the basis for the effective multilateralization of intra-CMEA trade. This represents a prerequisite for external trade to be based on more realistic prices, with qualitatively better products, and above all to be founded on that "commodity convertibility" which is the essential element for the development of trade.

Notes

1. "When deeply reformed, the CMEA could find its 'raison d'être' at least in order to keep a trade flow of products insufficiently fit for the world market from the qualitative point of view" (Jacques Delors, Presentation of the Programme of the European Commission to the European Parliament, 17 January 1990).
2. At the moment hard goods such as food, raw materials, and fuel constitute the bulk of USSR exports to other CMEA countries, whereas Soviet imports from these are primarily soft goods such as inferior quality manufactured products. But while Soviet exports to these nations are at prices around or below world market prices, Soviet imports from the other CMEA nations are paid at prices above world market prices.
3. As a matter of fact, the West European post-war experience, with the creation of the European Payments Union, was a means to make export profits gained in Europe equal in value to US dollars, so that corresponding incentives to exports inside or outside the area existed.
4. This condition would occur should a third partner external to the area enter the transaction and should, for instance, B sell its commodities against hard currency.

Economic Relations between Eastern Europe and the USSR: Bilateral Ties versus Multilateral Cooperation

Marie Lavigne

Synopsis

Soviet-East European economic relations are bound to display a decreasing trend in the nineties, due to several causes:

The impact of Soviet perestroika. The traditional Soviet foreign trade organization has been dissolved, and the new system is not yet working. The economy in general is suffering a crisis. Exports to the CMEA region are to be limited to the amounts needed to secure imports. The USSR is ready to accept from its partners only the goods which satisfy its priority needs, both in quantity and quality. The new rules on intra-CMEA settlements in world prices and convertible currencies, to be applied beginning in 1991 as decided at the 45th session (January 1990), are going to strengthen this trend.

The trends in world energy prices. With a lag, these trends influence intra-CMEA prices. Since 1986, the Soviet Union has experienced a decline in its terms of trade with the CMEA countries. In 1988 it developed a deficit with the European CMEA countries for the first time since 1974. As long as trade within CMEA is settled in transferable roubles, the partner countries will limit their surplus on the USSR through a decrease in their exports. Once this trade is settled in convertible currencies, they may well reduce their imports. In both cases the trade turnover will shrink.

The westward trend in the foreign trade of most of the East European countries. The agreements concluded or in progress with the EEC, as well as the dramatic changes which have occurred in the political and economic régimes of Eastern Europe since the end of 1989, are strengthening this trend.

To these causes, one has to add the present state of disorganization and even decay of the CMEA itself.

The *traditional* mechanisms of trade and cooperation do not work any more. This is due to political causes, as well as to the contradiction between reform trends in domestic economies, calling for a "marketisation" of foreign trade, and the rigidity of the inter-governmental bilateralism which characterises the traditional model. The perestroika of the CMEA was in principle decided in 1988. A unified market is to be set up in the nineties according to this decision, with a reform in the mechanism of trade, price-fixing, and currency systems. Though this scheme was not totally discarded at the 45th session of the organization in 1990, the centrifugal tendencies at work may well jeopardize it. The CMEA will thus not be able to provide an adequate framework for the development of Soviet-East European economic relations. A different framework is to be built. This presentation will discuss the range of feasible alternatives.

I. *Introduction*

In the whirlwind of events which affected the East European scene in 1989, the CMEA as an organization seemed to be threatened with extinction.*[1] The 45th meeting of the CMEA in January 1990 apparently confirmed these expectations. Even before the meeting there were rumours from Czechoslovak officials that Czechoslovakia might retire from the CMEA altogether.[2] There is a growing perception that East European countries want to get rid of the CMEA as intensely as they reject Communism. They are supported in this determination by the feeling that the West urges them to get rid of an obsolete structure while offering them direct economic assistance or otherwise helping them to become more integrated into the world economy. This is supposed to be antinomic with a continuation of intra-CMEA links. There is such a consensus on this subject that any hint of a rationale of an integrative structure between the Soviet Union and Eastern Europe is considered preposterous. If anything, only loose models of a free exchange zone or customs union type between some East European countries, are envisaged. And even this only if it does not harm their inclusion in the Western international economy. In addition, the Soviet Union itself is showing an open indifference toward the issue, on the basis of the new so-called "Sinatra Doctrine": do it your way.[3]

We shall argue here that Eastern Europe, even more than the USSR, needs to reach a working arrangement on the way trade links between the present members of the CMEA are to be arranged. Otherwise, these countries are to suffer considerable losses, even in their attempts to become more integrated into the world economy. This does not mean trying to revive the CMEA in its traditional format. However, it would be very paradoxical to consider arrangements based upon bilateral ad hoc relations with the Soviet Union as the best solution, at a time when the Eastern countries are prompted to seek multilateral-type relations with the outside world.

To assess what may be useful now one has first to review what the CMEA indeed was, or rather was not, in the past, then to recall the various reform proposals which have been put together, including a final reflection upon the kind of trade (possibly cooperation) relations which might emerge between the USSR and Eastern Europe.

II. *Did the CMEA Exist?*

A line commonly found in the general press since 1989 is the following: the CMEA was meant to coordinate the national central plans, and as there is no more (or very little) central planning left, the very reason for the existence of the CMEA drops by itself. This is a misunderstanding of what the CMEA really was. One should make the effort to go back into history so as to try to assess the true nature of the organization.

A. *A plan coordination that never was*

The CMEA was created in 1949, in a political move to counter the Marshall Plan launched in June 1947, and the so-called boycott of Eastern Europe (as stated in the Declaration on the creation of the CMEA published on 25 January, 1949 in the Eastern press). In some sources it is mentioned that originally the CMEA was meant to be set up as a comprehensive economic pact, providing for a wide-range cooperation, but this was never ratified (see van Brabant, 1989, page 20). In actual fact, though some cooperation mechanisms were set up in the late fifties through the creation of Standing Commissions, the CMEA Charter detailing the aims of the organization was adopted only in 1959, and the CMEA itself was shaped into a fully-fledged permanent institution in 1962 with the creation of an Executive Committee. Finally, also in 1962, and following this institutional strengthening, the Basic Principles of the International Socialist Division of Labour (ISDL) were adopted. The concept of ISDL was clearly supranational in essence and assumed centralized plan coordination. This format could, however, never be put into operation. It should be remembered today that the country which was most opposed to this supranational scheme was Romania, for which it got great and long-lasting political credit in the West.

Following this first failure, the Comprehensive Programme for Socialist Economic Integration (SEI), adopted in 1971, meant to combine market and plan coordination (in the wake of domestic economic reforms in the mid-sixties) without any element of supranationality or intervention into domestic planning. A complicated system with different time-spans was then devised, with various methods of coordination according to the time range: for annual, five-year, and long-term plans. The aim was to reach a workable cooperation and specialization among the member countries, which would in every concrete case be based upon an agreement of all the interested parties.

The energy crisis which developed in 1973-74 had the effect of concentrating the operation of the CMEA almost exclusively upon the energy supply problem. This was done through the joint investment format, the most prominent case being the building of the Orenburg gas pipeline in 1974-78. Some ambitious schemes were set up, such as the Concerted Plans for Multilateral Integration Measures (the first one being launched for the period 1976-80) and the Target Programmes for Long-Term Cooperation, in energy and raw materials, machine-building, transport, agriculture and manufactured consumers' goods industry (signed for 10 to 15 years in 1978 and 1979). These schemes were not completely cosmetic, in the sense that some achievements have been put into these boxes. But the actual achievements would have been realized anyhow (and often were) on the basis of bilateral agreements between the USSR and the East

European countries. To quote just one example, the Orenburg gas pipeline was included in the first "Concerted Plan", and mentioned in the Target Programme for energy, though it would have been constructed quite irrespective of these arrangements.

Looking backwards, one may now realize that these schemes were very harmful to the Western perception of the CMEA. All the pompous phrasing about the "coordination of plans", the "socialist economic integration", etc., just fuelled the impression that the Soviet Union was successfully monitoring the planning process overall, so as to achieve a kind of supranational plan with provisions compulsory for all CMEA members. In reality, the Soviet leaders had long ago given up such an aim for the near future, even if some theoreticians still dream of an integrated planning as the ultimate format of the CMEA.

What the Soviets really expected from the CMEA has changed over time. If we limit ourselves to the past 20 years, in the seventies they clearly wished the CMEA countries to contribute to the development of Soviet energy and raw material resources. In the early eighties, they wanted to maintain at least a workable specialization format, being conscious that the East European countries were no longer able to provide a sizeable contribution to Soviet investments when their own domestic investments were drastically cut by painful adjustment programmes. And in 1984, when the East European economies began to recover, what the Soviets really wanted was to take advantage of this renewed growth so as to get good quality manufactured goods and additional food supplies. This would also allow their partners to repay a large debt in transferable roubles, then amounting (according to Soviet statistics) to more than 10 billion roubles.

B. *An inefficient specialization pattern*

The Soviet claim for better supplies from their partners, as formulated in 1984, was in itself an acknowledgement of the failure of the specialization pattern. But what does specialization exactly mean here? Again, we are facing large misunderstandings. For an economist trained in standard international economics, the theory of international specialization *is* precisely the basic layer of the discipline. Economic agents engaged in international trade automatically specialize on the basis of their comparative advantage, according to the logic of the market. The main developments in international economics since Ricardo are chiefly refinements of the original hypotheses, such as introducing factor mobility in addition to the movement of goods.

It is, therefore, very difficult to grasp what is meant by specialization in the CMEA context. Among the authors who devoted the greatest attention to this process, Sobell (1984) explored all the fields of intra-CMEA specialization and attempted to assess its results. The basic conclusion of Sobell is that the CMEA is indeed a "system", but not an "international trade system" comparable to market-type integrated groupings. It is an "international protection system" in which the members try to achieve an expansion of their production while protecting themselves from external disturbances. As a result, a network of inter-governmental specialization agreements emerges not on the basis of industrial links on the enterprise level, but on the basis of political coordination largely managed by the USSR. Is such a protection system efficient? The answer is yes (again, following Sobell's line): not in the sense that the achieved specialization is in any way close to what would have been reached through the market maximization of comparative advantages, but in the sense that it does *exist* at all.

In economic terms however, specialization in itself is hardly efficient, and this is widely acknowledged in CMEA countries' publications since the mid-eighties. The indicators of efficiency used in the East are very poor, as rightly mentioned by van Brabant (1989, page 281). They basically consist of (a) the number of specialization agreements for a given group of products; (b) the share of "specialized production" in trade for a given country and given goods. In addition to their vagueness, these indicators are inaccurate because the existence of a specialization agreement does not mean that specialization is indeed implemented (see Kolchin, 1988). This may explain why the measures submitted by various authors differ so widely.

Was this pattern imposed upon its partners by the USSR? The most common answer in Western literature (and nowadays in the Eastern one as well), is yes, from a whole set of evidence. First, the USSR is the only country which did not specialize or, what amounts to the same, "specialized" in everything. But this is a feature common to large countries richly endowed with resources, such as the USA in the Western world. Second, Soviet attempts in the early sixties to force a crude inter-branch specialization pattern on their partners, according to a preconceived idea of broad comparative advantages (in manufacturing industries for the GDR and Czechoslovakia, agriculture for Hungary, Bulgaria and Romania, petrochemical industry for Romania) provide additional evidence. As we know, Romania successfully fought the idea, but then chose for itself an obviously wrong type of specialization — in the steel industry — for which it had neither enough energy resources nor iron ore. Finally, the pattern which eventually emerged in the seventies and the eighties is said to serve Soviet interests while being disadvantageous to Eastern Europe. Is this really so? Yes, if by that we mean that the USSR may get large supplies of some finished goods (Hungarian Ikarus buses, Bulgarian forklift equipment, GDR railway wagons, Polish ships, Czechoslovak nuclear equipment) or parts (for instance, parts for the Lada car are being manufactured in East European countries in return for finished cars). These goods are of a poor quality, and the Soviet Union has repeatedly complained about this. The East European countries have complained as well, arguing that such goods are unexportable to the West. In fact when they were, it was indeed a different product which was specially manufactured for Western needs (see Marer, 1984, for the Ikarus buses). Should the Soviet Union be held responsible for the fact that it allowed its partners to dump large quantities of otherwise unsaleable goods on its market? This is a very common argument nowadays, on the grounds that the inefficient production structure of Eastern Europe originated from Soviet pressure in the fifties. Would it not have been possible to manufacture good quality goods for the Soviet market as well, as soon as there were skills to manufacture them for the West? Here the CMEA mechanism is blamed, in particular the system of settlements. The East European countries bitterly complained of not getting adequate payment when they shipped goods embodying parts or materials imported from the West for dollars, and exported to the Soviet Union against transferable roubles.

But the crux of the situation, as far as specialization was concerned, was that there existed no way of improving it for reasons pertaining to the functioning of the CMEA and of the domestic economies. The lasting flaw of the specialization agreements was that they could only be signed at inter-governmental level and could only be implemented by administrative means, the signatory countries often resisting this implementation. As long as the specialization agreements were not embodied in trade agreements, and despite all efforts to increase the responsibility of the committed countries, there was no way to prevent a country from walking out. This has happened often, thereby weakening all the signed agreements. As for the domestic field, the enterprises traditionally avoided any specialization, as this would have put them at the mercy of their suppliers in a sellers' market situation characteristic of a shortage economy. Even more so they avoided being dependent on foreign suppliers. In consequence, according to the specific "Socialist" wording, the GDR or Czechoslovakia were said to manufacture "more than 70% of the range of machinery produced in the world" (the statement was made at the Economic Summit of the CMEA in June 1984). This meant that both countries consciously avoided being dependent on foreign supplies. No surprise, then, that intra-CMEA specialization mainly worked for the Soviet Union. East European countries sought to avoid being dependent on supplies of their partners for manufactured goods. They were dependent, however, but on the USSR, and for energy and raw materials supplies which did not belong to the "specialized" items as currently defined. One may also say that in the long run they *became* dependent on the Soviet "market" for absorbing such goods.

C. *A rump market*

That the CMEA never was a market (the reason we have used the word between inverted commas) seems obvious enough. There has been no free movement of goods, services, labour or capital among the member countries. In fact there has been hardly *any* movement of labour and capital across the borders. In the case of labour, this was due to the severe limitations of individual freedom of travel if not for (mostly organized) tourism. These limitations, in turn, have impeded any intra-firm cooperation even when such a cooperation was declared desirable. The only cases of large labour transfers occurred in relation with joint investments such as the building of the Orenburg gas pipeline, and even then with great reluctance on the part of the countries supplying labour. True, especially at the end of the eighties, there were Vietnamese workers (and occasionally Cuban) in most of the CMEA European countries. The local population was largely unaccustomed to the presence of such *Gastarbeiter*, thus explaining ethnic intolerance,[4] but also evidence of the absence of a real labour market between countries, except on a limited scale on the borders. As for the capital market, one cannot reasonably qualify as such the movements of investment funds, be they bilateral or channelled through the International Investment Bank of the CMEA, which derived from the joint investments (see Graziani).

Here again, a comparison with the domestic setting is useful. In the centrally planned economies, there is no capital market: the monetary flows automatically follow decisions on physical flows, and this is the main reason for the traditional "soft credit constraint" in this system. Within the CMEA the credit constraint was equally soft, be it for credits linked with overdue settlements or with investments, as long as the corresponding physical flows had been decided upon (bilaterally or multilaterally) or had taken place. As far as labour is concerned, there is a quasi market in the domestic centrally planned economies. But here its extension to the CMEA area as a whole was limited by nationalism, red tape, and mostly the inconvertibility of the domestic currencies and the great wage differentials from one country to the other (translated into purchasing power parities). Finally the flows of goods and services were strictly regulated in physical terms on the basis of trade agreements and protocols. This was fully consistent with the rules applied within the "traditional" centrally planned economies, but it gradually became inconsistent with the operation of the domestic markets, imperfect as they were, in the "modified" planned economies such as Hungary after 1980 or Poland after 1986.

It should follow from this that the CMEA cannot be described in terms which are used for relations between market economies. In actual fact, nobody has ever attempted to call the CMEA a "free trade area", but in recent years the view of the CMEA as a "customs union" (indeed a stronger link) was reassessed by Franklyn Holzman who had developed it as early as 1962. This view has been expanded upon by other authors, such as Josef Brada or Padma Desai (see the survey article by Brada, 1985, and his elaboration of the same theme, 1988). I agree with many points made by these authors, but I do not agree with the definition of the CMEA as a customs union. Of course the first argumentation developed by Franklyn Holzman, and his subsequent refinements, are very strong in explaining in economic terms some of the features of the CMEA. But the wording itself is not satisfactory, mainly because one has to qualify this *sui generis* customs union in such a way that one abandons the very specificity of a customs union — its market operation.

Let us briefly deal with this point. When Franklyn Holzman first launched the idea in 1962, this was for a specific aim. He had to counter the widely held idea that the USSR was "exploiting" the East through the prices applied within the CMEA. He had the relevant figures, but this was not enough, especially when the West has just emerged from the Cold War. He had to explain the *rationale* for such figures in an economist's way, using standard theories. The same reason led him to reformulate the theory more than 20 years later, again to substantiate price levels and price movements which could otherwise be explained only on political grounds – the fact that the USSR was selling fuels at lower than world prices and buying machinery at higher than world prices. This debate has been called, among Sovietologists, "the subsidy debate". It emerged in the early eighties through the findings of Michael Marrese and Jan Vanous (1983). Holzman's approach (and also that of the quoted authors who supported it) is as follows: once we assume that the CMEA is a customs union where the common external tariff, as an instrument of trade promotion within the union, is replaced by a system of quotas on trade with non-members, we may apply the standard international trade theory which shows that within the union relative prices, as compared with relative world prices, display a pattern consistent with the factor endowments of the area as a whole and of the individual countries. Then there is a rationale for energy prices being relatively low and machinery prices relatively high: one does not need to go out in the hazardous world of politics.

D. *A club of the unwilling*

Recently, several authors have attempted to describe the CMEA in terms of political science or political economy concepts (see Comisso, 1986 and Brada, 1988). This research has been motivated by a desire to find a logical and acceptable explanation for the operation of the CMEA and its evolution over time, while relating it to existing theories. Josef Brada thus sees the CMEA as a *club* (as a form of international *régime*) whose members desire a public good (a mechanism for promoting trade and integration in a stable environment) and are willing to pay a price for it (in terms of foregone gains on world markets). I certainly do not do justice to the refined developments of Josef Brada by summing them up in this way, and I would advise the reader to go to the source.

But though the theory is quite coherent, I cannot adhere to the idea that in the CMEA régime the members have "voluntarily adher(ed)" (be it only "in part") "to a régime whose benefits outweigh the costs of membership" (Brada, 1988, page 658). However, I agree with him on the rejection of the "trade-off" approach suggested by Vanous and Marrese in the "subsidy debate" which also, for that matter, used political economy arguments to explain a situation described in standard economic terms.

E. *Unconventional gains from trade?*

The issue of price-fixing has provoked more discussions than any other issue related to the operation of the CMEA. It may be divided into several distinct questions: how are intra-CMEA prices fixed? How may these prices be compared with world prices? Who is gaining and who is losing from these prices?

Let me sum up the stages of this very complex discussion:

(i) In a long debate with Horst Mendershausen, Franklyn Holzman, as we have seen before, proved that the USSR was not systematically discriminating against its CMEA partners through the prices which it charged them (by comparison with selling prices to the West) or the prices it paid them (by comparison with prices paid to the West).

(ii) The debate re-emerged in the seventies, when since the end of 1973 (and despite changes in the price mechanism made in 1975) the Soviet price for oil appeared to be much smaller in CMEA trade than in trade with the West. The extensive econometric study by Marrese and Vanous (1983) provided evidence that the particular pattern of Soviet export *and import* prices with the CMEA led to substantial losses for the Soviet Union in terms of foregone gains from trade with the West. Also, the study sought to show that such losses were a permanent feature of Soviet trade with the CMEA, and that they had only been exacerbated after the rise in world oil prices in 1973.

The authors felt that they had to explain such findings, especially because the amount of the Soviet "subsidy" or "indirect transfer" was so large, and because it did not fit with the traditional picture of the Soviet Union as the political leader of the bloc. The answer was, then, that the USSR was granting subsidies for "unconventional gains", such as political and ideological allegiance and military security. In the West, the Marrese-Vanous theses have been widely discussed from the point of view of the accuracy of data, of the methodology, and of the substance. I myself entered into the debate, arguing that the Soviet Union was indeed tolerating (rather than deliberately granting) such subsidies so as to advance its own concept of socialist economic integration (Lavigne, 1983).

East European authors have never agreed upon the existence of such transfers. The few of them who entered the debate argued that the level of prices was not a substantial issue. One had to look, they said, at the substance of the CMEA mechanism, which was in the long run detrimental to all partners because it perpetuated an obsolete production structure and isolated the CMEA countries from the world economy (Köves, 1983).

(iii) Since 1985 the Soviet oil price for the CMEA countries is higher than the world price. While one of the authors of the initial study, Jan Vanous, argued that nevertheless it remains under the world price if one chooses a "realistic exchange rate"[5] (Vanous, 1989) the other, Michael Marrese, in a case study centred on Hungary, came to the conclusion that "the Soviet subsidization of Hungary had dramatically declined between 1982 and 1987" (Marrese and Wittenberg, 1989). In another study, Marrese discussed intra-CMEA trade in terms of "winners and losers", not as regards price relations but from the point of view of the commodity composition of trade, which brings him much closer to the East European view (Marrese, 1989).

Logically, the "subsidy theory" should be particularly strong today. Why could one not argue that the time has come when the Soviet Union is no longer interested in political, ideological, military and diplomatic "gains" in Eastern Europe and hence has stopped subsidizing Eastern Europe?

Indeed, in 1990 Eastern Europe almost unanimously complains about the losses entailed by the operation of the CMEA. But, significantly, it does *not* complain on the grounds of the price structure, and it does *not* acknowledge having been subsidized in the past.

To sum up: the CMEA has not been a supranational planning agency, or a mechanism promoting specialization, or a market, or a club, or a vehicle for subsidies. Perhaps it never existed? In fact, it is widely acknowledged that the most powerful links within the CMEA were those linking the USSR to each of its partners through a variety of bilateral trade and cooperation agreements, programmes and special currency arrangements. This "radial pattern" of intra-CMEA trade extends to relations among the Six East European countries, where basically every country offers the same selection of goods and barters these goods in a bargaining process aiming at a bilateral balance rather than at an expansion of trade or at gains from specialization. Why, then, reform the CMEA at all?

III. *Could a New CMEA Exist?*

Reform of the CMEA mechanisms was attempted, in two opposed moves, in 1984 and 1988. Both attempts failed. It is now widely accepted that the organization is no longer viable in its old format. But even if one believes that an economic integration is impossible among the CMEA members, should one aim to drastically cut trade relations between the USSR and East-Central Europe?

A. *The attempts that failed*

1. *The technological integration*

In 1984 the aim was undoubtedly to improve plan coordination as the main instrument for socialist economic integration. At the same time the Soviet purpose was to try and achieve, on a collective level, what not a single country had been able to achieve in the past, i.e. a shift to "intensive" growth relying on an increased productivity of factors. The launching of the Eureka programme within the EEC was widely invoked as an example and largely misunderstood in the East. One might easily compare the level of mutual misunderstanding in the CMEA and in the EEC. While in the West one considered the Eastern integration as significantly more powerful than it actually was, the East tended to overestimate the degree of scientific-technical coordination within the Eureka framework, overlooking the fact that Eureka represents just a small fraction of industrial research and development in Europe and is heavily concentrated on a few sectors.

The Eastern "Eureka", i.e. the "Comprehensive Programme for Scientific and Technical Progress" (STP Programme), decided upon in 1984 and launched in December 1985, which now appears as a stillborn child, originated from a reasonable idea but had two main flaws. The reasonable idea was to shift away from an obsolete production structure based upon the primacy of heavy industry. The first mistake of the USSR was to impose this on their partners so as, or so it seemed, to reap the benefits of a modernized structure in terms of better supplies. East European countries could not forget that initially the now obsolete structure had been forced upon them by the USSR, and they could not agree to reverse it forcibly just to meet Soviet needs, be it in their own interest as well. The second flaw was to expect a rise in joint research and development while retaining a basically inter-governmental type of cooperation. True, the need for "direct links" between enterprises was noted, but without the preconditions for such links to develop, i.e. a genuine market both within each country and on the CMEA scale. Anyhow the leverage that the USSR had on its partners in 1984, in terms of a large surplus in transferable roubles, was soon to disappear. At its maximum the surplus reached (in the years 1975-86) an amount of almost 16 billion transferable roubles, which in dollar terms might be translated to about 25 billion. The USSR was clearly wishing to recuperate part of this surplus in goods. However, due to the fall in world oil prices which were gradually affecting Soviet prices for oil sold to the CMEA, and also due to a reduction in Soviet supplies, the Soviet surplus began to shrink and in 1988 went into deficit. This new situation was clearly experienced as a loss by the East European countries. But the puzzling question is: where did the past surplus go? One has individual answers: with Romania trade was always more or less balanced; Poland has indeed a debt, both in hard currencies and in transferable roubles, which has been rescheduled. But what about the other cases? The usual answer is that the USSR was traditionally in deficit on its services account, and thus in fact the overall balance was close to even already in 1986. But until we have the complete data on goods and services trade for both the rouble and the non-rouble trade between the USSR and each of the Six, the picture cannot be accurate.

2. *The unified market*

In 1988, at the 44th session of the CMEA in Prague, all the CMEA members but Romania agreed to take steps toward "the gradual formation of conditions for the free movement of goods, services and other production factors among them, with a view to forming a unified market in the long term" (quoted from the Communiqué of the 44th session). This was understood as a response to the EC '92 deadline, as well as an attempt to bring the evolution of the CMEA closer to that of the countries which were implementing market-type economic reforms. It soon became obvious that intra-CMEA trade could not be liberalized in a situation when all the partners were not heading toward the same type of reform, and when even in reforming countries there was still a great deal of central regulation in the field of foreign trade. To help offer a picture of "decentralized" intra-CMEA trade the USSR had to arrange villages-of-Potemkin-like "trade fairs" between Soviet and CMEA enterprises, where there was something to buy because it had been provided for centrally through the wholesale trade Soviet organization, the *Gossnab*.

The failure of the scheme is also due to the fact that all things remained equal in the CMEA framework, i.e. the price system with the traditional rules of price fixing, and the currency system based upon settlements in transferable roubles, a non-convertible accounting unit.

Concerning *prices,* the CMEA countries have such different price structures, and such different approaches to their own price reforms, that any "own" CMEA price system based upon average domestic prices was unthinkable. Thus it was decided to remain within the "Moscow rule" for price-fixing (prices being changed every year on the basis of an average of the world prices for the five previous years). In fact, except in the case of raw materials and especially oil, CMEA prices are more the result of bilateral bargaining than of a deliberate attempt to follow the "world" prices, and anyhow they do not matter much in comparison with what matters most, i.e. the nature and the quantities of the goods supplied.

As for the *settlements,* it was decided to retain the transferable rouble though acknowledging its drawbacks, but to introduce a partial convertibility of domestic currencies so as to use these currencies in bilateral inter-enterprise cooperation. Indeed several agreements were concluded to that effect between the USSR and Czechoslovakia (1988), later on Bulgaria, Poland and Mongolia. But according to a Soviet author such settlements never amounted to more than 0.1% of bilateral trade flows (Sergeev, 1989). Such arrangements may probably be considered as altogether obsolete by now.

A very puzzling point about this blueprint is not just that it failed to be implemented, it seems to have utterly fallen into oblivion. When the 45th session of the CMEA gathered at the beginning of January 1990 in Sofia, with an unprecedented number of journalists flocking in, the necessity of a radical reform of the CMEA was underlined without mentioning the 1988 scheme which was, after all, intended as a significant reform as well. True, this scheme had been proposed at a time when the Communist Party was everywhere in power: a good reason to forget about it.

B. *1990: the CMEA in limbo*

Beginning in 1990 there was a feeling that nobody needed the CMEA except the Soviets, and that even they held to the CMEA as a matter of principle than for any other reason. The decisions which were taken at the 45th session of the CMEA in January are of a conservative type. They leave open the question of the future of the organization (if any). But whatever the members' feelings, some institutions and arrangements are still left.

1. *A quasi dissolution*

Two ideas emerged from the 1990 meeting. The first was that one should get rid of any idea of multilateralism and revert to bilateral links. This is really very strange because there has hardly ever been any multilateralism in the functioning of the CMEA, which has basically rested on bilateral arrangements. The second decision, already agreed upon in principle between Hungary and the USSR earlier, in September 1989, was to shift to trade in "world market prices" and in convertible currencies, beginning in 1991. This has been presented as a Soviet proposal, although the Soviet Union has also been said to favour the transferable rouble system.

The old "subsidy debate" thus attains a new dimension. Let us sum up. Just *before* the January 1990 meeting the USSR was blamed for having a deficit in transferable roubles, that is delivering its partners less than it was getting (of course, at the specific CMEA prices). But calculations made as to the impact of a shift to world prices and hard currency settlements showed that, in this case, the USSR would be in *surplus* (by about 2 billion dollars vis-à-vis Hungary, while it is now in deficit by the same amount in roubles for 1989). The same would occur in trade with Czechoslovakia, and Czechoslovakia was already asking in January for some compensation (*Financial Times*, 11 January 1990).

Is this evidence that in the traditional system the Soviet Union was indeed subsidizing its partners? Partly yes, especially at a time when in *addition* it was maintaining a trade surplus. The effect of (relatively) low prices of oil (in terms of prices of Eastern machinery sold to the USSR) were compounded by the free credit extended by the USSR through the sole existence of a surplus in an inconvertible currency. But, though we do not know how the calculations on the impact of the new system were made, these estimates have probably taken into consideration that in the new system the USSR would deliver less raw materials and would rather use its hard currency gains for buying machinery in the West.

For the time being CMEA trade is shrinking. According to Soviet data for 1989 trade with the socialist countries diminished (by 1% for Soviet exports while Soviet imports increased by 2.7% in value terms), while trade with the capitalist countries increased by 7.6% on the export side and 23.6% on the import side.[6] Trade with the European CMEA countries decreased overall, Soviet imports growing by 1.7% and Soviet exports decreasing by 3.3%.[7] At the beginning of 1990 the USSR announced a decrease in its supplies of fuel to Poland (by one third for the first three months of the year), Czechoslovakia (by 20% in January) and Bulgaria (by an undisclosed amount in January: see the *Financial Times*, 14 February 1990), following the trend which began in 1988. Though supplies to Romania increased in January 1990 this was meant as an emergency aid measure and not as a new basis for trade. Also in 1990, Hungary decided to revise all its export licenses on a case-by-case basis, so as to "divert" as little goods as possible to the CMEA market and to prevent the export of goods saleable to the West. This is only the latest instance of what emerged earlier in 1988 as a "customs war" conducted by Czechoslovakia against its neighbours and first and foremost the USSR. Arguing that the Soviet and other East European tourists were plundering the domestic market due to a favourable exchange rate, Czechoslovakia imposed exorbitant duties on most of the goods exported by tourists. This was followed by other countries, including the USSR itself, which introduced quotas for the export of consumer goods at end 1989.

The CMEA "non-market" thus appears as an area of shrinking trade, increasingly segmented. Never was the phrase of Franklyn Holzman on "trade aversion" more true. This was also, at the beginning of 1990, a rather general feeling. Before the CMEA meeting in January several officials from East European countries suggested that their countries should leave the CMEA. The strongest voice was that of the Czechoslovak Minister of Finance, Vaclav Klaus, but in a more conditional way Hungarian and Polish officials expressed the same idea. A month later, however, the picture was already different. The Hungarian Vice-Premier, Peter Medgyessy, who was also then the Chairman of the Executive Committee of the CMEA, rejected the idea in an interview, saying that one should maintain the existing advantages of integration (*Le Monde*, 10 February, 1990). The new Czechoslovak Ambassador to Moscow, Rudolf Slansky, stressed the importance of the Soviet link (*New York Times*, 15 February, 1990). But to begin with, what still remains of the old system?

What is left? We do not know that precisely. The Communiqué published at the end of the 45th session states that a new Statute is to be drafted, and the whole system of cooperation is to be revised. The 1959 Charter (several times amended) is thus in force only for a few months perhaps. What about the whole system of multilateral agreements which have created intergovernmental organizations (such as the MIR system which links the power grids of Eastern Europe and Western USSR, the INTERMETAL organization for trade and cooperation in some steel products, and some others) or defined rules for the organization of mutual trade and settlements? Reports on the session hinted that Czechoslovakia (and perhaps also Poland and Hungary) wanted to pull out of the so-called Karl-Marx-Stadt agreement signed in 1973, regulating the exchange rate between the national currencies and the transferable rouble for the operation of joint investments. What about such agencies as the CMEA banks, the IBEC (the International Bank for Economic Cooperation) and the IIB (the International Investment Bank)?

The new system of pricing and settlements is due to enter into force in 1991. Is "business as usual" going on in 1990, with prices formally set according to the "Moscow rule" of 1975? Is there some transition to be envisioned? What about the operation of the CMEA "joint enterprises", of which there were a hundred cases or so at the beginning 1990 (most of them not really operational)?

Rather than going on with unanswerable questions we may state some hypotheses. Existing multilateral institutions are probably going on at a low level. All multilateral actions in progress are likely to be frozen, in particular those deriving from the 1985 STP programme. Bilateral trade agreements were the strongest feature of the CMEA (precisely because they did not require the CMEA as such to function). They should remain in force, but one cannot exclude that other countries might follow the Hungarian example and reconsider existing agreements by introducing a system of domestic licensing for exports to the other CMEA countries (with likely retaliation on the part of the latter).

One must not forget that the legal rules of the CMEA require that each member country implement any "recommendations" of the organization by incorporating it into its own domestic legal system, or by ratifing the multilateral agreements signed. Otherwise the CMEA rules do not apply to this country: this is the "interested party principle" which is one of the principles of the organization. Thus, CMEA member countries are tied not by virtue of any supranational rule, but by their own acceptance: this is a cornerstone of the CMEA. To undo these ties the countries would first have to change their own legislation according to their domestic law. This will in all cases require some time.

The network of five year trade agreements will probably not survive the present five year period which ends in 1990. But if we assume that there will remain some trade among the CMEA members, how will it be conducted? The domestic reforms have not gone so far as to allow, in all countries, all enterprises to trade on their own account. Bilateral trade contracts involving the ministries of foreign trade and/or sectoral ministries may take care of that. The institutional arrangements on the implementation of foreign trade contracts, in particular the conditions for delivery which may be seen as a kind of CMEA international contract law, should in any case be preserved.

As to cooperation in general, CMEA instruments are presumed dead. Coordination of planning is condemned as is planning itself. But here, too, some institutions might remain. We have already mentioned some international organizations such as the MIR system. The transport-related cooperation (in a broad sense, including the transport-by-pipe systems) has to remain if serious disruptions are to be avoided. These are not small matters, but probably too technical to get wide attention.

But should these arrangements be considered as essentially temporary, to last only until the East European countries achieve their integration into the Western economy? Should they just belong to the "limbo" where these countries are waiting for such an integration? Or should one think of a new organization replacing the CMEA? The general view in the West rather favours the first scenario: an overall shift to the West is indeed what Eastern Europe needs.

C. *The sought after alternative: an overall shift to the West*

In this scenario each East or Central European country should develop its trade with the West and reduce commerce with the East to a minimum level. This is based on a very strong desire of the Eastern countries to enter the European Community as soon as possible; any move which might suggest that an alternative solution is viable is considered as harmful.

Several arguments are usually quoted in support of this thesis.

(i) The present pattern of trade is obsolete. It is based upon Soviet deliveries of energy and raw materials, which are needed because the area is consuming large quantities of such goods due to the "Stalinist" mode of development which was imposed upon Eastern Europe after the war. It is better to cut down this trade to a minimum level so as to force structural changes which may hurt but which should adapt the Eastern economies to the requirements of the Western markets. Even if one has to close the plants which manufacture goods especially for the Soviet market it will be beneficial in the long run, as it will compel the enterprises to become more competitive. In this respect trade in hard currencies and at world (market) prices, which is to become the rule between the USSR and Eastern Europe as from January 1991, will have the same effect.

(ii) Trade among East European countries and between them and the USSR is not "natural". The pre-war situation is referred to. But was it more "natural"? The USSR was discriminated against, since in East Central Europe there was a network of trade and payments accords centred on Nazi Germany.

(iii) As the ultimate aim is membership in the EEC, any new regional arrangement might be taken as a pretext to delay the granting of membership status. One should look for an associate status vis-à-vis the EEC and for links with EFTA. Any hint of a revival of the previous "bloc autarky" must be resolutely avoided.

(iv) There is a fear of the USSR. This country is no longer looked upon as a superpower dominating or exploiting the bloc, but as an unstable country not really engaged in reform. Thus it would be harmful to associate with it in the transition period.

(v) Each East European country wants to assert its sovereignty and would not accept any derogation of it to a grouping with supranational powers. The argument is inconsistent with the wish to join the EC: any East or Central European country joining the EC would surrender part of its economic sovereignty with, presumably, less control on the process than in a specific grouping.

(vi) Each East European country is a special case and has to be treated as such (was this not the situation in Western post-war Europe)? Each has to play its game with its assets. (The implicit line of thought behind this is the following: let each country secure as much aid for itself from the Western community as possible). Moreover, there are strong nationalistic antagonisms among all these countries and one should not risk a revival of these nationalisms, which might be the case if the Eastern countries were to be compelled to any kind of association. Here I have two questions. Were not national antagonisms strong in Western Europe after the war? Still, the USA thought it wise to advocate regional cooperation as a quid pro quo for Marshall Plan help. Would the existing antagonisms (be it within or among the countries) automatically wither once the given countries have joined the EC? The experience of the EC itself shows that this would hardly be the case.

The last argument is the less sustainable, but perhaps the strongest. Exacerbated political feelings are hard to control. The situation may be likened to that of a difficult divorce. The marriage is disolved, the parents are estranged, and suddenly the children find out that they strongly dislike each other. There may be tactical alliances among them but there is no family; everybody just wants to walk out.

Should these arguments prevail the trend which began in 1990 might well become permanent. As an alternative, and assuming that the ex-CMEA countries pursue the same goal, i.e. to join the EC as soon as possible, a milder variant would be to maintain a reasonable amount of trade within the (ex) CMEA area. This variant takes into account that the reorientation of trade to the West will take time, even with such favourable conditions as the lifting of quantitative restrictions by the EEC and the United States, the granting of generalized preferences, etc. This delay is due to several reasons:

- there is no large supply response in the short run to the domestic adjustments, neither for the domestic market nor for exports;
- integration in the world market requires structural adaptation (greater productivity, sectoral industrial restructuring, modernizing). In the meantime, the same type of goods are to be manufactured, and these goods are not adapted to the world market;
- a large part of the East and Central European industry is still geared to the Soviet market, both as a supplier and a buyer. To disrupt these links would entail bankruptcies of the firms selling to the Soviets and domestic disorganization of supplies.

Thus, as a transition, trade with the USSR and also among East European countries would remain as a large share of total trade. But nothing should remain of the former "socialist economic integration", and all intergovernmental agreements and multilateral arrangements should be cancelled. Some countries have already attempted this dismantling on their own account, such as Czechoslovakia, which has renounced most of the multilateral arrangements of which it was a partner.

D. *For a new regional grouping replacing the CMEA*

Among the suggestions made in this sense, the most popular idea is now an OECD-like format, i.e. an organization mainly concerned with providing information and supplying forecasts (without the "D" component of development aid and even without any real "C" in terms of cooperation!)

My point is the following: I think that a new regional grouping among East European countries would be highly useful during the transition to a market economy, and even after. The present stance of these countries – discarding the idea of any institutional grouping – should not be encouraged by the West because ultimately it would be costly to the West.

Before turning to the discussion on this scenario, one should state that there is no way of reviving a "global" CMEA with non-European members. Already in the USSR aid to Cuba, Vietnam and Mongolia has become a controversial issue (see *Moscow News*, 3 December, 1989, "Soviet Economic Aid: Generosity or Waste?"). This is even more so from the point of view of Eastern Europe. The Vice-Premier of Czechoslovakia, Vladimir Dlouhy, was quoted as saying that his country, as well as Hungary, had refused to go on pledging assistance to these countries (*Financial Times*, 15 January, 1990). In fact, the USSR was bearing most of the aid effort to these countries. If even Soviet aid is withdrawn this will be an additional problem to the international community, at least as far as Cuba and Vietnam are concerned, compounded by the uncertainty of the evolution of these countries.

Turning to realistic alternatives, some blueprints have been suggested, the most popular being a sub-regional grouping among Poland, Czechoslovakia, Hungary, possibly extended to Austria, Slovenia and even northern Italy. A meeting of these countries took place in April 1990, mainly devoted to security issues; there was little enthusiasm for strengthening economic cooperation. In any event, the case of the GDR has to be put aside as it depends on the future of the country as a state. The cases of Bulgaria and Romania seem very dim: would these countries seek a closer link with the USSR, with the other Balkan states? Finally, one must not exclude the idea of an economic grouping of the countries of the former Soviet Union if several Soviet republics secede.

As noted above, a more ambitious pattern is rarely advocated. I would, however, like to mention the suggestion made by President Jacques Delors (speaking at a session of the European Parliament on 17 January 1990, a few days after the Prague session of the CMEA) for a radical reform of the CMEA, and for the commitment of the European Community to provide its expertise on international economic cooperation, should the idea be pursued.

A preliminary question is: would such an arrangement include the USSR? I personally think that this would be advisable. But the West and the East have such strong reservations about anything resembling the old CMEA that it would probably be better to start on a more modest scale, with the three Central European countries, who might later on be joined by Bulgaria and Romania, depending on the state of the reforms there. One might, in addition, envisage variable groupings according to the aim pursued: trade, industrial policies and monetary arrangements.

1. *Trade*

This is not to say that we want to revert to administered, state trading forms. If we assume that Hungary, Poland, Czechoslovakia, and later on Bulgaria and Romania, are to become genuine markets, why not facilitate movements of goods, labour and capital across the borders? This would be an exercise in free trade. Often economists from the East, especially the most market-oriented among them, assume that in a market economy international trade is just the business of the companies who make the relevant arrangements among themselves. But then, why do we in the West have common markets, free trade areas, etc?

Should one have just a free trade area as in EFTA or a customs union? I would favour the latter. Some protectionism would be useful for the new “infant” industries of the East, and it would also give a quid pro quo in trade negotiations with foreign partners or organizations such as GATT and the EC. This would not be tantamount to a resumption of autarky; following the standard international trade theory, we would have net trade creation along with some trade diversion, and if only market instruments are used we would not witness the “trade destruction” effect as analyzed by Franklyn Holzman with reference to the old CMEA. International trade theory convincingly shows (cf. the gravitational models of trade) that trade among neighbours is rational. Why should Eastern Europe be an exception? If the USSR evolves into a market economy the benefit of such a union would be greatly enhanced by Soviet participation. The attractiveness of the East to Western businessmen is largely due to the access they expect to the Soviet Union when trading with East Central Europe. Why should Eastern Europe neglect such opportunities for its own sake?

The economists of the East are fond of perfect markets. In this sense free trade is the optimal solution. But if it is not attainable a customs union is second best. In any case it is preferable to bilateral trade with all kinds of restrictions, from national tariffs to quotas.

The East European countries also overstate the degree of openness of the West. They are confident that the full benefit of the MFN clause from the United States, the relaxation of trade barriers on the side of the EC as part of the aid package, will make it easier to enter Western markets. But if the Eastern enterprises are not competitive enough and/or if they have to face new barriers such as a surge of anti-dumping actions, would their governments reconsider the *rationale* of a large common market which would include the USSR?

2. *Industrial policy*

Here I see at least three fields of application:

- Antimonopoly policies. The Eastern countries are very keen on dismantling their formidable domestic state monopolies. Are they right? One may say that the Western industrial world is a world of large companies, mergers, etc. The answer would probably be here that the old monopolies should be dismantled so as to clean the slate for new, efficient entities. Let us assume that to be true. But then, why not fight the monopolies together, looking at Articles 85-86 of the Treaty of Rome?
- Restructuring obsolete industries. The experience of the European coal and steel community might be useful, as well as that of later policies such as the Davignon Plan, which enabled the EEC to organize cuts in the steel capacities of the member countries, a very urgent problem indeed for the East.
- Protecting the environment. The East looks forward to cooperation with the West, but cooperation with Eastern Europe may be a beginning. In this sense, the orderly increase of Soviet gas supplies might be crucial so as to reduce the polluting effects of energy balances still based on coal (and still worse, brown coal). This in turn would point to some cooperation with the USSR in the field of energy, again along a new format.

Finally, I would like to mention in this respect the development of direct foreign investment and joint ventures among Eastern *partners.* This is certainly not a popular issue as all these countries mainly pursue the goal of attracting Western capital. Here again the emergence of market economies should trigger intra-branch cooperation and specialization based upon a market rationale. The expertise of the West might be highly useful to help to devise the ways of such arrangements.

3. *Monetary arrangements*

Though with some reservations, I agree with Western experts who suggest a new "European Payments Union" for the East. True, the 1990 conditions in the East are not comparable with the post-war conditions in the West. I do think, however, that helping each East European country in isolation to achieve convertibility of its currency is not apt to solve all the problems. First, what we call "convertibility" (when, for instance, we say that since the beginning of 1990 the Polish zloty may be considered as convertible) is mainly an organized access of residents (enterprises and private persons) to foreign convertible currencies, i.e. a limited internal convertibility. Second, there is a point in trying to make the East European currencies convertible among themselves in a concerted way. The shift to settlements in hard currencies among these countries is not an adequate response, first because it cannot be applied to all settlements, second because it will inevitably act as a restricting factor in trade. In fact, such a shift will not take place immediately in 1991, contrary to what has been announced in January 1990. For some time there will be instead a system of bilateral clearing arrangements, the main difference with the former system being that the clearing currency will be the dollar (or some other convertible currency), the balances being settled in hard currency.

The West is mainly interested in the convertibility issue because convertibility in Western currencies will solve problems such as the repatriation of profits generated by joint ventures, and will decrease countertrade demands. But should we be happy with the lack of any concerted monetary policy among the East, with artificial exchange rates between Eastern currencies, distorting rational decisions in commercial matters? Can we really stick to such a stance while we are advocating a monetary union in the West? Here again one has to be innovative: there is no question of recreating a "transferable rouble".

IV. *Conclusion*

The challenge to the West, and particularly to the EC, is enormous. The EC has never liked the CMEA much. The June 1988 agreement between the two "communities" was more an act of goodwill toward Gorbachev than a whole-hearted agreement over the prospects of coperation, and the European Commission has never concealed its preference for a bilateral approach and for trade (and cooperation, the latter being added rather reluctantly) agreements. The EC has had to alter its policy once already, revamping the concluded agreements in line with an assistance-type approach, first to Hungary and Poland and then to most of the other East European countries. It has now to ponder the consequences of the disaggregation of the CMEA. Obviously, the EC is mainly concerned with making it clear that the issue of individual CMEA countries' membership in the European Community is not to be raised. The East European countries should not, either, put too great hopes on EFTA. The European Free Trade Association countries play their own game. The European Economic Space is more appealing to them than any "European Common House", the short-lived concept of Gorbachev which has lost the little credibility it might have had. And there is no doubt that the EFTA countries would be little enthusiastic about moves of Eastern Europe to get nearer to the EC through the EES.

The June 1988 agreement between the EC and the CMEA is soon to be totally obsolete. The question of whether to replace it with a new agreement concluded with any new organization is not essential. The main issue is how to treat trade relations with the East. New bilateral trade agreements are not enough. Somebody has to teach these countries not only how to build market-type economies, but also how to come to terms among themselves. One might object that this is not the West's business. But I believe that this might be the most useful lesson to learn from the Marshall Plan. One should remember that an essential condition of the Marshall Plan was an organized cooperation in Europe: this was how the OECE was born, becoming later on the OECD. The West viewed the CMEA as a Soviet dominated organization which it was in part only: the CMEA was rather a sort of negative-sum game binding a reluctant Eastern Europe to a Soviet Union which was never in control of the game but had, like the others, to abide by irrational rules damaging to all members. Now the time has come when potentially a new economic grouping might emerge if properly assisted. Integrated Western Europe cannot be satisfied with a disintegrated Eastern Europe at its side.

References

* This article is the continuation of a work in progress on the CMEA perspectives following the 1988 44th meeting of the CMEA Council, which decided upon transforming the organization into a "unified market". Most of this work has been done during a research stay at the BIOST (*Bundesinstitut für ostwissenschaftliche und internationale Studien*), Cologne, Federal Republic of Germany, on the basis of a fellowship extended by the Volkswagen Foundation, whose help is gratefully acknowledged. See also my articles "Intra-CMEA Relations and Domestic Reforms: Some Interactions", *Recherches Economiques de Louvain*, 1990, nº 2, pp. 147-168 and "The Perestroika of the CMEA and the Challenge of the '92 Western European Single Market", in *Trade and Economic Reform: North, South and East*, Essays in Honour of Bela Balassa, edited by Jaime de Melo and Andre Sapir, 1990, forthcoming. As all researchers in the field, I had to address a whole range of new questions following the events of the last months of 1989 and the beginning of 1990. In this, I greatly benefitted from the stimulating environment of the Harriman Institute at Columbia University in New York, and of the excellent working facilities which were available to me there.

Notes

1. The CMEA (Council for Mutual Economic Assistance, also called Comecon) regroups ten countries. This paper is concerned with the European members of this community, i.e. the USSR itself, and the Six East European countries (Bulgaria, Czechoslovakia, the GDR, Hungary, Poland, Romania), hereinafter designated as the Six, leaving aside the three developing countries (Mongolia, Cuba, Vietnam, by chronological order of joining the organization).
2. Statement by the Czechoslovak Minister of Finance, Vaclav Klaus. See the *Financial Times*, 5 January 1990.
3. This already famous saying has been attributed to Gennadi Gerasimov, the Soviet Foreign Ministry spokesman (see the *New York Times*, 26 October 1989).
4. It was announced in February 1990 that many East European countries wanted to send the Vietnamese back. See the *Financial Times*, 20 February 1990.
5. This statement is quite surprising. It would imply that Jan Vanous does not really believe in the actual implementation of the price rule. If one reckons that annual prices are actually fixed on the basis of world prices of the five previous years (with many technicalities not to be mentioned here), then one has to admit that the *same kind* of exchange rate is to be used both ways, first to convert the initial world prices year by year into transferable roubles, and then to compare the actual resulting price in transferable roubles with the current price in dollars.
6. *Ekonomika i Zhizn'* (formerly *Ekonomicheskaia Gazeta*), no. 6, February 1990.
7. *Ekonomika i Zhizn'*, supplement to no. 15, April 1990.

Bibliography

Brada, Josef C. (1985), "Soviet Subsidization of Eastern Europe: The Primacy of Economics Over Politics?" *Journal of Comparative Economics*, Vol. 9, no. 1, March, p. 80-92 (review article).

Brada, Josef C. (1988) "Interpreting the Soviet Subsidization of Eastern Europe", *International Organization*, Vol. 42, no. 4, Autumn, p. 639-658.

Comisso, Ellen (1986), "Introduction: State Structures, Political Processes, and Collective Choice in CMEA States", *International Organization*, Vol. 40, Spring, p. 19-62.

Desai, Padma (1986), "Is the Soviet Union Subsidizing Eastern Europe?" *European Economic Review*, Vol. 30, no. 1, p. 107-116.

Graziani, Giovanni (1980), "Les mouvements de capitaux au sein du CAEM", *Economies et Sociétés*, série G, Economie planifiée, no 40, p 45-77.

Holzman, Franklyn D. (1985), "A 'Trade-Destroying' Customs Union?", *Journal of Comparative Economics*, Vol. 9, no.4, December, p. 410-423.

Holzman, Franklyn D., (1986), "The Significance of Soviet Subsidies to Eastern Europe", *Comparative Economic Studies*, Vol. 28, no. 1, Spring, p. 54-65.

Kolchin, S. (1988), "Integratsia v ramkakh SEV: problemy kolichestvennoi otsenki" (Integration in the framework of the CMEA: problems of a quantitative assessment), *Voprosy Ekonomiki*, no 10, p. 109-117.

Köves, Andras (1983), " 'Implicit Subsidies' and Some Issues of Economic Relations Within the CMEA (Remarks on the Analyses Made by Michael Marrese and Jan Vanous)", *Acta Oeconomica*, Vol. 31, no. 1-2, p. 125-136.

Lavigne, Marie (1983), "The Soviet Union Inside Comecon", *Soviet Studies*, Vol. 35, no. 2, April, p. 135-153.

Marer, Paul (1984), "The Political Economy of Soviet Relations with Eastern Europe", in Sarah Miklejohn Terry, ed., *Soviet Policy in Eastern Europe*, New Haven and London: Yale University Press, p. 155-188.

Marrese, Michael (1989), "Future Developments in the CMEA: Likely Winners and Losers", June, mimeo.

Marrese, Michael, Vanous, Jan (1983), *Soviet Subsidization of Trade with Eastern Europe, A Soviet Perspective*, Berkeley: University of California, Institute of International Studies, 254 p.

Marrese, Michael, Wittenberg, Lauren (1990), "Implicit Trade Subsidies with the CMEA: A Hungarian Perspective", January, mimeo.

Sergeev, B. (1989), "Skvoz' valiutnye zavaly" (Through Currency Gluts), *Ekonomicheskaya Gazeta*, no. 29, July.

Smith, Alan (1989), "Can Comecon Survive?" *Centrally Planned Economies Service, The WEFA Group*, December, 10 p.

Sobell, Vladimir (1984), *The Red Market, Industrial Co-operation and Specialization in Comecon*, Aldershot: Gower, 265 p.

van Brabant, Jozef M. (1989), *Economic Integration in Eastern Europe, A Handbook*, New York, London: Harvester Wheatsheaf, 452 p.

Vanous, Jan, ed. (1989), "Soviet Energy Trade During 1986-88: Combined Exports of Crude Oil and Refined Oil Products Reach a Record 205 MMt in 1988", *PlanEcon Report*, 18 August, Vol. V, no. 32-33.

The Current State of Relations between the CMEA-Countries and the European Community

Marc Maresceau

I. *Introduction*

Up to the end of 1974 the framework of trade relations between CMEA countries and Western Europe was largely determined by bilateral agreements between the individual Member States of the European Community (EC) on the one hand and the CMEA countries on the other. In 1974 the EC invited the CMEA countries to conclude bilateral trade agreements in order to replace the existing ones.[1]

It appeared that the Eastern European countries were not willing to follow this procedure. Instead, the CMEA, as an organization, proposed to conclude an inter-institutional general framework agreement. On political, as well as legal, grounds the EC refused to follow this proposal, and this explains why the framework of trade relations since the end of 1974, from the point of view of the Community, was mainly based on autonomous commercial policy measures. It is true that in a limited number of sectors "agreements" were concluded by means of exchanges of letters.[2] These sectoral agreements, however, could by no means be considered as a sufficient framework for trade relations.

The first general trade agreement which the EC concluded with a State trading country was that with the People's Republic of China in 1978.[3] In 1980 — a period of almost complete stagnation in relations betweeen the EC and Eastern Europe — the EC concluded an agreement on trade in industrial products with Romania.[4] While the economic repercussions of this agreement are not to be overestimated, it nevertheless had an undeniable symbolic effect: for the Community it constituted a breakthrough of the deadlock situation while, for Romania, the agreement was a clear demonstration of its independence vis-à-vis the USSR and CMEA.

The stagnation in relations between the EC and CMEA or CMEA countries lasted until 1985, the year in which Gorbachev came to power. During that year the new CMEA Secretary, Mr. Sychev, took the initiative to resume contacts with the Community. The basis for his initiative was largely that proposed by the Community in the seventies, namely that trade matters were to be discussed directly between the EC and the CMEA member countries whilst, on an inter-institutional EC-CMEA level, official relations ought to be established. These two types of contacts had to develop on a parallel basis. For a number of reasons, it took somewhat longer than expected to reach an inter-institutional agreement,[5] but finally on 25 June 1988 the Joint Declaration on the establishment of official relations between the EEC and CMEA was signed.[6] Whereas the content of the Declaration was not of great substance — not one area for co-operation between the two organizations was mentioned — its legal and political significance was important: it implied recognition of the EEC by the CMEA member countries. Since the signing of the Joint Declaration all Eastern European CMEA countries have accredited missions to the European Communities.[7]

It was also in 1988, soon after the signing of the Joint Declaration, that the first bilateral trade and economic co-operation agreement was signed with a CMEA country, Hungary. Similar agreements were concluded with Poland and the USSR in 1989, whilst in 1990 it is expected that co-operation agreements with all Eastern European countries will be signed.[7bis] Before we examine these bilateral frameworks of trade and economic co-operation it is necessary to first examine briefly the autonomous Community (commercial) policy measures which have governed imports from Eastern Europe. The (autonomous) specific Community measures introduced recently or planned as a result of the political and economic reforms in Eastern Europe are mentioned in a separate section of this paper, since they form a category different from the "classical" autonomous Community commercial policy measures. The last part of this paper contains some short reflections on prospects for future trade and economic relations.

II. *The Autonomous Community Régime vis-à-vis Eastern Europe*

Until recently, because of the lack of bilateral agreements, the autonomous Community régime has, since 1 January 1975, been the leading Community framework for trade relations with Eastern Europe.

The first main legal instrument to be mentioned is *Community Regulation 1765/82 on imports from State trading countries.*[8] The basic provision of this regulation is that products included in the annex to the regulation are not subject to quantitative restrictions. However, the practical importance of this regulation should not be overestimated since the great majority of potential exportable products originating in State trading countries are not listed in that annex. For products not liberalized in Regulation 1765/82 one has to refer to Regulation 3420/83 of 14 November 1983[9] and to the subsequent annual Council decisions laying down the import quotas to be opened by the Member States. The last application of this procedure is to be found in *Council Decision of 6 November 1989 on import quotas to be opened by the Member States in respect of State trading countries.* The expression "quotas to be opened" should not hide the fact that it implies that, for the products mentioned, quantitative restrictions do exist in the Member States. The structure of that Decision is as follows: for every country labelled as a "State trading country", that is to say Albania, Bulgaria, Hungary, Poland, Romania, Czechoslovakia, USSR, GDR, People's Republic of China, North Korea, Vietnam and Mongolia, the quotas to be opened by each Member State are enumerated. The Decision of 6 November 1989 contains a listing of quantitative restrictions of more than 300 pages.[10]

This system, laid down unilaterally by the Community, has in the past been under constant attack from State trading countries. They argued, *inter alia,* that these quantitative restrictions were discriminatory. Also, from a Community point of view, the system resulting from the combined application of Regulation 3420/83 and the subsequent annual Council Decisions determining the specific quotas is not without practical and legal problems. Indeed, it leads to a splitting up of the "Common market" along national borders and it may also lead to applications of Article 115, EEC Treaty.[11] Clearly, it is particularly difficult for the current system to survive after 1992 since it, as such, constitutes the very negation of the Internal Market. It is not astonishing therefore that, to date, there has been a growing awareness in Community circles that fundamental changes in the existing legal pattern are necessary. It must be said that some important modifications, which will be discussed later on, have already taken place or are envisaged as a result of the bilateral co-operation agreements signed or recent specific Community actions taken to stimulate reforms in Eastern Europe.

The description of the Community import régime as determined by Regulations 1765/82, 3420/83 and the annual decisions implementing the latter regulation is not complete without mentioning the Community's anti-dumping policy towards Eastern Europe. It is impossible to examine here in detail the Community anti-dumping policy, but it cannot be ignored that the anti-dumping mechanism has frequently been used against imports from Eastern Europe. If one considers that trade with Eastern Europe represents only about 6-7% of total Community external trade, it is obvious that imports from Eastern Europe have been relatively frequently hit by anti-dumping actions.[12] The main issue here, of course, is the existence of the specific provisions in Community law on dumping from State trading countries. It is well known that in Community anti-dumping law the concept of "normal value" is a key notion. Community law starts from the assumption that "normal value" cannot be determined according to a cost analysis in the exporting State trade country. In this reasoning "normal value" must be determined on the basis of comparison in market economy non-EC countries. This, naturally, has in practice often caused problems.[13]

Be that as it may, the current anti-dumping law vis-à-vis imports from State trading countries will also need to be reviewed. Nowadays, not one Eastern European country, including the USSR, any longer accepts the designation "State trading country", and there can be no doubt about the fact that the general and indistinctive label "State trading", to qualify Eastern European countries, has become totally inappropriate and outdated.

III. *Bilateral Agreements between the EC and Eastern European Countries*

As mentioned previously, the first bilateral agreement concluded between the EC and an Eastern European country was that concluded with Romania in 1980. It was only in the second half of 1988 that a new bilateral agreement with an Eastern European country could be concluded. On 26 September 1988 the Agreement on Trade and Commercial and Economic Co-operation between the EC and Hungary was signed. Since the conclusion of this agreement there has been a big move towards a further development of bilateral framework agreements with Eastern European countries.

The Agreement with Hungary was in many respects an interesting piece of work. For the first time a Community agreement with an Eastern European country contained a chapter on "co-operation", while, as far as the trade side was concerned, the principle of abolition of quantitative restrictions was incorporated. The years of difficult negotiations between the EC and Hungary had mainly been devoted to this last issue. Clearly, it was with very great reluctance and only through the incorporation of several stages in the procedure for the gradual elimination of quantitative restrictions — with 1995 as the ultimate deadline — combined with the possible use of a kind of reinforced safeguard mechanism for imports of very sensitive products, that the Community had finally been prepared to accept the principle of total elimination of specific QR's. Indeed, such QR's are in Community law the very characterisation of the treatment of imports from State trading countries. On the other hand, Hungary, referring to GATT and to its Protocol of Accession to GATT, strongly claimed that the Community was already for a long time legally bound to withdraw the existing quantitative restrictions.[14] Of course, the provisions in the Agreement on "co-operation", covering commercial as well as economic co-operation, were innovative. It is impossible here to examine these provisions in detail but they contain, for example, explicit references encouraging the use of arbitration for the settlement of disputes among firms. The Agreement also considers countertrade as a temporary and exceptional practice. The chapter on "economic co-operation" is of a general nature and, *inter alia*, aims at promoting a favourable climate for investment, joint ventures and licensing arrangements. Arrangements for investment promotion and protection will be stimulated, in particular for the transfer of profits and repatriation of invested capital on the basis of the principles of non-discrimination and reciprocity.

It is interesting to note that the Community strongly felt the need to justify the far-reaching contents of the Agreement with Hungary. It did so by stressing very emphatically the specificity of the Hungarian case. It is certainly true that at the moment of negotiating and concluding the Agreement, Hungary was *the* CMEA country where the development of political and economic reforms was most evident: Hungary had indeed clearly taken the lead in reforms. The emphasis on specificity, however, also necessarily implied that the Community had not the intention to use the Agreement as a model for negotiating agreements with other CMEA countries.

A classic example for the application of this approach is to be found in the Agreement with Czechoslovakia on trade in industrial products, signed on 19 December 1988.[15] Its scope was very limited and its structure and contents were closer to that of the agreement with Romania of 1980 than of that with Hungary.

In 1989, political and economic reforms in other Eastern European countries took such a form and intensity that the original Community approach was indeed no longer workable. Hungary no longer was a unique case in the CMEA world, and it became therefore more and more difficult to maintain the Community's original strategy of first signing "trade agreements", which could then later, if everything went well, develop towards "economic co-operation" agreements.

Obviously, the Agreement on trade and commercial and economic co-operation with Poland which was concluded on 19 September 1989, was largely inspired by the Agreement EC-Hungary.[16] Only as far as the elimination of quantitative restrictions was concerned did the Agreement with Poland somewhat differ from the Agreement EC-Hungary. It did not contain the principle of total elimination in the same absolute terms as did the Agreement with Hungary.

However, the agreement which by no means attracted the greatest public attention was that with the Soviet Union, concluded at the end of 1989. Already at the end of 1987 it had become clear that the USSR was not satisfied with the possible conclusion of a classical trade agreement since, anyhow, a great deal of Soviet exports to the Community was not subject to customs duties. On the other hand the USSR was very eager to increase economic co-operation, transfer of technology, etc. in order to modernize its own economic structure. The original reluctance of the Community to initiate negotiations with the USSR on this basis was finally overcome and led to the conclusion of a co-operation agreement on 19 December 1989.[17]

There can be no doubt about the fact that the Agreement with Hungary had been a very useful point of reference for structuring the agreement with the USSR. It also contains the principle of elimination, by 31 December 1995, of specific QR's, however "with the exception of those concerning a limited number of products which might be deemed sensitive at that time". Besides the classical procedure for taking safeguard measures, the Agreement furthermore provides for the possibility of taking action, if necessary, justified on grounds of protection of essential security interests relating, *inter alia*, "to the traffic in arms, ammunition and implements of war and to such traffic in other goods and materials as is carried on directly or indirectly for the purpose of supplying a military establishment".

As far as co-operation is concerned it is worthwhile noting that the Contracting Parties will provide natural and legal persons of the other Party with guarantees for their individual and property rights, including non-discriminatory access for that purpose to the courts and appropriate administrative bodies of the Community and USSR. An identical clause as in the Agreement with Hungary concerning counter-trade is included in the Agreement with the USSR, and the same holds true as far as the encouragement of arbitration for the settlement of disputes among firms, enterprises or economic organizations is concerned.

Finally, it should be mentioned that in the enumeration of the potential areas for economic co-operation reference is made to energy, including nuclear energy and nuclear safety (physical safety and radiation protection).

IV. *Specific Community Actions for Eastern Europe*

Since the middle of 1989 the Community has taken a considerable number of specific initiatives supporting reforms in Eastern Europe. Moreover, within the Group of 24, the Community plays an important coordinating role, particularly in the area of food aid, access to markets, management programmes, investment promotion and environmental protection. These actions within the Phare-programme, originally only aimed at stimulating reforms in Hungary and Poland, will soon be extended to other countries such as the GDR, Czechoslovakia, Bulgaria and Romania. The extension of the programme to those countries is the result of the fulfilment of a number of conditions such as, for example, the organization of free elections, the establishment of a multiparty system, respect of human rights, introduction of a market economy. It is very likely that in June 1990 the Community will proceed to the extension of this programme to the countries mentioned.[18] This, however, does not mean that there will be a monolithic application of the Phare-programme to all these countries, since their economic and financial situation is not the same.

The most relevant specific Community actions are probably those concerning financial support and co-operation and those on the abolition or suspension of QR's.

As far as financial aid and co-operation is concerned the Community has made very serious efforts. The originally planned financial support for 1990 of 300 million ECU will be increased to 500 million. For 1991 the Community proposes 850 million ECU and for 1992 one billion. Another important initiative in which the Community and its Member States will play an important role is that of the Bank for Reconstruction and Development of Eastern Europe (BERD). At the moment of writing this paper there was still no agreement about the loan conditions for the USSR and the level of Soviet participation in the Bank. Nor was it clear what role, if any, should be played by the European Investment Bank in the BERD.[18bis]

Particularly interesting are also the measures taken by the Community to eliminate all specific QR's and those to suspend, for a period of at least one year, all non-specific QR's on all imports from Hungary and Poland. Of course, these measures have more than just a symbolic meaning, since they precisely cover products which, during the negotiations for the bilateral co-operation agreements, have caused so many problems and were considered so extremely sensitive that they could only through a long transitional period be allowed to be imported quota free into the Community. A number of Member States had been of the opinion that sudden quota-free imports from these countries could jeopardise a number of domestic industries considered to play a vital role in the country. It is therefore more than striking that, for example, the trade chapter of the Agreement signed with Poland in September 1989 was already virtually outdated before it ever even entered into force, since by 1 January 1990 the specific QR's had been eliminated unilaterally by the Community. How laudable this Community measure for the countries concerned may be, it will probably not increase the credibility of the Community and its Member States on the economic justification and necessity of the QR's. Finally, it should also be mentioned that the Community, through its unilateral measures, found a solution for the legal Gordian knot which it faced as a consequence of the 1992 constraints.

V. *Prospects and Conclusions*

At the moment of writing this paper it is totally impossible to make any serious prospective analysis of the future framework of trade and economic co-operation relations. Only some short term evolutions can be considered. It is well known that the Community wants to round off the negotiations for bilateral agreements on trade and economic co-operation with Eastern Europe. It has been mentioned repeatedly by Commissioner Andriessen that before the Special Dublin Summit on Eastern Europe and German unification — to be held on 28 April — all negotiations with Eastern European countries should be terminated. As far as the GDR is concerned the initialling of the co-operation agreement — an agreement of which nobody knows whether it will ever be applied — has already taken place (13 March) while the initialling of a co-operation agreement with Bulgaria and Czechoslovakia will, without doubt, also have taken place before the April date. Relations with Romania are less predictable, and it is very unlikely that any concrete results are to be expected before 28 April.[18ter]

The conclusion of "trade and economic co-operation agreements", however, cannot be considered as the final objective in the relations EC-Eastern Europe. Although not longer ago than 1988 the conclusion of these type of agreements with Eastern Europe was looked upon as very exceptional and as a maximalist goal, such agreements appear today partly outdated even before they enter into force. The QR's issue, as described previously, is a good example of this. Also at the signature of the Agreement EC-USSR, M. Dumas, the French Minister of Foreign Relations, already explicitly mentioned that the Agreement was a step towards the integration of the USSR in the international economic structure, while M. Shevardnadze, for his part, saw the Agreement as the beginning of a process towards a further economic integration of Europe as a whole.

It is now official Community policy that the co-operation agreements with Eastern Europe are not an end in themselves. Such agreements constitute a legal basis for further in-depth development. What form this development should take is to date still unclear, although the association-model, based on Article 238 EEC-Treaty, is most frequently mentioned. In an association-type framework a free trade zone could be established and joint institutions could elaborate joint policies or could coordinate those policies. It is generally thought that the association model would the least adversely affect the internal cohesion within the Community of the Twelve. It is also not excluded that a *sui generis* European model finds its way between an association and an accession to the Community and finally, one should not, in the long run, exclude even an accession to the Community of some Eastern European countries. Be that as it may, the deepening of links between the EC and individual Eastern European countries should not lead us to forget that there are still intra-Eastern Europe economic relations on an important scale. Existing trade patterns cannot be changed from one day to the other, and, it is moreover questionable whether a sudden disruption and complete change is at all desirable. The Community can certainly not replace the USSR in providing energy or raw materials. In this context an institution such as COMECON, adapted to the new political and, more in particular, the new economic realities in Eastern Europe, may have a serious role to play. It is indeed rather unrealistic to conceive that in the short or medium-term all Eastern European countries wishing to accede to the Community could be absorbed by the Community. This would have financial and economic implications which the Community and the Member States would not be able to bear. Moreover, the integration process within the Community of the Twelve, the decision-making and legislative Community potential, would be fundamentally hit by the process of Eastern European enlargement. Already now there are serious complaints about all the attention and energy put into the inter-German relations and into EC-Eastern Europe relations as a whole. Some consider this as detrimental to the Community's 1992 programme and, particularly, to the economic and monetary union which has to follow the achievement of the internal market within the Community of the Twelve. The developments in Eastern Europe should indeed not be an excuse to distract the Community from the goals which it has imposed on itself. At the same time, however, better forms of trade, economic and — why not? — political co-operation with Eastern Europe should be worked out. Free trade zones and common institutions, perhaps modelled on those established or to be established with EFTA, are potential options which could very well be worked out. However, whatever form this type of relationship may take, it will be for economic, political and security purposes necessary to incorporate in one way or another the USSR into this process. The deepening of EC-Eastern European relations may, by no means, lead to an isolation of the USSR.

Finally, in the light of our topic, a word should be said about the impact of all these evolutions on the application of export controls. To date, the Community, as such, has not been much involved in export controls. From a political view this may have been defendable, or at least understandable. From a legal point of view, it can be seriously questioned whether this was the correct approach. Be that as it may, taking into consideration the many changes in Eastern Europe, relaxation or abolition of these controls for dual use goods, including for export to the USSR, should be seriously considered. It cannot be accepted that institutions, such as COCOM, whose legal nature and structure disappears in a "flou artistique", can avail themselves of competence and power to retard or hinder the economic modernization process in Eastern Europe, including the USSR. Better economic development in Eastern Europe and particularly in the USSR will be a sounder contribution to peace and security than the maintenance or creation of obstacles to normal trade and economic co-operation relations.

Notes

1. See e.g. P. Benavides "Bilateral relations between the European Community and Eastern European countries: the problems and prospects of trade relations" and J. Maslen "European Community-CMEA: institutional relations", in: *The Political and Legal Framework of Trade Relations between the European Community and Eastern Europe* (ed. M. Maresceau), Dordrecht-Boston-London, 1989, pp. 21-37 and pp. 85-92; J. Pinder "The EC and Eastern Europe under Gorbachev: how normal could relations become?", in: *The Economies of Eastern Europe under Gorbachev's Influence* (ed. R. Weichhardt), NATO Colloquium 1988, p. 266; M.-A. Coninsx "Oost-West relaties, gezien vanuit economisch en handelsperspectief", in: *Vlaanderen, België en Europe in de wereld,* LSC Documenten no. 2, 1987, pp. 17-32.
2. Sectoral agreements cover areas such as iron, steel, textiles and some agricultural products. They had been concluded with virtually all Eastern European CMEA countries, except the USSR and the GDR.
3. See *O.J.,* L 123 of 1978.
4. See *O.J.,* L 352/1, 1980.
5. For example, one of the last obstacles which considerably delayed the signature was the reference to the inclusion of West Berlin as part of the territory of the Community
6. *O.J.,* L 157/35, see M. Maresceau "A general survey of the current legal framework of trade relations between the European Community and Eastern Europe", in: *The Political and Legal Framework of Trade Relations between the European Community and Eastern Europe* at note 1, p. 4-5.
7. On this topic see papers at the International Conference on Promoting CMEA-EC Cooperation, CMEA, 13-16 October 1989, Moscow.

7[bis]. After the completion of this paper cooperation agreements have been signed with all European CMEA countries, except Romania. The signature of this last agreement, which was due to take place in June 1990, was postponed by the Community as a demonstration of displeasure against the handling, by the Romanian government, of anti-government protest.

8. *O.J.,*L 195/1, 1982.
9. *O.J.,* L 346/6, 1983.
10. *O.J.,* L 354, 1989.
11. See F. Sarre, "Art. 115 EEC Treaty and Trade with Eastern Europe", *Intereconomics,* 1988, pp. 233-240.
12. There have been years where near to 50% of all Community anti-dumping actions were initiated against imports from State trading countries. The latest Commission report on the Community's anti-dumping activities reveal that the number of Community anti-dumping measures against imports from Eastern Europe have decreased, see e.g. *Sixth Annual Report of the Commission,* COM (89) 106 final.
13. See F. Jacobs, "Anti-dumping procedures with regard to imports from Eastern Europe", in: *The Political and Legal Framework of Trade Relations between the European Community and Eastern Europe,* mentioned at note 1 pp. 291-308, also J. Pinder, mentioned at note 1, p.1.
14. See on this issue A.M. Van den Bossche, "GATT: The Indispensable Link between the EEC and Hungary?", *Journal of World Trade,* 1989, pp. 141-155.
15. *O.J.,* L 88, 1989.
16. *O.J.,* L 339, 1989.
17. O.J., *L 68, 1990.*
18. See *Agence Europe,* 8 March 1990. However, as far as Romania is concerned, see observations under note 7[bis].

18[bis]. Since the completion of this paper these questions have been solved. The BEI will participate in the BERD capital for an amount of 30.000 shares, corresponding to 3% of the total number of votes. The EEC, its Member States and the BEI together, hold the majority of the capital and of the votes. The USSR will participate in the BERD capital for 60.000 shares, corresponding to 6% of the total number of votes; the USSR, however, will not be entitled to borrow from the BERD in excess of its participation. After 3 years, the decision to alter this restrictive régime can be taken only by a 85% majority (this means that the USA and Japan, which together hold 18,5% of the votes, have a blocking majority in this matter, see *Agence Europe,* 12 April 1990.

18ter. see note 7bis.

East European Reform: Synthesis and Prospects for External Competitiveness

Michael Kaser

Synopsis

The widening and deepening of competition will be the fundamental trend of the industrialized part of the world in the 1990s, and for the first time since the 1930s that part will include East Europe and the USSR.

The Great Depression had narrowed and restricted markets – through cartelization, exchange controls and bilateral clearing (which particularly affected Eastern Europe), government intervention (both as protectionism and to secure resources for rearmament) and the unsettling swings in the terms of trade; the USSR withdrew into autarky and East Europe's trade nadir in the crisis years was lower than that of Europe or of world turnover as a whole.

The conditions for five decades of East-West separation terminated in the very last months of the 1980s. The transition of the six East European states to market systems will require time and both material help (to ease disequilibria which inhibit market forces) and institutional support from the West (including the admission of non-members to the international economic organizations, improved access to the EC and EFTA, the moderation of strategic embargoes and the linkage of capital markets).

"Destatization" is a complex process with each element inter-locking with others: the sequencing and pace of each varies in the six countries. The starting point for all must be the legitimation of new governments by parliamentary elections at dates already set for the first half of 1990 (except for Poland, where a partial election in 1989 legitimated a Solidarity majority in the government). Competition is already being fostered in their markets for labour and for goods and services. As paternalism of the "ministerial system" for state enterprises is withdrawn, social support structures must be provided for those affected by redundancy, the need for greater labour mobility and the inflation needed to restructure both retail and wholesale prices. Only two states, Hungary and Poland, have so far established capital markets. A more intensive Western inflow from joint ventures (soon to be legal in the GDR, as already elsewhere in East Europe) and privatization of state industry will enhance the competitiveness of the investment process and the activation of a role for the rate of interest.

Finally, the rationalization of prices for labour and for current and capital goods will permit the introduction successively of realistic exchange rates and of convertibility.

I. *Ending Five Decades of Abnormality*

Two declarations by Polish statesmen of the Solidarity led government crystalize the essential East European economic objective of the 1990s. The Prime Minister, Tadeusz Mazowiecki, said that the intention was not "to reform the system", but to change the system, and the Finance Minister, Leszek Balcerowicz, added that it was to have "a normal market system of the Western kind". The six countries which terminated the political monopoly of the communist party during the closing months of the 1980s may now perhaps be termed "previously planned economies": they have in common revolutions aimed at a simple return to normality. This paper examines the pace at which existing mechanisms are being dismantled or restructured and new ones created. Such institutional changes support, and are supported by, democratization but the social processes involved in reestablishing a market run deeper than those freeing elections and parliaments. This is because the communist governments built for themselves, or adapted existing, agencies of constitutional democracy and continued formally to use them even under personal or clannish dictatorships. The institution of markets and the commercial and financial culture that permeates them were by contrast demolished, and a free market persisted only in peasant and craft sales or in informal or illegal dealings. It may thus be harder to overcome that alienation from commercial culture than to open up to political pluralism. Those aspects of dismantling the old system and those of constructing a market, which will enhance East European competitiveness towards the West, are also examined here.

Two paths may be safely forecast for the industrial market economies in the first half of the 1990s. Everywhere the globalization of competition will continue: markets for money, for goods and for services will mutually become still more sensitive on a world-wide scale. This trend is likely in pursuance both of the experience of the 1980s and as the Uruguay Round is completed and implemented. The Industrial West, as constituted by the OECD, will be enlarged by the admission of some of the "newly-industrialized countries" and (if present political developments are a guide) South Africa. For Europe the completion of the single market in the Community in 1992 will doubtless be followed by its enlargement and by its closer association with EFTA. The political revolutions in East Europe come just in time for their economies to participate in this evolution. German reunification, which is now certain, will integrate East Germany with the Federal Republic and hence with the Community. Other states not already in GATT, the IMF, the World Bank and the BIS will become members – the USSR formally posed its GATT candidature in March. If Comecon continues *in corpore* its nature will be more consultative (like the OECD) than integrative: whether or not it does, some of its members are likely postulants for the EC/EFTA "European economic space".

These expected articulations within Europe form part of the pattern which will distinguish the 1990s from the previous five decades. The year 1940 is the obvious dividing line: the Nazi *Grossraumwirtschaft* enveloped East Europe as it did much of the rest of the Continent, with just Britain and the few neutrals outside. No sooner had the war economy been relaxed than market relations were subordinated to reconstruction plans, and then, around 1950, to Soviet-type central planning. Yugoslavia broke with those practices in 1950 but despite some marketization from 1965, liberalization came only after the authorization of large-scale private enterprise from October 1988, the stabilization plan initiated in January 1990 and the renunciation of a communist political monopoly the following month. Hungary renounced directive planning in 1968 but retrogression in the 1970s and the persistance of "paternalism" and the "soft budget constraint" (Kornai's two evocative terms) in the 1980s insulated state enterprises from the bulk of competitive forces.

But competitiveness in Central and Eastern Europe had begun to be weakened by the Depression of the early 1930s. From then on East Europe was all but shut off from Western capital flows and, in common with most other states, confined its home markets behind protective barriers and exchange controls while fostering cartels and state industry and subsidizing private firms. In the later 1930s, although seriously only in some countries, trade was tied to Germany under bilateral clearing agreements. Domestic employment was enhanced by such measures, as also by expenditure on rearmament, and was thereby safeguarded from the adjustments that would have been imposed by swings in the terms of trade. Since it was well placed for commerce with the USSR, East Europe was also affected by the Soviet withdrawal into autarky. The nadir of East Europe's trade in the crisis years of the 1930s was lower than that of Europe or of the world as a whole. It is small wonder that, even without the political barriers of the Cold War, East Europe was signally uncompetitive on world markets. The Western restrictions and Eastern self-sufficiency ushered in by the Korean conflict worsened competitiveness. In 1965 the six member countries of Comecon accounted for only $1\frac{1}{2}$ % of the imports of the Industrial West; by 1988 and 1989 their share had sunk to little over 1%.

The circumstances which had marginalized the market were dissipated in the second half of 1989 by the deprivation of the ruling communist parties of their authoritarian power. Elections in all but two of the East European states in the first half of 1990 could confidently be expected to introduce non-communist parliamentary rule. The exceptions are Albania, where only modest liberalization has begun, and Poland, where the decisive national election took place in 1989 (although the local vote of 1990 would carry political significance because the general election was partial). Secondly, a new freedom for the mass media permitted the public discussion of issues such as environmental damage, the quality and availability of consumers' goods and services, and rejection of the state's monopoly of trade and ownership of non-farm productive assets. Finally, and as an outcome of the two first conditions, statistical information and economic documentation began to be overhauled along two lines. The official data supply became more accurate and comprehensive, being no longer required to serve only the government's purposes. It was also becoming more widely available, although the speed and volume of transmission was constrained by an antiquated communications network.

The measures which have to be taken to effect the desired transition from central planning (overt in five of the countries considered, more latent in Hungary since 1968) may be grouped into macroeconomic and microeconomic;[1] internal and external; institutional and policy-based; monetary and non-monetary; and into negative and positive. The latter grouping is adopted in the present paper: negative measures are those which correct or dismantle relationships or procedures which obstruct the operation of a competitive market, while positive measures are those which promote market activity. Such a grouping may help the analysis of the sequence of measures since, in general, demolition is required before construction. In both sets the Hicksian definition of an economic system as a "structure of rules and understandings"[2] has particular importance; on the one hand the communist party typically influenced many economic decisions by informal procedures, and on the other hand an essential element of a market economy is a "commercial culture".

II. *Demolition and Equilibration*

The simile used in international economic relations of a "level playing field" is apposite to the displacement of obstacles to market competition in any context. But it is especially useful to illumine the non-market practices of resource allocation and income distribution in East European practice until now. At the base of any societal structure is the individual, those of working age being potential or actual producers, and all being consumers. Rule by a communist party inhibited the occupation of persons in functions maximizing their productivity.

Farmers were restricted, for the ideological "gain" of collective or state agriculture, to small private homestead plots or to subordination within cooperative or state farms; in Poland peasants were in many ways "second-class citizens" until 1972, and in some ways thereafter. Cooperative farms were least restrictive on their members in Hungary and at their worst in Romania (and Albania). Steps are already being taken to enlarge the area of land cultivable on an individual basis, but none of the five countries had (at the time of writing this paper) followed the Chinese example of abolishing communes in agriculture as the first major step towards marketization. It is unthinkable, however, that freedom of choice in farm ownership would be restricted in the Eastern part of a United Germany. The CDU victory in the polls of 18 March 1990 ensures that only strictly voluntary cooperatives will be tolerated in the period preparatory to unification. Restitution of agricultural land to the owners immediately following the 1946 land reform was a campaigning point for the Independent Smallholders Party in the Hungarian elections of 25 March 1990 and of the Peasant Party in Romania.

Personnel in state enterprises and institutions were in all six countries subject to the system of *nomenklatura*. The practice must have been dysfunctional in terms of microeconomic efficiency whenever criteria of party loyalty or nepotism ranked higher than merit, experience or innovative ability in selection for responsibility. Its synchronous disappearance with the single-party monopoly of state power does not usher in a meritocracy but will facilitate the appointment of decision-makers capable of entrepreneurship. It is a moot point whether entrepreneurship existed outside the minor private sector in the Soviet-type system. The present writer has defended the view that in the USSR entrepreneurship was extinguished with NEP (and, by extension, in East Europe around 1950) because enterprise managers did not have the information (notably flexible scarcity prices) to exercise entrepreneurial ability and planners were overdetermined by being in control of each other.[3] The degree of extinction, and the persistence of its more broadly-spread concommitant, a "commercial culture", was less extreme in the six states of East Europe. Neither factor, however, is trivial in influencing those countries' path to domestic efficiency and external competitiveness.

For such personal talents and experience to be deployed in the interest of competitive efficiency two relationships associated with economic *etatisme* (a more mellifluous term than "statization") have to be withdrawn by deliberate action. One is the administrative concentration of enterprises in a hierarchy which fosters monopoly power and the other is the "paternalism" — Kornai's term[4] — of the supervising authority to the enterprise. The entity through which both relations mainly, but not exclusively, flowed was the "industrial ministry". Neither the abolition of branch ministries in Hungary in favour of a single Ministry of Industry nor the effective supersession of them by Combines in East Germany weakened the force of monopoly or of non-market interventions to modify a subordinate's conditions of supply. The central-planning procedures which favoured both monopolization and enterprise-specific intervention have either gone (in Hungary and Poland), have been renounced (in East Germany and Czechoslovakia), or are under threat (in Bulgaria and Romania).

All the new governments appreciate the imperfection in any prospective competition arising from the present form of industrial administration. Such economies of scale or internalization of externalities as were achieved by the creation of large single enterprises could be offset by modernization, since the technology in use is often antiquated.[5] Moreover, as Czechoslovak and Polish economists have pointed out since the revolutions, much more of Western European and North American manufacturing output comes from small firms (less than 500 employees) than currently in Eastern Europe. Where East European governments differ is on the sequence of "destatification" and deconcentration: should it precede or follow the decontrol of prices? Poland has already chosen its schedule. Its policy is to open up the market first through flexible pricing and the withdrawal of subsidies and force the inefficient firms to reduce output, change their product-mix or close, leaving monopoly profits to be dealt with by progressive corporate taxation and by competition (the external dimension furnished by zloty convertibility). In Czechoslovakia the issue is controversial within the new government, but a weighty argument is the country's experience of 1968, when "enterprises apparently managed to 'sell' their padded costs to the price authorities. The inflated prices disrupted the working of some important subsystems of the reform .... and hampered its unfolding."[6] Such price "padding" had two decades ago been facilitated by an earlier reorganization which had concentrated all industry into one hundred branch associations. "Under such conditions, the reform brought decentralization only to the level of associations. It was a very curious 'market game' indeed, played amongst one hundred large monopoly partners."[7] In Hungary the liberalization of pricing has been given precedence over deconcentration, but the policy of the interim governments in Bulgaria and Romania is the maintenance of price control. In East Germany the new government has yet to enunciate a programme, but free pricing is a *sine qua non*; approaches made by West German concerns to associate themselves with existing state-enterprises or combines suggests that it will leave the degree of concentration to market forces.[8]

The prospect of German unification removes a second institutional obstacle in East Germany which persists in widely varying degrees elsewhere in East Europe. The GDR government had forbidden the entry of foreign firms, even as joint ventures, into domestic economic activity,[9] whereas the five other governments even before the revolutionary changes of 1989 had admitted joint ventures, and the Hungarian and Polish governments had permitted 100% foreign ownership. Decisions on full foreign ownership have still to be taken in Bulgaria and Czechoslovakia but are imminent in the GDR.

The issue of "destatization" is of course not only one of ownership and pricing; it also embraces a range of interventions which influence resource allocation and welfare. All must be regarded as transitional after the round of elections in 1990 and some have already disappeared. They include the rationing of both producers' and consumers' goods; the supply priority for certain branches of production (such as military goods or foreign tourism); pressure on trade unions and management on conformity to national norms in wage settlements and grading; privileged access to selected buyers (generally on the *nomenklatura*) for purchasing scarce consumers' goods, services and accommodation for permanent residence or for vacations; and discrimination against certain groups (private traders and craftsmen, and the clergy) in taxation and supply.

To complement the dismantling of procedures and regulations which inhibit marketization the new governments must "level the playing field" by bringing various sets of nominal incomes and expenditures towards equilibrium and by reducing the outstanding money balances arising from past disequilibria. It is obvious that marketization itself should effect some of the equilibration: the Polish and, less radically, the Hungarian governments have decided to rely on inflation for the adjustment of price relativities and the clearance of inflationary overhangs. Those overhangs and the disparities arising from inflation long repressed remain serious in the four other countries.[10] Nowhere does the problem seem to be so large as to require a currency reform whereby, as in some East European states in the early 1950s, excess money balances were confiscated: the aggregate of involuntary saving and cash hoards does not exceed one year's disposable personal income. The Federal Government's promise to convert East German savings deposits at a ratio of one Mark to one Deutschmark was limited to a relatively low maximum balance thereby effectively halving (at a 2:1 rate) the inflationary pressure of the residual. Proposals for a "heavy lev" which would circulate alongside and gradually replace the present unit, were being drafted in Bulgaria even before the demonstrations of November 1989. Currency reform is ruled out in Czechoslovakia but is a remote possibility in Romania.

As Brus and Laski (and others) have pointed out, state retail prices "were supposed to balance supply and demand to provide freedom of choice (but not consumer sovereignty, because market signals were not transmitted automatically to producers). However, in practice open or disguised rationing and queuing prevailed, because even under the political conditions of mono-archy it is difficult to bring about the desired rate of surplus by effective control of money incomes alone".[11] The control of personal income is one which cannot be relaxed while the household sector is becoming equilibrated, but the instruments previously deployed – centrally-set limits on wages funds or on employment and wage-rates – are unsuitable. Rather, as Czechoslovakia, Poland and Hungary have chosen, the tool is the progressive taxation of wage increments seeking to keep these below the rate of productivity growth and, for a transitional period, below retail price increases. On the demand side other measures include the widening of the tax base for all incomes (from private, cooperative and state employment and from self-employment); a rise in the rate of tax to GNP; a rise in interest rates to foster voluntary saving; and the elimination (fast in Poland and Czechoslovakia) of the budget deficit. The "shake out" of high-cost production and plant is also cutting disposable income in Poland and can be expected to be effective elsewhere. On the supply side the volume and mix of the goods and services on offer to households will in the long run be assured by the normal processes of the market, but in the short term a number of measures can accelerate the achievement of equilibrium. Unrequited imports are already being supplied under the "food aid" and other programmes of the European Commission and other OECD governments, and some consumer supplies can be financed from part of the various stabilization loans. The extension of foreign-trade authority, linked to foreign-earnings retention, to state enterprises has resulted in some diversion of consumers' goods from the home to the external market and such reductions have to be offset. In the medium term the moderation of government orders (for military administrative and political requirements) combined with the "shake out" will release capacity for consumer-goods production. The dilution of the sellers' market for consumers' goods and services will assist external competitiveness, but the motive force for fundamental change in the producer sector comes above all from positive action.

III. *The Positive Measures*

The extent to which East European governments have adopted legislation or initiated procedures for market institutions varies from much advanced in Hungary and Poland to little in Bulgaria and Romania. The East German case is quite distinct and is not treated further in this paper: the negotiations engendered by the victory of the Alliance for Germany and by declarations of the Federal Government will form the framework in which market structures are created in preparation for unification.

The fundament of all the changes in prospect is the diversification and equal treatment before the law of property rights in productive assets. Both Hungary and Poland before the demission of communist governments had enacted legislation on the private ownership of enterprises – in Hungary with a limit of 500 employees, but unlimited in Poland. These are today the two governments with an accelerated programme of privatization of state productive establishments, available to both domestic and foreign purchasers. The speed of the programme and the inadequate experience of valuation (exacerbated by market imperfection and the heritage of fossilized prices) has led to some underpricing. A particularly unfortunate consequence is termed "wild" privatization in Hungary and "spontaneous" privatization in Poland – buy-outs by existing managers or local party officials at unrealistically low prices. The tempo and extent of privatization is at the time of writing in dispute within the Czechoslovak Council of Ministers – the Minister of Finance, Vaclav Klaus, urging speed and comprehensiveness, the Deputy Premier in charge of the economy, Valtr Komarek, opting for a slower and narrower path. Decisions await parliamentary elections in Bulgaria and Romania.

Allied with privatization is decollectivization in agriculture. It is not required in Poland, where, as already noted, private farming predominates, and no definitive action seems to have been taken in the other four countries. In Romania, where collectivization and the procurement regime was the harshest in East Europe, the sole concession so far has been an extension (albeit substantial) of the homestead plot. In Bulgaria the regimentation of the agro-industrial complex was broken with effect from 1 January 1988, but cooperative farms have not been authorized to disband.

In the non-farm sector cooperatives and the leasing of state concerns have always been legal, but they were fostered only in Hungary and only in the 1980s. There seems little public pressure for the conversion of state enterprises into cooperatives or other forms of self-management, probably because of the economic crisis of the late 1980s in Yugoslavia, to which worker management contributed. Corporate ownership in which employees have the non-exclusive right to shares is a more promising avenue, and a stock exchange exists in both Hungary and Poland. The other principal structure of a capital market, the commercialization of banking, has ostensibly taken place in four of the five states, Romania as yet being the exception. Further enactments in all areas of ownership, notably on joint-stock companies and on foreign participation, are of course still required. As markets set scarcity prices for capital goods and as accountancy services become more sophisticated (including depreciation accounting), the valuation of a firm's assets will become more realistic. Because there are as yet no commodity markets and a seller's market still prevails, a Walrasian auctioneer should be invented. Foreign transactors are that very auctioneer – either coming onto the domestic scene as buyers of assets or of current goods and services or available abroad for trade.

In domestic production and distribution a revived stratum of specialized sub-contractors or traders is urgently needed. Governments, in breaking up monopolistic or market-dominating entities, can assist the revival by specifying some sub-entities as potential contractors and by encouraging foreign trade in components. The share of intra-industry trade in all the six East European imports/exports is far lower than that among Western countries; an increase in the ratio would indicate enhanced competitiveness.

The labour market requires the revival of only one institution, the labour exchange, not merely to reduce search cost but also to verify unemployed status for the payment of social security insurances or benefits. An extension of social security protection against the increased risk of unemployment is correspondingly required and will add slightly to labour costs. But on balance, competitiveness will be improved by the shake-out.

The final market for which a structure is needed is in foreign exchange. In the short term a disequilibrium exchange rate is being tolerated, save in Hungary and Poland (where the zloty has been internally convertible from 1 January 1990). Czechoslovakia abandoned a multiple exchange rate (except between commercial and non-commercial transactions) on 1 January 1989, but they persist as currency coefficients in Bulgaria and Romania. Foreign exchange auctions continue in Bulgaria and Czechoslovakia, but are no longer needed in Poland. Membership of the IMF is essential for Bulgaria and Czechoslovakia to operate their exchange-rate mechanisms in accordance with Western practice. The Czechoslovak government has signified its intention to denounce the Karlmarxstadt Agreement on exchange rates among CMEA members. Its representative at the Sofia Session of the CMEA (and doubtless at the committee which began work in Moscow in February) was prepared to demolish the agency altogether. The bilateral treaties of each country with the European Commission (that with Romania is still being renegotiated and awaits the Community's political confidence) as well as membership of GATT (still lacking for Bulgaria) will assist the penetration of East European goods on to their main Western markets. Their dependence on themselves and on the USSR has undermined their competitiveness and has especially rendered their products excessively energy- and material-intensive. Much of this trade (the terms of which will worsen for them as world prices obtain within CMEA from 1990) will persist. How far their low labour costs are offset by low factor productivity remains to be tested under the new conditions.

Notes

1. This grouping was chosen by the Policy Forum Editor of the *Economic Journal,* Professor David Greenaway, for the June 1990 issue: Professor Paul Hare was invited to write the microeconomics and the present writer the macroeconomics.
2. J. R. Hicks, *A Theory of Economic History,* Oxford: Oxford University Press 1969, p. 141. The definition and content of an economic system is thoroughly examined in T. Shiraishi and S. Tsuru (eds.), *Economic Institutions in a Dynamic Society,* London: Macmillan 1988.
3. M. C. Kaser, "Russian Entrepreneurship", *The Cambridge Economic History of Europe,* vol. VII, part 2, Cambridge: Cambridge University Press 1978, pp. 416-93.
4. J. Kornai, "The Hungarian Reform Process: Visions, Hopes and Realities", *Journal of Economic Literature,* vol. 24, no. 4, 1986, pp. 1687-737.
5. See the OECD studies, *East-West Technology Transfer:* G. D. Holliday, *Survey of Sectoral Case Studies,* 1984; H. Wienert and J. Slater, *The Trade and Economic Aspects,* 1986, Paris: OECD. These have been reinforced by much recent evidence from the countries concerned. The Western strategic embargo contributed to East Europe's technological lag, but was exacerbated by the planning system itself and by the tie to their own region's, and the Soviet, lower technology clients and suppliers.
6. J. Adam, *Economic Reforms in the Soviet Union and Eastern Europe since the 1960s,* London: Macmillan 1989, p. 60.
7. O. Kyn, "Czechoslovakia" in H.-H. Höhmann, M. Kaser and K. C. Thalheim (eds.), *The New Economic Systems of Eastern Europe,* London: Hurst 1975, p. 141. This paper was the first to stress the significance of the sequence of marketization measures.
8. It is relevant that the former East German government perceived the Combine as a factor in the demarcation *(Abgrenzung)* of the GDR against the Federal Republic (H. Betz, "Recent Changes in the System of Management in the GDR" in Adam, op. cit., p. 224).
9. The interim government of the PDS (January to March 1989) had authorized minority equity participation with majority ownership to be considered on a case-by-case basis.
10. Data are cited in my *Economic Journal* paper for Czechoslovakia, East Germany and Romania (vol. 100, pp. 596-615); discussions in Sofia in October 1989 convinced me of the problem in Bulgaria, but without quantification.
11. W. Brus and K. Laski, *From Marx to the Market: Socialism in Search of an Economic System.* Oxford: Oxford University Press 1989, p. 40.

Analysts Face a Moving Target as They Examine the Economies of Eastern Europe*
Summing Up

Richard F. Kaufman

The 1990 NATO Colloquium on the economies of Central and Eastern Europe was held at the Alliance's Brussels Headquarters in April, just a few months after the historic events of the Fall and Winter of 1989 and while the momentum of change was still going forward. The region had not only been altered, it had been turned upside down politically, economically, and ideologically. The Stalinist system of central planning, which had been under serious attack in the Soviet Union since 1985, and the leading role of the Communist Party, were simply swept away in most of the region. Leaderships were replaced and most committed themselves to the establishment of democratic, multi-party governments and market-type economies.

The challenge to the community of experts on the economies of the region could not have been greater. Events which many thought might happen some time in the distant future, if at all, were suddenly *faits accomplis* — significant withdrawals of Soviet military forces, disintegration of the Warsaw Pact, and the start of German reunification, to only name three. If ever a group of analysts were faced with a moving target, they were in this instance. Events were literally unfolding during the Colloquium itself.

It was the good fortune of the Colloquium, thanks to the foresight of the organizers, that those who made presentations were long time students of the area and able to adjust quickly to the new situation. Some, including those from the region under examination, were both scholars and active participants in economic policy. The impression during the proceedings was that one was both observing and engaging in the process of change.

The papers which were presented and the discussions can be ranged around three questions concerning the domestic economies and reforms, international factors, and future East-West relations. The following article attempts to summarize what transpired under each of these questions.

Economic Reforms

All the countries of the region have experienced economic deterioration and are struggling to arrest decline in the wake of political upheavals and the disruptive effects of changing their economic systems. In essence, they are having to shock themselves to arise out of the ossified state imposed by rigid central planning. The costs of the transitional shocks are high in terms of production and income foregone. Those countries attempting to bring inflation and hyperinflation under control must add to their discomfort with stabilization policies. All face the difficult task of meeting unfamiliar standards of performance.

The major steps towards systemic economic reform in Eastern Europe probably would not be under way now were it not for the actions of Mikhail Gorbachev. It was his call for restructuring in the Soviet Union, and the pressures he placed on his Warsaw Pact allies to reform their economies, together with the unilateral military force withdrawals from Eastern Europe, that encouraged the populations in those countries to press for change. Ironically, up to the time of the Colloquium, the USSR was among those who had done the least to restructure their economic systems.

As Oleg Bogomolov said in his oral presentation, so far perestroika has mostly raised public expectations. There has been no real improvement in agriculture or industry, and no improvement in daily life. The deficit is 10-11% of GNP, the government continues to mismanage the economy, and foreign debt is growing.

John Hardt painted an even grimmer picture of the Soviet economy in crisis, with the possibility of a major recession in 1990, more severe monetary disequilibrium, and a rising and record level of inflation. Unless there is radical change, there will be less food, more inadequate housing, and further deterioration of health care and the environment.

Both Hardt and Bogomolov agreed that the Soviet Union is at a turning point, facing a choice between transformation of the economy through radical change or deep recession and political instability, and that time is running out. Both urged that steps be taken towards a market system with diverse forms of ownership, free enterprise and competition, increased glasnost, multi-party pluralistic democracy, and integration with the world economy. The two urged the central government to do more to implement restructuring. But they acknowledged that the government's lack of public support, and the unhappiness of consumers and workers with the results thus far of perestroika, made it more difficult for the necessary actions to be taken.

The papers on the smaller CMEA countries presented clearer images of the directions of current policies because the situations in most of them are less ambiguous. In most of these countries, changes have been forced from below, as opposed to the top-down process in the Soviet Union.

Michael Kaser's two-step approach to the process of change is helpful to an understanding of where each country stands. Kaser stated that, to effect the transition from central planning, there must be, first, negative measures to demolish the old system, followed by positive measures to construct a new one. For example, Communist Party rule and the nomenklatura must be eliminated so that individuals can function up to their potential productivity; central planning and fixed pricing must be discarded in order for market forces to operate. Positive measures include legislation to assure property rights and private ownership of enterprises. Logically, Kaser wrote, demolition is required before construction.

This sequencing may help explain why partial attempts at reform proved ineffective in Poland and Hungary, as well as the USSR, where the Communist Party and central planning were left intact. In those previous efforts, not enough of the old system was dismantled to allow a new one to be built. Looked at from this perspective, the East German case is not as paradoxical as may first appear. It came late to the process of change, and as Doris Cornelsen stated, as recently as one year ago it was considered "An orthodox but still working model". Today, it is seen as the centrally planned economy most likely to be transformed successfully. The obvious reason is the Federal Republic of Germany, which stands ready to finance the operation.

Using Kaser's taxonomy of change, the GDR's approach to the problem of systemic reform has been logical and efficient. In just a few weeks, it got rid of the old leadership (with the encouragement of Gorbachev) and demolished the Communist Party in a free election. The remaining steps to be taken seem mere details, although actual economic and financial costs can still be debated. The positive task of creating a market economy will be accomplished by incorporation into the Federal Republic of Germany, although there will, of course, be hardships and transitional problems. Unfortunately, the process will not be so easy nor the outcome so predictable in the other five countries.

Poland and Hungary have long histories of economic reform efforts which have been only partially successful. Both have initiated programmes of change that are more comprehensive and qualitatively different from what was done previously. As Marek Grela and Jan Bielawski wrote in their paper on Poland, "one has to differentiate between partial reforms within the existing system and reforms or rather transformations changing the system itself".

The Polish government's *shock therapy* programme is intended to achieve transformation by, first, eliminating hyperinflation and stabilizing the economy. The premise behind the decision to quickly decontrol most prices while curbing wage increases, reducing government spending, and tightening the money supply and credit, was that a gradual approach to very high inflation would not work. In the second phase of the programme, state owned enterprises are to be privatized, monopolies broken up, a private banking system established, and tax reforms introduced. Although the programme may fail for a variety of reasons, reaction "to the failures of socialism has been so deep that the pleasures of burying it for the moment compensate for many of the discomforts of the encumbent capitalism".

The Hungarian case is, in essence, similar to Poland's. The Communist Party is being replaced through elections, and the non-communist leaders intend to install a market economy. Tamás Bauer argued in his paper that Hungary has the same objectives as Poland but Hungary's chances are better because of more than 20 years of market-type changes. But optimism about the prospects for establishing a market economy in Hungary must be restrained by the knowledge that many difficult steps remain to be taken in a weak economy hampered by foreign debt and a shortage of hard currency.

Czechoslovakia and Bulgaria are similar to one another in that past economic reforms have been more narrowly focused and equivocal than in Poland and Hungary. In addition, the present leaderships in both countries are committed to instituting market type economic systems but more gradually and less comprehensively than in Poland or Hungary.

In Czechoslovakia, the economic reform process has not kept up with the sweeping political changes. This was probably a result, in part, of the relative stability of the Czechoslovakian economy, where the standard of living is the second highest in the region. Franz-Lothar Altmann stated in his paper that the relative stability of the economy retarded reforms, but it was stability at a low, stagnation level. The dispute within the government over the pace of reforms has been intensive. For now, it will try a "smoother transition" to a market economy, carrying forward the reforms of the previous government in such areas as banking, foreign currency, and prices, and applying tight anti-inflationary monetary and budgetary policies. But not all subsidies will be cut or all prices freed, because of concerns about unemployment and living standards.

The pace of change has been even slower in Bulgaria where the economy has been among the worst in Eastern Europe. As a result of the recent elections, the former Communists (now the Socialist Party) won a majority and it is not yet clear that free elections and political pluralism will be institutionalized. The present government has stated there is no alternative to a market economy and has adopted some measures toward that end. For example, private property rights have been broadened and some restrictions on small businesses have been removed. However, it has indicated that progress will be gradual.

Romania, in most respects, lags the rest of the region and is the furthest behind the reform curve. Under the recently elected regime, there has been little progress toward political or economic decentralization, and because of the decimation of society under Ceaucescu little will and few resources to move forward. Alan Smith constructed an optimistic scenario, based on the experience of the newly industrializing countries of Asia, in which Western investment is attracted following a series of market type reforms. But he stated that Romania is not likely to take this course. A gradualist approach will probably prevail.

International Factors

If one were doing an economic forecast of the region based on the papers and discussions in this conference, the outlook would, in general, be favourable but certain risks would have to be noted. Political instability is one, and there are uncertainties implicit in stagnation and recession and in stabilization efforts. Perhaps the most serious risks are in the external sector, although there are promising developments there as well. For example, Norman Scott linked the disruption of supplies within the Soviet Union in 1989 to interruptions in exports to Eastern Europe which produced "a near breakdown in the intra-CMEA trading system". Of particular importance was the drop in Soviet energy deliveries. The difficulties in the smaller CMEA countries were compounded by this external shock from the USSR, their principal trading partner.

One of the region's most difficult challenges will be to integrate their trade with the West while simultaneously reducing their dependence on the USSR. The immediate prospects for integration with the West are not bright; the competitiveness of the region's manufacturers has continued to fall, and its share of Western markets has declined since the 1970s. Foreign investment offers a potential source of financing of industrial restructuring and modernization but, except in East Germany where Federal German investment will be concentrated, this source of capital is not likely to be substantial for the foreseeable future. It is possible that specific investments can have important sectoral or regional effects. Data on joint ventures with Western partners indicates that actual levels of investments from this source have been relatively low.

While Western investors show interest in the region, East Europe's external imbalances are a major source of uncertainty. It may be as difficult to solve this region's foreign debt and balance of payments problems as it has been in other areas. Western governments are providing substantial financial and technical assistance, and have responded to Eastern Europe's desires for closer ties with trade concessions, eased restrictions on technology transfers, and support for East European membership in the GATT and other multilateral institutions. The more important question is how private investors respond. According to Alberto Chilosi, until relief is found from the crushing hard currency debt, the most helpful aid would be official credits and guaranties so that there can be greater access to foreign capital which the debt problem now obstructs.

Piero Zaino discussed the seriousness of the external balances from a Western commercial banker's perspective. He pointed out that net hard currency debt of the region rose again in 1989 to $120 billion, and that in the past three years, debt maturities became longer. The prospects are favourable for new credits for the USSR and Czechoslovakia where debt ratios are manageable but for the more highly indebted countries — Poland, Hungary, and Bulgaria — the situation is problematic and will become even more difficult with the current increases in international interest rates. Zaino stated that the forecast is for an increase in East European debt, and that based on experiences with certain non-European countries, where new credits served more to back up the existing structure rather than to change it, banks have to be particularly careful.

Future East-West Relations

Two Western perspectives and a Soviet view were presented on the changing international institutional structures and arrangements between East and West Europe. Marie Lavigne explored the question of possible future relations by putting forward three scenarios. In the first, the trend for Eastern Europe was towards minimum trade and minimum links, in which all recognize that present trade patterns are obsolete and the countries force themselves to reorient their trade with the West by reducing trade among themselves and the Soviet Union. A second possibility was that reasonable levels of trade are maintained but without any special new arrangements. In this scenario, new regional groupings are not formed, allowing for more gradual reorientation to the West and also to the Soviet Union when it becomes a real market.

In the third scenario, a new regional grouping is formed of the East European CMEA members, except for East Germany, in something like a free trade area or customs union. Some form of economic grouping among the East Europeans would be desirable, Lavigne said, because "Integrated Western Europe cannot be satisfied with a disintegrated Eastern Europe at its side".

Oleg Bogomolov's assessment was consistent with Lavigne's third scenario. He stated that as a result of the criticism directed at CMEA by East European officials and the threats of some to leave the organization, a new consensus has formed to shift cooperation to market principles. While prospects for a market-type integration are still indefinite, and subregional groupings of some member countries and associations with West Europe are possible, cooperation within the CMEA framework will continue.

Viewing the subject from the vantage point of the European Community, Marc Maresceau came to surprisingly similar conclusions. Concerning future cooperation with Eastern Europe, the association model is more frequently mentioned. In such a framework, a free trade zone could be established, although accession to the European Community of some East European countries, or something between association and accession, should not be ruled out. However, Maresceau said, existing East European economic relations cannot be quickly changed, nor would it be realistic for the Community to absorb in the short or medium term all those who wanted to accede. For this reason, CMEA may have a serious role to play.

A Final Comment

A major underlying premise of the Colloquium concerned the easing of East-West tensions as a consequence of the winding down of the cold war. While assessments of the military threat were not explicitly considered, the idea that it had diminished was implicit. It was under this circumstance that individuals from the Soviet Union and East Europe participated in the conference.

There were some references to the security issue. For example, Maresceau suggested relaxation or abolition of controls on dual use goods, including those for export to the Soviet Union. He said that better economic development in Eastern Europe and the Soviet Union will be a sounder contribution to peace and security than the maintenance of obstacles to normal trade.

Ambassador Henning Wegener addressed the relationship between security, defence and economics in a speech during the Colloquium. The Ambassador said in his remarks that because free, democratic, and prosperous countries will not wage war, the security policy of the Alliance must be to help the Warsaw Pact nations reform their economic and political systems. The task of reform, he concluded, is mostly the responsibility of the Eastern nations, but the West can hold out the fruits of its efficient, functioning societies in a spirit of solidarity to help the process along.

Ambassador Wegener's statement captured the prevailing sentiment of the Colloquium. There was a strong sense that the idea of national security needs to be redefined to give greater weight to economic factors, including living standards and international competitiveness. It was also understood that it is in the West's interests for the reforms to succeed and that the outcomes cannot be taken for granted.

* This article was first published in the NATO Review, No. 3, June 1990.

Biographies of Authors

Name:	**Franz-Lothar ALTMANN**
Current position:	Deputy Director Südost-Institut; Editor-in-Chief, *Südosteuropa* and *Osteuropa-Wirtschaft*
Main field of work:	Economic systems; East-West trade; economic development of Middle-East and South-East Europe.
Publicatons during last two years:	"CSSR", in: H-H. Höhmann, G. Seidenstecher (Hrsg.): *Die Wirtschaft Osteuropas und der VR China 1980-1990. Bilanz und Perspektiven,* Verlag Weltarchiv, Hamburg 1988, S. 191-258.

"Zu den Versuchen der 'Vervollkommnung' des Aussenwirtschaftssystems in der CSSR", in: M. Haendcke-Hoppe (Hrsg.): *Aussenwirtschaftssysteme und Aussenwirtschaftsreformen sozialistischer Länder,* Duncker & Humblot, Berlin 1988, S. 129-142.

"Bilaterale Aussenwirtschaftsbeziehungen zwischen der Tschechoslowakei und der Bundesrepublik Deutschland" in: *Osteuropa,* 7-8/1988 (Festschrift zum 70. Geburtstag von Otto Wolff von Amerongen), S. 726-736.

"Wirtschaftsreformen in Südosteuropa und der CSSR - Versuch einer vergleichenden Gegenüberstellung", in: *Südosteuropa,* 6/1988, S. 280-294.

"Probleme des Verkehrs- und Nachrichtenwesens in der CSSR", in: *Infrastrukturprobleme in europäischen RGW-Staaten* (=Wirtschafts- und Sozialwissenschaftliche Ostmitteleuropa-Studien 13), Marburg an der Lahn 1989, S. 73-84.

"Restructuring of Czechoslovak Economic Mechanism", in: J.S. Berliner, H.G.J. Kosta, Masumi Hakogi (Hrsg.): *Economics of the Socialist Countries,* Maruzen Company, Japan 1989, S. 103-116.

Name:	**Tamás BAUER**
Current position:	Professor of Economics, University of Frankfurt am Main; Senior Research Fellow, Institute of Economics, Hungarian Academy of Sciences, Budapest
Main field of work:	Comparative analysis of Soviet and East European economic systems, reforms and performance.
Publicatons during last two years:	"The Firm Under Perestroika". *Berichte des Bundesinstituts für ostwissenschaftliche und internationale Studien,* Cologne 1989; auch gekürzt in Russisch in *Eko,* 6/1989.
	"Reforming or Perfecting the Economic Mechanism", *Social Research,* Vol. 55, no. 4, Winter 1988.
	"Deceleration, Dependency and Depaternalization. Some Considerations Concerning the Chances of the Soviet Union and Eastern Europe in the Coming Decades", *Acta Oeconomica,* Vol. 39, Nos. 1-2, 1988.

Name:	**Oleg BOGOMOLOV**
Current position:	Director, Institute of Economics of the World Socialist System, USSR Academy of Sciences
Main field of work:	Political and economic problems of East European countries; political economy of socialism; theory of international labour division.
Publicatons during last two years:	"Socialisme & Compétitivité", Presses de la Fondation Nationale des Sciences Politiques, Paris 1989.
	"Perestrojka und die Aussichten für die Wirtschaftsbeziehungen zwischen Ost und West", *Europa-Archiv,* 16/1988, pp. 444-450.
	"Die Erneuerung des Sozialismus und der gesamteuropäische Prozess", pp. 115-131, in: *Europas Aufstieg,* Europaverlag, Wien-Zürich 1989.
	"Socialist Economies at the Turning Point" in: *Economic Growth Policies. Theory and Reality,* pp. 177-188.

"Toward Ruble Convertibility", *World Link,* Nos. 11-12/1989, pp. 53-54.

Name: **Alberto CHILOSI**

Current position: Professore Ordinario di Politica, Economica e Finanziaria; Director, Institute of Economics and Finance, Faculty of Political Sciences, University of Pisa

Main field of work: Economics of socialism; comparative economic systems.

Publicatons during last two years:

"Rates of Growth of Stocks and Flows in Discrete and Continuous Time", in: Gerhard Fink, Günther Pöll and Martin Riese (eds.), *Economic Theory, Political Power and Social Justice,* Springer, Wien-New York 1987, pp. 173-189.

"Una breve guida alla letteratura rilevante per l'analisi della questione distributiva nel socialismo (reale e ipotetico)", in: L. Marcolungo, M. Pugno, F. Targetti (eds.), *L'economia mondiale in trasformazione,* Franco Angeli, Milano 1988, pp. 129-136.

"Libero accesso e pieno impiego in economie partecipative e non partecipative", in: Bruno Jossa (ed.), *Autogestione, cooperazione e partecipazione agli utili,* Il Mulino, Bologna 1988, pp. 149-157.

"Nessi e Interpretazioni causali nella macroeconomia di Kalecki", *Quaderni di storia dell' Economia Politica,* 1988, pp. 361-370.

"Kalecki's Quest for the Microeconomic Foundations of his Microeconomic Theory", in: M. Sebastiani (ed.), *Kalecki's Relevance Today,* Macmillan, London 1989, pp. 101-120.

"Alternative Models of Market Socialism", *Acts of the VI AISSEC Conference,* Vol. 1, Urbino 1989, pp. 182-191.

Name: **Doris CORNELSEN**

Current position: Head of Department of the GDR and East

	European industrial countries (German Institute for Economic Research)
Publicatons during last two years:	Contributions to the *Deutschland Handbuch,* Bonn 1989. Bundeszentrale für politische Bildung. *Wochenberichte des DIW:* 5/1988; 30/1988; 5/1989; 31/1989; 6/1990.
Name:	**Marek GRELA**
Current position:	Senior Research Fellow, Polish Institute of International Affairs; Counsellor to the Foreign Minister, Ministry of Foreign Affairs, Warsaw
Main field of work:	European security and East-West relations.
Publicatons during last two years:	*Polska a stosunki Wschód - Zachód w latach osiemdziesiatych,* Warszawa 1989 (Poland and East-West Relations in the 1980s). *European Polyphony: Perspectives beyond East-West Confrontation,* Macmillan Press, London 1989 (co-author).
Name:	**John P. HARDT**
Current position:	Associate Director and Senior Specialist in Soviet Economics, Congressional Research Service, Library of Congress, Washington D.C.
Main field of work:	Soviet economics.
Publicatons during last two years:	John Hardt has edited, coordinated, and contributed to many volumes on the economies of the Soviet Union, East Europe and the PRC for the US Congress. *Gorbachev's Economic Plans,* two volumes released in December 1987. *Pressures for Reform in the East European Economies,* November 1989. *Perestroika: A Sustainable Process of Change* (with Sheila Heslin, Commentary by Oleg Bogomolov), released by Group of Thirty in October 1989.

Name:	**Michael KASER**
Current position:	Director, Institute of Russian, Soviet and East European Studies, University of Oxford
Main field of work:	Transformation of planned into market economies.
Publicatons during last two years:	"Comecon as an Instrument of Change under Gorbachev", *Österreichisches Jahrbuch für Internationale Politik,* Vol. 3, 1987 (Bohlau Verlag, Vienna), pp. 146-152.
	"The Economic Dimension" in: E. Moreton (ed.), *Germany Between East and West,* 1987 (Cambridge University Press), pp. 123-140.
	"Soviet Economic and Social Change" in: *Gorbachev and Glasnost: Implications for Atlantic Area Nations,* 1987 (Chicago Council on Foreign Relations), pp. 112-126.
	"Soviet Restructuring in Relation to the Chinese Reform", *Asian Economies* (Seoul), December 1987, pp. 68-78.
	" 'One Economy, Two Systems': Parallels between Soviet and Chinese Reforms", *International Affairs,* Summer 1987, pp. 395-412.
	"Reform in the USSR and China", *Pacific Quarterly,* No. 1, 1988, pp. 38-49.
	"The Impact of Technological Change on East-West Relations" in: F.S. Larrabee (ed.), *Technology and Change in East-West Relations,* 1988 (Institute for East-West Security Studies, New York), pp. 147-163, reprinted with amendments in *Prace naukowe Akademii Economicznej we Wroclawiu,* No. 454, 1988, pp. 137-147.
	"Ziele und Grenzen der sowjetischen Perestroika" in: K. Vak and H. Zilk (eds.), *Europas Aufstieg,* 1989 (Europaverlag, Vienna), pp. 73-81.
	"Economic Problems Facing Gorbachev and his Possible Solution" in: C. Donnelly (ed.), *Gorbachev's Revolution: Economic Pressures and Defence Realities,* 1989 (Jane's, London), pp. 35-48.

"The Conference in Perspective" in: T. Shiraishi and S. Tsuru (eds.), *Economic Institutions in a Dynamic Society: Search for a New Frontier,* 1989 (Macmillan, London), pp. 237-240.

Name:	**Richard F. KAUFMAN**
Current position:	General Counsel, Joint Economic Committee, Washington, D.C.
Main field of work:	International law and economics.
Publicatons during last two years:	"Industrial Modernization and Defense in the Soviet Union", 1988.
	"Economic Reform and the Soviet Military", 1988.
	"US-Soviet Trade Policies in the 1980s", 1989.
	"Resource Flows to Developing Countries: An Economic Overview", 1989.
	"Pressures for Reform in the East European Economies" (co-editor 1989).
	"Economic Environment for Investment Opportunities in Eastern Europe", 1990.

Name:	**Marie LAVIGNE**
Current position:	Professor at the University of Paris I, Panthéon Sorbonne
Main field of work:	USSR and Eastern Europe: domestic and international economic developments.
Publicatons during last two years:	*Economie internationale des pays socialistes,* Paris, Armand Colin, 1985, 256 p. (update 1988).
	"Entreprises conjointes et coopération Est-Ouest" in: *Coopération entre entreprises, entreprises conjointes, stratégies industrielles et pouvoirs publics,* Alexis Jacquemin and Bernard Remiche (eds.), Bruxelles, De Boeck Wesmael, Association Internationale de Droit Economique 1988, pp. 175-194.

"La modernisation des activités productives dans les pays europées du CAEM et l'intégration socialiste: conflits ou interaction?", *Economies et Sociétés, Cahiers de l'ISMEA* 1988, no. 2, série G "Economie planifiée" no. 43, pp. 175-201.

"The Evolution of CMEA Institutions and Policies and the Need for Structural Adjustment" in: *Economic Adjustment and Reform in Eastern Europe and the Soviet Union, Essays in Honor of Franklyn D. Holzman,* Josef C. Brada, Ed. A. Hewett and Thomas A. Wolf (eds.), Durham and London, Duke University Press 1988, pp. 147-169.

(Avec Krystyna Szymkiewicz) "Les pays à commerce d'Etat et le GATT" in: *Conflits et négociations dans le commerce international, l'Uruguay Round,* Patrick Messerlin and François Vellas (eds.), IVè colloque du Greco-Efiq, Paris, Economica 1989, pp. 55-74.

"Prospects for Soviet Foreign Trade Reform" in: *Gorbachev's Agenda, Changes in Soviet Domestic and Foreign Policy,* Susan L. Clark (ed.), Boulder, Co., Westview Press 1989, pp. 129-160.

"CMEA Relations with the Third World", *Pressures for Reform in the East European Economies,* Study papers submitted to the Joint Committee, Congress of the United States, Vol. 2, Washington, USGPO 1989, pp. 444-467.

Relaciones Economicas Este-Oeste, *Informacion Comercial Espanola,* Revista de Economia, numéro spécial *Reforma y apertura de la economias del Este,* no. 674, octobre 1989, pp. 13-36.

International Political Economy and Socialism, Cambridge University Press, 1990 (forthcoming).

Name: **Marc MARESCEAU**

Current position: Professor of EEC law, Universities of Ghent and Brussels; Director, European Institute, University of Ghent

Main field of work: EEC law; legal framework of trade policy of the European Communities.

Publicatons during last two years: "The effect of treaties in domestic law: Belgium" in: *The Effect of Treaties in Domestic Law* (ed. F. Jacobs and Sh. Roberts), London, Sweet & Maxwell 1988, pp. 1-16.

"A general survey of the current legal framework of trade relations between the European Community and Eastern Europe" in: *The Political and Legal Framework of Trade Relations between the European Community and Eastern Europe,* 1989, pp. 3-20.

(Ed.) *The Political and Legal Framework of Trade Relations between the European Community and Eastern Europe,* Dordrecht-Boston-London, Martinus Nijhoff Publishers, 1989.

"Les compétences des Communautés et des Régions en matière de relations internationales et l'application du droit communautaire européen", *Chambre des Représentants de Belgique* 1989, pp. 15-32.

Name: **Marie-Claude MAUREL**

Current position: Professeur de Géographie, Université de Montpellier

Main field of work: Changement social et réformes en Europe de l'Est

Publicatons during last two years: *Les paysans contre l'Etat. Le rapport de forces polonais.* L'Harmattan 1988, 230 p.

"Administrative reforms in Eastern Europe: An Overview". Chapter 7 in: *Territory and Administration in Europe: Comparative development of regional and local government in Socialist and West European countries* (ed. by J.R. Bennett), Pinter Publishers, London 1989, pp. 111-123.

"L'agriculture soviétique sur le front de la perestroïka". *Historiens-Géographes* 1989, no. 323, pp. 143-153.

"Un succédané de la perestroïka. La nouvelle réforme de l'administration territoriale en Bulgarie". *Le Courrier des Pays de l'Est,* mai 1989, pp. 34-43.

"Sociétés locales, territoires, pouvoirs en Europe de l'Est". *Espace rural,* no. 20, pp. 27-49.

"Les paysans polonais dans la bataille politique". *Le Monde Diplomatique,* janvier 1990, p. 10.

"Quel avenir pour les paysans polonais ?" *Revue Autrement,* no. spécial Pologne 1990 (à paraître), 10 p.

"Economie parallèle et travail polymorphe dans les pays de l'Est" in : *Espaces et travail clandestin.* Collection Recherches en géographie, Masson 1990, à paraître.

"Local societies and territoriality in East Central Europe", *Geoforum,* Vol. 21 (2) 1990, 30 p.

Name : **Norman SCOTT**

Current position : Director, Trade Division, United Nations Economic Commission for Europe; Visiting Professor, Graduate Institute of International Studies, Geneva

Main field of work : East-West economic relations; international trade procedures; comparative economic systems.

Publicatons during last two years : *East-West joint ventures : economic, business, financial and legal aspects* (Collective secretariat authorship by team led by Norman Scott), UN/ECE 1988.

"Establishing and financing a joint venture" in : *La Co-entreprise à l'Etranger,* University of Ottawa 1989, pp. 61-96.

Name : **Alan H. SMITH**

Current position : Senior lecturer in East European economics, School of Slavonic and East European Studies, University of London

Main field of work:	Soviet foreign economic relations; economic transitions in Eastern Europe; the Romanian economy.
Publicatons during last two years:	"Gorbachev and the World. The Economic Side" in: *The Soviet Union under Gorbachev,* edited by David Dyker. Croom Helm.
	"Debt Repayment and Romanian Economic Prospects". *WEFA Group,* June 1989.
	"Can Comecon Survive?" *WEFA Group,* December 1989.
	"Can Gradualist Economic Reforms Succeed in Eastern Europe?", Centrally Planned Economies Outlook. WEFA Group, April 1990.
	"The Implications of Change in the Central East European Economies for the Balkan Socialist Economies". *Stockholm Institute of Soviet and East European Economics Working Paper,* 1990.
	Economist Intelligence Unit. Country Reports on Romania.
Name:	**Piero ZAINO**
Current position:	Senior Vice President, Istituto Bancario San Paolo di Torino, Turin
Main field of work:	Projects in Eastern Europe